Legendary Hawai'i and the Politics of Place

Legendary Hawai'i and the Politics of Place

Tradition, Translation, and Tourism

CRISTINA BACCHILEGA

PENN

University of Pennsylvania Press

Philadelphia

10 9 8 7 6 5 4 3 2 1

Published by
University of Pennsylvania Press
Philadelphia, Pennsylvania 19104-4112

Library of Congress Cataloging-in-Publication Data

Bacchilega, Cristina, 1955–
  Legendary Hawai'i and the politics of place: tradition, translation, and tourism /
Cristina Bacchilega.
      p.   cm.
  ISBN-13: 978-0-8122-3975-1 (cloth : alk. paper)
  ISBN-10: 0-8122-3975-X (cloth : alk. paper)
  Includes bibliographical references and index.
  1. Legends—Hawaii—History and criticism.   2. Oral tradition—Hawaii—History
and criticism.   3. Folk literature—Hawaii—History and criticism.   4. Hawaiians—
Folklore. Politics and culture—Hawaii.   5. Culture and tourism—Hawaii.
6. Heritage tourism—Hawaii.   7. Public opinion—Hawaii.   8. Hawaii—Colonization.
9. Hawaii—Folklore.   10. Hawaii—Foreign public opinion.   I. Title
GR110.H38 B33   2007
398.209969—dc22   2006050050

To defiant and loving women
including Shanta and Bruna

Contents

Preface

This could have been, in someone else's mind and hands, a much larger-scale book, along the lines of Paul Lyons's *American Pacificism: Oceania in the U.S. Imagination* (2005) or Vilsoni Hereniko and Rob Wilson's collection *Inside Out: Literature, Cultural Politics, and Identity in the New Pacific* (1999)—projects I very much admire for their capacity to bring knowledge of so many different fields to bear on our understanding of Pacific studies and Oceania, and with which I see an affinity of purpose. The scope and focus of my project are much narrower: I have studied how Hawaiian stories were presented as "legends" in English at the beginning of the twentieth century to promote what I call *legendary Hawai'i*, a construct buttressing—at a crucial time in the history of Hawai'i—those "sanctioned ignorances" that Paul Lyons identifies as having contributed to the "collective or structured 'misrecognition'" of Hawai'i and more generally of Oceanian cultural systems (*American Pacificism*, 8–9).

While this is not a book about Hawaiian legends and I am not of these islands, taking Hawaiian knowledge and epistemology seriously is my starting point, one that enables me to question the persistent popularity of *legendary Hawai'i* today. Thus, learning from a "Hawaiian view," as I trace my own transformation in Chapter 2, is also to counter a "deeply invested ignoring of Oceanian epistemologies, political institutions and forms of cultural and intellectual tradition and performance" that has long inflected Euro-American everyday and scholarly perspectives on the region (*American Pacificism*, 8–9). Learning from Hawaiian narrative tradition and scholarship involves a willingness to acknowledge and unmake a powerfully damaging mistranslation or misrecognition.

Jack Zipes's oeuvre historicizing the genre of the fairy tale, unmasking its mythification, documenting its appropriation of lower-class values and later commodification in mass-culture industry, and highlighting its changing ideological functions within varying sociohistorical contexts and nations is perhaps the most profound inspiration for my methodology and project. But the spotlight in this book is on Hawaiian scholarship—on what we *malihini* (newcomers) can learn from it—because it has too often been dismissed or marginalized from the production of discourses about Hawai'i. "Can one, should one, always take Native scholars at their word, always giving them the last word?" asked an otherwise enthusiastic anonymous reader of an earlier draft of my manuscript. The way I see it, I work hard to give Hawaiian scholars the authority of the "first" word. In a text where Henry Glassie, Mary Louise Pratt, Gayatri Chakravorty Spivak, and Raymond Williams, among others, are also invoked as authorities, this is a challenge of its own—and attending to that tension is important to me on scholarly, personal, and political levels. As far as adjudicating who should have the "last word" about Hawaiian cultural production, that is definitely not within the scope or goals of my project.

What Hawaiian cultural practitioners and scholars have to say about Hawaiian traditions is not monolithic—how could it be? One 'ōlelo no'eau (saying) goes, "Ua lehulehu a manomano ka 'ikena a ka Hawai'i," or "Great and numerous is the knowledge of the Hawaiians" (Pukui 309, no. 2814); another specifies "'A'ohe pau ka 'ike i ka hālau ho'okāhi," or "All knowledge is not taught in the same school" (Pukui 24, no. 203, glossed "One can learn from many sources"). This multiplicity of interpretations and perspectives is evident when we watch the splendid variety of styles at the annual Merrie Monarch hula competition; it is also evident in the self-representation of the great many sovereignty groups in Hawai'i today. But in their insistent and varied performance of Hawaiian knowledge, the different hula hālau (dance schools) participate in the common goal of revitalizing Hawaiian culture and performance art. Similarly, sovereignty is a common goal for very different groups of Hawaiians today, however differently they pursue it. My excavation of the narrative logic and political implications of legendary Hawai'i aims to reinforce the legitimacy of this struggle, not to intervene in the struggles among Hawaiians and within Hawaiian or Pacific studies. From my position, somewhat analogously to men supporting feminism, I seek to be a student and ally. This need not entail taking Hawaiian cultural and scholarly production wholesale as "truth," but it does involve realizing how much is lost by either ignoring it or rescripting it before we malihini even take it seriously.

At the outset of this book is a reflection on place—on how, when, and why we experience a specific location as familiar or unfamiliar—in relation to other places and on the narrative production, in place, of subjectivity as well as social memory and history. In 1997—the year of the 'Īlio'ulaokalani successful protest led by hula practitioners against a state bill that would have limited their customary gathering rights—as I was about to leave for an extended stay in Europe, I received a gift: Anne Kapulani Landgraf's book Nā Wahi Pana O Ko'olau Poko. The friend who gave it to me asked that I take it with me; she must have known how much I'd miss Hawai'i, even though my stay in London and Rome could easily be read as a "return home," and she also knew how much I had—and have—to learn about the place I'd lived in since 1983. Six months later, in Hawai'i and still on sabbatical, I started researching for a paper entitled "Notes Towards Understanding 'Place' in Adaptations of Folk Narratives in Hawai'i," which I delivered in Göttingen at the 1998 International Society for Folk Narrative Research (ISFNR) meeting. From that paper, the presentation I also gave in my department in 1998, and the plenary address I delivered in Melbourne at the 2001 ISFNR meeting, this book project evolved.

Not as consciously, also in 1997, I started a complementary lifelong project by joining Hālau Hula o Maiki, where hula, in the words of founder Maiki Aiu, is defined as "the art of Hawaiian dance expressing all we see, hear, smell, taste, touch and feel." This is a noncompetitive *hālau* led by *kumu hula* (hula teacher) Coline Aiu, one of Maiki's daughters. Thanks to my *kumu*'s teachings, the stories in the songs we learned became actively connected with specific places in my mind—Hi'ilawe Falls in Waipi'o Valley, Pi'ihonua also on the island of Hawai'i, Kīpū Kai and Kō'ula on Kaua'i, Lanihuli in Nu'uanu, O'ahu—and they in turn acquired for me a felt history. So it was and is through my experience of hula that I continue to live most vividly the contrast or tension between my *malihini* sense of nature and landscape and a Hawaiian poetics of place, as well as my desire to acknowledge and understand the latter, both in spirit and action.

Some clarifications about terminology, language use, and diacritics are necessary.

I use Hawaiian and Native Hawaiian interchangeably in the book and as distinctive from Hawai'i-based, "local," *haole* (formerly meaning "any foreigner" and now referring to Caucasians), and *malihini.*

Individual Hawaiian words, such as *malihini* and *mo'olelo,* are italicized in my text. Often they are not italicized in texts by Hawaiians who rightly want to foreground that Hawaiian, *'ōlelo Hawai'i,* is not a foreign language in Hawai'i. However, I expect that Hawaiian will be a foreign language for most readers of this book outside Hawai'i. And, perhaps more to the point, what I know of *'ōlelo Hawai'i* comes from a few classes with *kumu* Carole Silva, hula instruction, *mele,* and reading on my own. Due to no fault of the teachers, I am learning Hawaiian all too slowly and, while I hope to make more time for it, I come to it definitely as a foreign language.

No diacritical marks are used in nineteenth-century Hawaiian-language texts, while it is standard use to include them in contemporary Hawaiian-language writing; following such practice, for instance, *kaao* will be *ka'ao* when I refer to it in my text. When diacritics are not included in a nineteenth or twentieth-century text, I do not add them.

For proper names, I use the more common orthography, whether it includes diacritics or not. In particular, I include no diacritics in Naku-ina so as to allow for multiple understandings of the name.

Chapter 1
Introduction

> [W]hat constitutes "tradition" to a people is ever-changing. . . . The Hawai-
> ian relationship to land has persisted into the present. What has changed is
> ownership and use of the land. . . . Hawaiians assert a "traditional" rela-
> tionship to the land not for political ends, . . . but because they continue to
> believe in the cultural value of caring for the land. That land use is now
> contested makes such a belief political.
>
> —Haunani-Kay Trask

This book focuses on the representation of Hawai'i as a legendary space
in modern and contemporary narratives that, via verbal and visual translation, have adapted Native Hawaiian traditional stories. This is not a
book about Hawaiian legends. It is a study of how Hawaiian stories
labeled as "legends" have been translated to produce a *legendary Hawai'i*
primarily for non-Hawaiian readers or audiences; and it is a study of how
some historical and contemporary Hawaiian counternarratives offer an
invitation to unmake this imaginary construction and re-envision
Hawai'i as an indigenous "storied place." Put differently, this book
documents the uses to which "legendary traditions" have been put to
reinforce a tourist-oriented image of Hawai'i in the twentieth and
twenty-first centuries, and argues for a re-cognition of Hawai'i as sustained by indigenous conceptions of place and genre.

Narrative Tradition

My general task is to investigate narrative tradition within a framework
that rejects the popular understanding that what is "traditional" is conservative and uninventive, and instead considers tradition as an ongoing
"process of cultural construction"—a process situated in the preoccupa-
tions and negotiations of the present, a process where every teller
engages with the past and interprets it so as to affect listeners or readers.
In this view, as folklorist Henry Glassie elucidates, tradition is "the cre-

ation of the future out of the past" (395) so that both responsibility (to the past, community, audience) and creativity (the opportunity to affect change) are active ingredients of any telling.[1]

Let me state from the start that this focus on change in "tradition" is not to be simply equated with the "invention of tradition," which quite apart from its scholarly genesis has in journalistic and popular usage been read as "fakelore" and as such has impacted indigenous peoples in negative ways. Rather, as Glassie points out, tradition is akin to history, both being an "assembly of materials from the past, designed for useful-ness in the future"; and its "continuity" effect is a dynamic, rather than static, aspect of culture: tradition commonly operates and persists via change (395). [2] Tradition is thus "to be understood as a process of cul-tural construction" (398), an *ongoing* process rather than a naturalized inheritance, and one that hinges on the complex negotiations charac-terizing its individual recollections and performances—negotiations that play out both the performer's responsibility to the past as source and the performer's responsibility to the present as audience or partici-pants.

Performance, then, whether it is the retelling of a narrative or the staging of a ritual, is the opportunity for an individual or group to "take control" (404) through an engagement with the past and to act so as to affect the future. Preventing us from reading this opportunity as unbound creativity, Glassie's language, "take control," also alerts us to the power dynamics—political, institutional, social, economic, gen-dered—that are inescapably at stake in the uses we make of both tradi-tion and performance.[3] It follows that the opposite of tradition "is not change but oppression" (396). Historical violence, in other words, is at the core of the rupture of tradition, a rupture that, at the hands of a new power, may take the form of translation (as recontextualization and recodification) or unequivocal suppression. In its record of continuous change, then, tradition is "a key to historical knowledge" (398), a docu-mentable site for a "better history" that speaks "of the engagement of wills, of the interaction among traditions, each fraught with value, all driving toward their different visions of the future" (396).

What guides my investigation is this understanding of tradition, and in particular its relation to colonialism—certainly one of the most sig-nificant violent agents of change on this planet. How does colonialism rupture the (narrative) traditions of colonized and/or indigenous peo-ples? Clearly it others them; at times it violently seeks to erase them; but even in doing so it represents them.[4] In rupturing tradition, colonialism then simultaneously delegitimizes the narratives of the colonized *and* constructs them as representative of the colonized "culture." Scholars in various disciplines, Edward Said, Johannes Fabian, Gayatri Chakravorty Spivak, have convincingly argued that the "culture" of the colonized people is not, however, the origin of this kind of narrative representation, but its effect. To keep that reversal in mind, I believe, makes researching the simultaneously delegitimizing and creative role that colonialism plays in the retelling of tradition a significant tool for undoing the colonial fictions that still shape our social imaginaries. At the same time, researching rupture in the context of change as the operative force of tradition can be a way out of the oppressor/victim dynamic that characterizes some studies of colonialism and dispossesses colonized peoples of agency. How so? By focusing on the dynamics of multiple versions and single performances—just as a literary scholar may focus on carefully contextualized close reading—it is possible to assess change as a negotiation of the performer's position within what Glassie calls "a complex nexus of responsibility" (402) and sociopolitical constraints. In other words, we can attend to the work of resistance and contestation that can inform retelling within colonial, and thus violently conflicted, dynamics of tradition.

I have found this approach to investigating tradition—*within* history and cultural politics and with an eye to the dynamics of change and rupture—helpful as I researched the politics of staging "legendary traditions" in late nineteenth-century and early twentieth-century Hawai'i. Most obviously, I use the phrase "legendary traditions" to acknowledge that, like "myth" and "folktale," "legend"—a narrative that across generations articulates cultural or historical knowledge and poses questions of belief—is commonly identified (and not exclusively by Western disciplines) as a "traditional" genre.[5] But given my preamble, "legendary traditions" is not, of course, to be read as "belonging to the past" or "unchanging." In particular, when inflected by Hawaiian scholar and activist Haunani-Kay Trask's assertion in the epigraph to this chapter, this approach entails being attentive to how the retelling of a "legend"—its performance as a social and artistic act—is not necessarily a "traditional" sign of change, but one of rupture.

This rupture for Hawai'i can be traced to—as Hawaiian historian Jonathan Kay Kamakawiwoʻole Osorio cogently writes—"a story of violence," in which colonialism "worked . . . through a long, insinuating invasion of people, ideas, and institutions" and "literally and figuratively dismembered the *lāhui* (the people) from their traditions, their lands, and ultimately their government" (*Dismembering Lāhui* 3). The "story" of colonialism in Hawai'i may not have been sudden or bloody, but Hawaiians have nevertheless suffered its "violence" and also resisted and protested it. If we focus on the nineteenth century alone, the story of this "disruption" developed through many painful sociopolitical and cultural changes, which included the continued and devastatingly massive

Native Hawaiian depopulation due to post-contact epidemics (Bushnell, *Gifts of Civilization*; Crosby; Silva, *Aloha Betrayed* 24–27; Stannard, *Before the Horror*), the spread of alcoholism, the introduction of new laws that were based on Christian morality and devalued expressions of Hawaiian religious and cultural tradition such as hula, the division and privatization of land (Kameʻeleihiwa, *Native Land and Foreign Desires*), the move to a representational political system, "a systematic destruction of the relationship between chiefs and people" (Osorio 13), the forceful annexation of Hawaiʻi to the United States at the end of the century, and the ensuing process of Americanization.

My goal then is to think through the transformations, ruptures, and negotiations of "legendary traditions" in close relation to issues of displacement in post-annexation Hawaiʻi, a place where to date the question of land rights is inextricably linked with Native Hawaiian sovereignty, where immigration until recently was supporting a plantation economy, and where development—as plantation, militarization, and tourism—puts into jeopardy the very survival of "local" sites.

The annexation of Hawaiʻi as a territory of the United States of America took place in 1898 against the will of the majority of Hawaiians, whose petitions and resistance were to no avail. This annexation followed the 1893 overthrow of the Hawaiian monarchy, a violence for which the 1993 bill signed by President Clinton has officially apologized to the Hawaiian people. Following the overthrow of Queen Liliʻuokalani, missionary descendant Sanford Dole became president of the interim republic, mostly run by Euro-American businessmen. As powerfully documented by Hawaiian political scientist Noenoe Silva in her groundbreaking and detailed study *Aloha Betrayed: Native Hawaiian Resistance to American Colonialism*, there was strong Native resistance to this takeover, a resistance that was ignored until recently by historians and other scholars whose work relied primarily on English-language sources. In a July 3, 1894, speech that Silva translated from the Hawaiian-language newspaper *Ka Leo o ka Lahui* (*The Voice of the Nation*), Hawaiian patriot Joseph Nāwahī had thus articulated his protest against the overthrow and the impending republic: "The house of government belongs to us, just as the Kamehamehas built it. We have been ousted by trespassers who entered our house and who are telling us to go and live in a lei stand that they think to build and force us all into" ("Kanaka Maoli Resistance to Annexation" 54).[6]

What had been already in many ways—cultural, racial, economic, and social—a challenging and complex interaction between the indigenous people of Hawaiʻi and settlers, both European and North American (along with the large numbers of Asians who had come to the islands for work), was sealed certainly by the time of annexation as an unmistakably hierarchical power play in which Native Hawaiians were no longer considered, by the Euro-American businessmen whose interests had become dominant, to be political interlocutors. In 1896, by law the English language became "the medium and basis of instruction in all public and private schools" in Hawai'i (*Laws* 189; Nee-Benham and Heck 102–11), resulting in the elimination of the few remaining Hawaiian-language schools and cutting down a public debate on language and education. Hawaiian petitions against annexation had some impact on the American Senate in early 1898, but were then ignored when Congress—pressured by the volatile situation in Cuba and the Philippines—passed a joint resolution to annex Hawai'i. Hawaiian lands were ceded to the United States without any vote taken among Hawaiians or Asian immigrants, the largest population groups on the islands.[7] "Hawaiians," Haunani-Kay Trask writes, "suffered a unilateral redefinition of our homeland and our people, a displacement and dispossession in our country. In familial terms, our mother (and thus our heritage and our inheritance) was taken away from us. We were orphaned in our own land. . . . As a result of these actions, Hawaiians became a conquered people, our lands and culture subordinated to another nation."[8]

Legendary Hawai'i and the Politics of Place

There is no need for me to politicize cultural production about and in Hawai'i: the colonization of Hawai'i does it for me. It follows that attending to the political and ideological dynamics of this colonization is both necessary and enabling when analyzing cultural and narrative production. Specifically, annexation politics and ideology are inextricably linked with the construction of what I am calling *legendary Hawai'i*, a cultural product that, I argue, is not to be simply equated with Hawaiian "legendary traditions." Thus, a large part of this book documents how, after annexation, Hawaiian *mo'olelo*, or connected (hi)stories that were identified as "legends," served—like raw materials—to imagine and market within popular and scholarly venues a new product, *legendary Hawai'i*: a space constructed for non-Hawaiians (and especially Americans) to experience, via Hawaiian legends, a Hawai'i that is exotic and primitive while beautiful and welcoming. This new product of the imagination was at the turn of the twentieth century valorized through the ubiquitous colonial practice of translation and the new technology of photography. And, most crucially, it was the budding tourist industry of the territory of Hawai'i that motivated, shaped, and sustained the production of this *legendary Hawai'i* especially for the benefit of American tourists and potential settlers. If (linguistic and media) translation is the modus operandi of the immediately post-annexation cultural phenome-

non I am calling *legendary Hawai'i*, the novelty of photography provides it
with a technological edge (while visually translating many of its narrative
topoi), and tourism is its economic and ideological motor.

Late nineteenth- and early twentieth-century English-language translations of Hawaiian *mo'olelo* and the uses of photography in these collections of "legends" to promote Hawai'i as a tourist destination are my
central focus of analysis (Introduction, Chapters 3 and 4). I do not mean
to identify *legendary Hawai'i* as a cultural production exclusively *by* non-
Hawaiians or *only for* non-Hawaiians, but to delineate how as a cultural
product it served primarily non-Hawaiian interests at a crucial political
juncture.

Later chapters—4 and 5 especially—raise issues of agency and performance in ways that should complicate a simple colonizer/colonized
dichotomy and grapple more closely with the complex dynamics of
power and knowledge as well as continuity and discontinuity in a colonial context. As Silva documents, from the eighteenth century on,
Hawaiians "often took the tools of the colonizers and made use of them
to secure their own national sovereignty and well-being" (*Aloha Betrayed*
15–16). I do sketch in Chapter 5 some transformations of Hawaiian "legendary traditions" in the nineteenth century to show how Hawaiians
exercised agency and creativity in print: the technologies of writing and
print had changed Hawaiian *mo'olelo*, but not disrupted and dislocated
them in the ways that the production of *legendary Hawai'i* would. And I
do examine two, very different from one another, recent twentieth-
century performances of Hawai'i's "legendary traditions": Anne Kapulani Landgraf's Hawaiian-centered view of "storied places" and Glen
Grant's representation of a multicultural "supernatural" Hawai'i—the
first powerfully countering *legendary Hawai'i* and the other adapting it to
the 1990s. But the core of this study is the examination of how the production of post-annexation Hawaiian legends in English delegitimizes
Hawaiian narratives and traditions *and* at the same time constructs them
as representative of Hawaiian "culture." This is not to say that all of
these narratives simply did the bidding of the tourist industry.

To pursue a documentation of Native Hawaiians' continued resistance
and contestation against their colonial representation, it is important to
identify and discuss within the varied performances of *legendary Hawai'i*
what Mary Louise Pratt calls "autoethnographic expression," that is,
"instances in which colonized subjects undertake to represent themselves in ways that *engage with* the colonizer's own terms" (*Imperial Eyes*
7). Today, thanks to the Hawaiian Renaissance that began in the 1970s
and the ongoing sovereignty movement, this resistance is more clearly
in the public eye, and strong re-visionary artistic practices animate much
of the Hawaiian literary, visual, and performance arts—but this resis-

tance never had subsided.[9] Ample evidence is to be found in Hawaiian-language sources, but scholarship resting on what Marvin Puakea Nogelmeier labels a "discourse of sufficiency" has often dismissed it in favor of a very limited selection of nineteenth-century Hawaiian documents that have in English translation been canonized to represent "Hawaiian culture."[10]

While I discuss only a few Hawaiian-language narratives, in this study, Emma Kaili Metcalf Beckley Nakuina's stories (1904) and Anne Kapulani Landgraf's photography (1994) serve as the primary examples or performances of a Hawaiian autoethnographic "legendary tradition" that articulates the tradition of *moʻolelo* and centers on "storied place." *Moʻolelo* most basically is a story, or a sequence of stories, but its social uses and artistic protocols signal the workings of Hawaiian epistemology and connect it with history. As per Lorrin Andrews's 1865 *Dictionary of the Hawaiian Language*, history, connected story, and tradition are all part of a Hawaiian understanding of *moʻolelo* or *moʻo-ʻōlelo*.[11] Today, for Osorio—a historian who articulates his project as writing *moʻolelo*—*moʻolelo* "literally, . . . means a fragment of a story" (250), not the whole story, but one located in the teller's/writer's history and yet participating in his people's larger history ("Our history owns us, shapes and contextualizes us," ix). Originating from *moʻo* and *ʻōlelo* (meaning "connected story" [Andrews 399] or "succession of talk" [Pukui and Elbert, *Hawaiian Dictionary* 254]), *moʻolelo* translates into English as "story" and "history" both; "tradition" and "literature"; specific modes of storytelling including "myth," "legend," "fable," "yarn"; and specific approaches to recording events including "journal," "essay," "chronicle," and "minutes" (Pukui and Elbert *Hawaiian Dictionary* 254). The relationship between the *ʻōlelo* (word) and the *moʻo*—as "succession," "generational line," "ridge" and "lizard," or "dragon," as well as "small fragment" or "narrow path" (Pukui and Elbert *Hawaiian Dictionary* 253)—is mutually constitutive and metonymically encapsulates the connection in Hawaiian thought of genealogy, land, and (hi)story. Furthermore, as the embodiment in some cases of a transformed *moʻo*, or dragonlike lizard, "ridge" suggests the emplacement of story. In this study, Emma Nakuina's work documents the affirmation of Native genre, authority, and place-centered knowledge in a now regrettably obscure early twentieth-century English-language publication. Landgraf's bilingual and multimedia text projects "legendary traditions" into the present in artistically and politically transformative ways that bring the *moʻo* into view. In fact, Landgraf's artistic intervention enables and frames my own readings of *legendary Hawaiʻi*; and this re-framing is necessary because even nowadays the dominant representations of Hawaiʻi are not "autoethnographic" or centered on a Hawaiian view of "storied place."

In the process of analyzing the historical production of *legendary Hawai'i* and its counternarratives, I will focus on the dynamic of "space" versus "place" as applicable to two related problematics: the making of Hawai'i itself into a legendary space for the benefit of post-annexation tourism; and the translation of narratives about Hawai'i's *wahi pana*, or "storied places," in print. By documenting the disruptive force of the former and the varied effects of the latter, I aim to work at the intersections of the politics of narrative and the politics of place.[12]

Focusing on the representation of "place" makes sense methodologically. In most, if not all Hawaiian *mo'olelo*, "place" situates events, heroes, tellers and listeners, memories and emotions in ways that connect the creation and transformation of landmarks with familial or genealogical relations. Indeed, animated, specific, and emotionally charged localization is the backbone (not the descriptive ornamentation) of Native Hawaiian narrative traditions. Furthermore, place continues to be at the heart of twentieth- and twenty-first-century *mele* (poetic song) and hula compositions, contemporary Native literature—as most evident in the issues of *'Ōiwi: A Native Hawaiian Journal*—and, though conceptualized differently, of Hawai'i's multiethnic literatures (to the point that many refer to "local" literature). And, within a Western classification of traditional narratives, "place" is a distinctive feature of the "legend." But the focus on how "the affective bond between people and place" (Tuan 4) needs "to be understood through the lens of social and cultural conflict" (Cresswell 29) takes priority for me also because historically Hawai'i has been, since contact with the West, violently translated into an exotic landscape that has provided a (self-)redemptive site for missionaries, raw materials (sugar most prominently) for enterprising colonialists, an *aloha*-filled paradise for moderately adventurous tourists, and a real-estate playing field for both state and global economies. The post-annexation construction of a *legendary Hawai'i*, I will argue, has played an important ideological role in enabling and perpetuating this violence—a symbolic one that nevertheless has real consequences.[13] Thus, while the process of endowing place with special meanings is universal, I believe that the charged conflictuality of meanings that continues to inform the narrative representation of *legendary Hawai'i* today calls for a historicizing and passionately intellectual—in the Gramscian sense—exploration.

Disciplinary Responsibilities: Folklore and Literature

Such an exploration involves not only explaining my use of concepts such as tradition, legend, *mo'olelo*, and place, but reflecting on my investigative framework and terminology. Is a "folklore and literature" approach appropriate when considering Hawaiian narratives and more generally literary and cultural production about Hawai'i that purports to adapt Native genres? I intend to keep this question active throughout the book. To consider colonialism as an agent of rupture in Hawaiian narrative traditions, as I proposed in the beginning of this introduction, constitutes the first step in addressing this question. But there are specific problems with using the categories of "folklore" and "literature" that I must also take into serious consideration.

We know that, historically, both folklore and literary studies have been and are active participants in the discursive formation and consolidation of nation-states. The discipline of American folkloristics in particular—as it emerged officially in 1888 in the United States—was obviously implicated in the knowledge we have of Hawaiian culture and, almost indistinguishably, its past as a nation. The study of British and American literature in Hawai'i's educational system has just as obviously served important purposes of acculturation against which many Hawai'i-based writers have rebelled especially since the 1970s. This kind of complicity is to be productively investigated, but it does not release those of us who have been trained as scholars in European and American folkloristics and literary studies from these disciplines. This, then, is my attempt, as a scholar of folklore and literature, to take on the challenge of working from within this framework to reevaluate and reorient it.

Naming—always already a renaming—has been a powerful tool of colonial rule and cultural appropriation. From early on, Native Hawaiian narratives, or *mo'olelo*, were for the most part identified by Western travelers, scholars, and popularizers as "legends," or "myths" and "folktales" interchangeably, and thus seen as "folklore," a newly formed category in European and American nineteenth-century thought. Because "folklore" was and is often viewed in the science-centered West as an outmoded or "false" way of knowing, this classification has unfortunately also provided an opening to view the *mo'olelo* as "untrue." As belief narratives, legends and myths maintain a relationship with history for scholars, but more generally "legend" is interpreted as fanciful or undocumented history. This has resulted in erasing the meaning of "history" carried in the Hawaiian word and genre, with *mo'olelo* being translated and understood only or primarily as "story."

This dismissive use of the term "folklore" is rightly suspect among Native Hawaiians and colonized peoples in general, and my study seeks to work against it. In commenting on how nineteenth-century Hawaiian historian Samuel Mānaiakalani Kamakau uses "*mo'olelo*," Nogelmeier notes that it "is a single concept in Hawaiian conveying multiple meanings, encompassing what in English would be considered as history, ethnography, myth, legend, account, description, tradition" (193). Within this epistemological framework, then, it makes sense nowadays for Hawaiian historian Osorio to write his history of the "dismemberment" of the Hawaiian nation in the shape and name of *mo'olelo* as (hi)story. Similarly, Lilikalā Kameʻeleihiwa's history of the privatization of land *Native Land and Foreign Desires: Pehea Lā E Pono Ai?* begins with *mo'olelo* to reframe her readers' understanding of Native Hawaiians in relation to their land. And Noenoe Silva turns to the *mo'olelo* in nineteenth-century Hawaiian-language newspapers to document how these narratives, for instance "He Moolelo no Hiiakaikapoliopele" (The legend of Hiʻiakai-kapoliopele), asserted Hawaiian epistemology in the face of the mission-aries' dismissal of their knowledge as savagery and ignorance (*Aloha Betrayed* 58–59, 76–79, and passim). *Mo'olelo* tells history in ways that Western scholars like myself need to learn to recognize, hear, and listen to.

Mo'olelo is thus a significant counternarrative to "folklore" in its popu-larized and belittling meaning, but for me to do away with the label "folklore" entirely could entail an a priori dismissal of the historical role it has played in facilitating the appropriation of these *mo'olelo* narratives for what I have called *legendary Hawaiʻi*. For instance, as Noenoe Silva and Kuʻualoha Hoʻomanawanui have pointed out, approaching Hawai-ian narratives as "folklore" in the nineteenth century meant that collec-tors and translators like Nathaniel B. Emerson could dismiss issues of authorship and lump Hawaiian tellers as anonymous "native infor-mants" ("This Land").[14] Though the Hiʻiaka *mo'olelo* I just referred to was signed by M. J. Kapihenui of Kailua, Koʻolaupoko, Oʻahu, Emerson's 1915 *Pele and Hiiaka: A Myth from Hawaii* could rely heavily on it without crediting Kapihenui (Silva, *Aloha Betrayed* 77) precisely because the folk-loric labels of "myth" and "legend" bring with them the assumption of anonymity. It is thus worth exploring such dynamics and investigating the historical role of "folklore" and amateur "folklorists" in Hawaiʻi.

Some Pacific writers and scholars have proposed "orature" as an alter-native indigenous paradigm to "folklore" (though still highlighting "mythology" within it). Since my study deals with Western as well as Native cultural productions in a "contact zone" and my primary focus is on unmaking a *legendary Hawaiʻi* produced for non-Hawaiian readers or audiences, I have not done away with "folklore": juxtaposing it to the *mo'olelo*, and "legends" to *wahi pana* (storied places), enables me to dis-cuss narratives within both frameworks and to foreground their histori-cal strife. I am not arguing against the frameworks of "orature" or "oral literature."[15] Rather, I want to push at the seams of "folklore"—in the case of Hawaiʻi both a colonial construct and a form of verbal expression that is not narrowly "literature" in its Western and dominant meaning. Perhaps I am working to turn the tools of folkloristics against some of the expropriative uses they have been put to. Certainly, I am working to document that appropriation. And, being attentive to performance— the creative, contestatory, and at times subversive, dimensions of folk-lore—I am also seeking to document or recover sites of resistance to the forces of Americanization and tourism that were the engine of this appropriation in the twentieth century.

Why talk about "folklore and literature" in discussing what I have described as the multimedia production of *legendary Hawai'i* and the retelling of Hawai'i's storied places? Some may have chosen to label all the narratives I am about to discuss as "folklore" either in its popular meaning of "untruth" or in its association with a cultural past that stands for tradition. But it is not (lack of) authenticity as such that I am pursuing. Folklorists increasingly acknowledge the "need to see how folklore is re-situated in a vast number of nonfolk contexts" (de Caro and Jordan 272) where it serves a range of interests. If as a "contact zone," Hawai'i has been "the space of colonial encounters, the space in which peoples geographically and historically separated come into con-tact with each other and establish ongoing relations, usually involving conditions of coercion, radical inequality, and intractable conflict" (Pratt, *Imperial Eyes* 6), within it the search for "authenticity" as such has been arguably more a symptom of the newcomer's or researcher's assumptions and anxieties than anything else.[16] These are not my tradi-tions and I have only rudimentary knowledge of the Hawaiian language.

Others may have chosen to label all the narratives I am about to dis-cuss as "literature" either in its older European meaning of "all printed matter," or in the framework of "oral literature" and "literature in per-formance." But there is much to be gained, I hope to show, from not reaching for "literature" as an umbrella term before having *worked* the differences that mark—socially and artistically—"folklore" from "litera-ture" and, methodologically, "folkloristics" from Western "literary studies."

Far from suggesting the autonomy of textual fields or disciplines, I would argue for an intertextuality that does not ignore how social func-tion and status play out in today's predominant understanding of what makes "literature." While marked by the creative agency and talent of individual tellers, "traditional" narratives function as part of a group (though not necessarily anonymous) repertoire and are often seen as articulating some form of accepted knowledge.[17] While also belonging to historical traditions, novels, poems, and essays are "literature" that bears the copyright mark and grants a special aura to "authorship." Thus, I am arguing for this differentiation in order to explore works of the imagination in ways that will not be limited by a strictly modern and Western definition of literature that often extols creativity as exceptional and purely individual. Surely, it is repetition that ensures the survival of legends: this is the "traditional" dimension of folklore, its always already "secondhand" or collective status once an individual's creativity is accepted and shared; at the same time, as noted earlier, every perform- ance or folklore "text" is an event that plays out specific social and artis- tic dynamics. It is this interplay of repetition and variation, or tradition and creativity, that folklore studies have been attentive to, especially in the last thirty some years; and, when researching—as I am—changes within a legendary tradition, this experience matters and can be produc- tively tapped into.

Two among the methodological tenets of modern Western folkloris- tics should be recognizable throughout this book: folklorists consider the multiplicity of versions through which any "one" narrative is experi- enced; and we foreground the performance and performative elements that make an individual telling "emergent, the product of the complex interplay of expressive resources, social goals, individual competence, community ground rules for performance, and culturally defined event structures" (Bauman, "Conceptions of Folklore" 13–14).[18] Two among the tenets of modern literary theory equally come into play: literary scholars read a text not as an insulated creative act, but as framed by specific institutions—including that of literature itself—and more gen- erally sociocultural and historical dynamics; and we explore fiction as an argument and the breakdown of that argument. Combined, the perspec- tives of folklore and literature support a consideration of texts in inter- textual conversation with one another and as located in their production and (re)telling/(re)reading, that is, tradition and history. This interdisciplinary perspective works to foreground the dynamics of performance and ideology in both folklore and literature. It seeks to rec- ognize a "web of intertextuality" where folklore is not set apart from literature and, at the same time, the social, historical, and artistic differ- ences between folklore and literature are not erased.[19]

Adopting this kind of folklore and literature perspective to pursue an understanding of narrative tradition within the politics of culture then allows me to take advantage of tools offered by performance-oriented folkloristics, located theories of literary narrative, and close reading. Centered on communicative *events* as well as correcting the misconcep- tion that "folklore" is exclusively preliterate or anonymous and that "lit- erature" is limited to Western genres and stylistics, this folklore and literature approach also makes for productive engagement with the diverse narrative media (orality, print, and image) through which *legend- ary Hawai'i* and Hawaiian "storied places" have been and are claimed.

To take a self-reflexive approach to folklore & literature in a colonial context involves denaturalizing the analytical tools of the disciplinary trade. In seeking to reach for or move toward an understanding of Hawaiian "storied place," I problematize "visual illustration" (Chapter 2) and "localization" (Chapter 5). Another structuring category of Western narrative, "time," comes into play in my observations of how pervasive the "ethnographic present" (Fabian) is in *legendary Hawai'i*, but also in the realization that the "from primitivism to civilization" narrative of development that structures early promotions of *legendary Hawai'i* is not only alien but counter to the Hawaiian perspective on the relationship of the present to the past and the future (Chapters 3). And I resist a homogenizing view of "collectivity" by insisting on a close reading of how the writer Emma Nakuina negotiates her responsibilities when it comes to ethnographic knowledge and family history (Chapter 4).

Overall, my ambition is threefold: to pursue the possibilities of reflexive folklore and literary studies as relevant to a specifically contested politics of place and tradition; to read the production of *legendary Hawai'i* and autoethnographic representations of Hawai'i's "storied places" as emplaced *events* themselves so as to articulate the multiplicity of their sociopolitical meanings and artistry without falling into a dehistoricized, flattening pluralism; and to contribute an analysis of works of the imagination that can also resonate within political land struggles in Hawai'i and more general ideological and institutional controversies, thus refusing to locate folklore or literature in an ahistorical and apolitical realm.

Translation Tales: Tourism and Photography

In the process of a historical documentation of *legendary Hawai'i*, three modes of cultural production emerge as important sites of investigation: translation, from the Hawaiian language into English, but also from one culture to another, from one genre to another, and from one medium to another; photography, as the technology that foremost contributed to the initial formation of a Westernized imaging of *legendary Hawai'i*; and tourism, as a determining post-annexation economic and ideological machinery of development.

Even though "translation studies" came officially into being as a discipline only in 1978, translation has been practiced and debated over for centuries, and is operative every day in our lives, often in ways that we do not stop to consider.[20] Translation facilitates communication, but is not synonymous with it. I may know this, but like many I find it more efficient and reassuring to go through my day as if translation and its problems were invisible. The discipline of translation studies, as described by pioneering scholars André Lefevere and Susan Bassnett, counters such a utilitarian approach to translation and considers, from a variety of perspectives, its intra- and intercultural dynamics. Since translation studies is a rich and rather fragmented field, my focus here is on what I understand as an emergent project within it: a critical intervention into the politics of *colonial* translation, considered in its production and reception as well as its linguistic, cultural, and institutional contexts. Within this project, thanks especially to the work of Gayatri Chakravorty Spivak and Lawrence Venuti, colonial and postcolonial uses of translation have become an important site for analysis, and this analysis in turn has affected the questions asked within the discipline at large. I will point here to three working ideas taken from these developments in translation studies that have helped me to understand post-annexation translations of *moʻolelo* into English-language "legends."

First, as Venuti synthesizes and several individual studies have shown, "Although the history of colonialism varies significantly according to place and period, it does reveal a consistent, no, an inevitable reliance on translation" (*Scandals of Translation* 165). As missionaries, administrators, educators, and anthropologists translated the texts of the colonized, these translated texts discursively strengthened colonial governments and constructed representations of the colonized subject that justified the "civilizing" project of the colonial power.[21] Such translations "enact a process of identity formation in which colonizer and colonized . . . are positioned unequally" (Venuti, *Scandals* 165). Often perceived as faithful or innocent documentation paradoxically *because* they are translations, these texts go unquestioned in the Western context and become the dominant representations of colonized peoples. I am using the present tense because, as my reading of *legendary Hawaiʻi* will confirm, the power of these translations—even if they originated in the nineteenth or early twentieth centuries—is still with us. Several consequences follow: authoritative Western translators become known as "experts" in non-Western cultures—their customs or literatures—while Natives are recognized as "informants" only; texts selected for translation become canonical and determine the construction of non-Western literary traditions and, by extension, comparative literature; the translated texts that form these selective "indigenous literary traditions" are often devoid of political content or strife.[22]

Second, because Western and non-Western languages are not equal, what Gayatri Spivak calls "translation-as-violation" (*Critique of Postcolonial Reason* 162) is operative in moving from the colonized or Native language to that of the colonizer. This violation operates in stark contrast with the faithfulness versus freedom debate that dominated early and Renaissance translation in Europe because on either side of the argument the authority or complexity of the original "classic" language and text was assumed. With translation from colonized languages, it is instead common for the target language—English in the cases I discuss—to dictate its cultural logic. The rewriting that all translation involves is thus driven in colonial translation by a discursive strategy of containment or domestication that requires re-writing the other in the dominant language's terms.[23] This violation is "epistemic" in that the colonized or Native world is recodified in terms of the colonizers'.[24] Within the discipline of folkloristics, Lee Haring has critically documented, in early twentieth-century French translations, the "reframing" of Malagasy narratives into a different generic shape. "What the west calls myth has no genre attached to it" in this region, he writes, but Western researchers took "the privilege of naming certain narratives as myth" (Haring 191 and 192). In folklore as in literature, this recoding has significant implications, and that is why I have been referring to Hawaiian "legend" in quotation marks: the early twentieth-century translation of *moʻolelo* (history *and* story) into "legend"—sliding into "myth" and "folktale," and away from "history" and knowledge— exemplifies this domesticating interpretive strategy.

Third, the violence of colonial translation was never successful in its totality. Translation was not a one-way street in nineteenth-century Hawaiʻi, where highly literate Hawaiians translated all kinds of foreign texts for Hawaiian-language newspapers. Their selections and strategies are symptomatic of a Hawaiian agency that is otherwise obfuscated. To identify the localized dynamics of translated texts and agency in colonial contexts helps to correct what Eric Cheyfitz calls "a foreign politics of forgetfulness" and undo the workings of that insidious narrative politics in the present.[25] Thus, attending not only to the logic, publishing history, and institutional uses, but also to the rhetoric of translations into the colonial language can be particularly productive if one's reading strategy is to seek the "remainder." This is what Venuti sees as the staging of linguistic, cultural, and generic power relationships in a translated text; it is "a clue to the workings of gendered [and indigenous] agency," what Spivak articulates as the "disruption of figuration in social practice" ("The Politics of Translation" 179, 187).[26]

In contrast to the "fluent" one, the translation that "releases the remainder" is "demystifying" in that it opens itself to the incursion of the foreign, "the substandard and the marginal" (Venuti, *Scandals of Translation* 10, 11), even if this foreignness is *within* the "domestic" culture or language. "Cultivating a heterogeneous discourse . . . does not so much prevent the assimilation of the foreign text as aim to signify the autonomous existence of that text behind (yet by means of) the assimilative process of the translation" (*Scandals* 11). Spivak's practice and theory have for a long time now been similarly advocating a translation that, by bearing traces of "the protocols of a text—not the general laws of the language, but the laws specific to this text" ("Translating into English"

94), would invite the reader "to push through to the original" (95). The reading dynamics of intimacy, love, and responsibility that Spivak names as the core of the translator's task—and significantly for her "becoming-human is an incessant economy of translation" ("Questioned on Translation: Adrift" 14)—are hardly the stuff of "translatese," but they do work toward being "able to discriminate on the terrain of the original" ("The Politics of Translation" 189). In my understanding, Spivak and Venuti offer no guarantee for the successful communication of an indigenous or "Third World" woman's text through these translation and reading practices. Rather translation itself is further problematized, not in the service of a hopeless untranslatability but of an ethics of reading—for the translator and for the reader of translations—that reaches toward learning (from) the language and "protocols" of the other. I have found this approach particularly useful in reading *Hawaii: Its People, Their Legends*, published by Emma Nakuina in 1904, since this Hawaiian woman's rather obscure collection bears the marks of *moʻolelo* in sharp contrast to the colonial and better-known translations of Thomas G. Thrum and William D. Westervelt. Thus, I read her translations for clues of Native and gendered agency that defy *legendary Hawaiʻi*.

Thinking about translation in these critical *and* utopian ways is useful while I seek to explore and resist the culture of tourism as it has affected the representation of Hawaiʻi. As Dean MacCannell put it in 1992, "tourism is not just an aggregate of merely commercial activities; it is also an ideological framing of history, nature, and tradition; a framing that has the power to reshape culture and nature to its own needs" (*Empty Meeting Grounds* 1). Tourism operates as a form of translation. Within this frame, "tourism stages the world as a museum of itself" (Kirshenblatt-Gimblett, *Destination Culture* 7) in which the tourist is encouraged to perceive everything as a sign of itself.[27] Through building up what makes a place different from the tourist's habitual space and often through putting on display "heritage," that mode of cultural production that Barbara Kirshenblatt-Gimblett defines as "the transvaluation of the obsolete, . . . the outmoded, the dead," tourism seeks to "convert a location into a destination" (*Destination Culture* 148, 7). This is a form of translation that, rather than attending to the protocols that are "in place," often thrives on visual and verbal performances of "hereness" or "staged authenticity" that collectively—thanks to advertisements, literature, performances—reinforce the "destination image" of that culture or place for the purposes of export.[28]

As identified in studies of tourism, a "destination image" is "a set of visuals and ideas associated in the tourist's mind with a particular locale, and it acts both as a lure for potential customers and as a framework for perception and evaluation of the tourist's experience once she or he is on site."[29] The ingredients of a "destination image" provide locations that are potential "getaways" or "escapes" with distinctive and thus competitive features (Kirshenblatt-Gimblett, *Destination Culture* 152–53). For Jane C. Desmond, whose book *Staging Tourism* focuses on the initial phases of the tourist industry in Hawai'i, that "destination image" for Hawai'i is best identified with the "hula girl," "the most ubiquitous symbol of Hawaiian culture" (xxii). It's hard to disagree, and Haunani-Kay Trask had already powerfully named this metonymy in her 1991/1992 groundbreaking essay "'Lovely Hula Hands': Corporate Tourism and the Prostitution of Hawaiian Culture."[30] In Trask's words: "Mostly a state of mind, Hawai'i is the image of escape from the rawness and violence of daily American life. Hawai'i—the word, the vision, the sound in the mind—is the fragrance and feel of soft kindness. Above all, Hawai'i is 'she,' the Western image of the Native 'female' in her magical allure. . . . Thus, Hawai'i, like a lovely woman, is there for the taking" (*From a Native Daughter* 136, 144). While Desmond documents the development of tourism in the early twentieth century, Trask presents striking statistics and facts to bring into view the manufacturing of a "soft" image of Hawai'i for corporate profit and its contrast with as well as impact on the "hard, ugly, and cruel" life that Native Hawaiians face in the "political, economic, and cultural reality" of the 1990s (137). She also recognizes that "many Hawaiians do not see tourism as part of their colonization" (145). Similarly I must recognize that in-class discussion of this essay has often begun with how off-putting Trask's request is: "If you are thinking of visiting my homeland, please do not" (146).[31] But it is important for that first reaction not to be legitimized as the final one. For isn't saying "no" to corporate tourism and its sale of "heritage" and land just as right as it is for a woman or any human being to say "no" to intrusion, commodification, or rape?

I am not saying that tourism can only oppress Native peoples or that there is no room for negotiation and creative agency as Native Hawaiians participate in the display of their culture. Hardly confined to commercial venues, hula, with its many *hālau*, or schools, plays—and has played—an important role not only in preserving and cultivating Hawaiian language and narrative traditions, but in authorizing a culture of Native resistance based on the habitus that comes from transmission of specific cultural competencies and the practice of embodied performances.[32] Nevertheless, tourists remain often ignorant of these talents and of their political edge, while the metonymic image of the "hula girl" continues to lure them into the potential of an exotic and sweet romance.[33] While she offers a complex narrative of its developments, historicizing the emergence of the "hula girl" image is only a small part of Desmond's project when she notes that "In the earliest period of the fledgling tourist industry, natural features of the islands, like volcanoes, were most heavily promoted. The place, not the people, predominated. However, the figure of the hula girl first appeared in advertising in the teens, and, by the twenties, images of Native Hawaiians and specifically hula iconography had become an integral part of tourist promotions" (6).[34] Lynn A. Davis points out that in the early twentieth century, "the lei sellers were the most frequently reproduced image of Hawaiian women in promotional publications. The hula girl, although common in early postcards, was not featured until the 1930s" ("Photographically Illustrated Books About Hawai'i, 1854–1945" 290). My point, as I will make it in the ensuing chapters, is that *legendary Hawai'i*—and not simply Hawai'i's "natural features"—is the antecedent and supplement of the "hula girl," the backdrop against which her performance is loosely placed and justified as "culture" even when it is commodified "entertainment for sale."

What surely has emerged in the very language of my discussion of tourism is the role that story or narrative plays in it. As Regina Bendix puts it, "any advertisement is ultimately a quick story, offering just enough imagery and text for the viewer or reader to insert themselves as potential buyers" ("Capitalizing on Memories Past, Present, and Future" 474–75). Narration frames our expectations as tourists, anticipating our longings and constructing our experience, *and* offers—in the personal stories of individual tourists—the potential for unique recovery and transformation of that experience, which of course also lends itself to commodification once it is communicated.[35] It is important to examine the narrative component of tourism because this most powerful industry "needs to supply a great deal of material satisfaction," but "what ultimately carries the business is the *intangible experience* of the customer" (Bendix, "Capitalizing on Memories" 471). As Trask remarks of Hawai'i as a tourist destination—being on holiday is largely "a state of mind." The English-language publication of 4,000 copies of the first *Hawaiian Guide Book, for Travelers* by Henry M. Whitney dates to 1875. A "search for authenticity," to be understood here as the "probing comparison between self and Other" (Bendix, *In Search of Authenticity* 17), on the one hand, and the new political status of Hawai'i as a territory of the United States, on the other, contribute at the turn of the twentieth century to the rapid multiplying of narratives promoting Hawai'i as a destination site. These narratives were particularly prominent in the *Paradise of the Pacific* magazine and the *Hawaiian Annual* that began circulating in the late nineteenth century, and they were naturally the stuff of the booklets and advertisements of the Hawaii Promotion Committee first formed in 1903. I will be examining their role in the production of a *legendary Hawai'i* for tourists.

But stories were not alone in impacting potential tourists: it is not acci-
dental that the first publisher of *Paradise of the Pacific* was a commercial
photographer, James J. Williams, since during that period Hawai'i and
Native Hawaiians were mostly introduced to people outside of Hawai'i
through visual representations, especially photographic ones. Colonial
photography is another form of translation, a particularly powerful one
because at the time it was a novelty. If in the second half of the nineteenth century "the ability of the camera to bring the world back home
astonished, excited and enthralled" Europeans and Americans, it is also
true that "photography became a lynchpin in the trade in foreignness
and fuelled the new discourses of the other—from anthropology and
ethnography to popular accounts of travel and colonial life" (McQuire
193). During a particularly aggressive phase of European and American
expansionism both south and east, photographs of Native and colonized
peoples circulated in the public sphere as part of "scientific" presenta-
tions, international exhibitions, and pornographic sales, thus traveling
widely but primarily one way toward the north and the west, and often
ending up in private albums and collections in Europe and the United
States of America. As postcards especially, they moved across oceans and
social contexts to foster "civilizing" missions and later tourism via the
titillation of the individual's visual imagination and desires. In *Colonial
Photography & Exhibitions: Representations of the "Native" and the Making
of European Identity*, Anne Maxwell has documented how, together with
international exhibits, colonial photography "was in the business of confirming and reproducing the racial theories and stereotypes that assisted
European expansionism" (9) and focused on how colonized peoples
were represented differently depending on varying sociopolitical
agendas in the colonizing countries.[36] She has also emphasized how in
contrast to exhibitions, "photographs of the colonized encompassed a
wide range of forms and genres" (cartes-de-visite, daguerreotypes, collo-
types, postcards, stereocards, travel photos, portraiture, ethnology) and
"sustained a greater variety of ideological positions" that could be a
function not only of the photographer's politics, but the "consumers'
interpretation of images" and "the maker's own relationship to the
dominant culture" (9).

By employing "reductive tropes," most anthropological and commercial photographs of Native peoples produced during that time
"uph[eld] the binary opposition of civility versus savagery" (Maxwell
14). This is not to say that savages or primitives were all alike, and in fact
the theory of cultural evolution that was dominant then depended on
their documentation and classification, but that overall these images fed
Europeans' and Euro-Americans' sense of righteous superiority, erotic
fantasies, and commercial or political expansionism. What is distinctive

about photography as a new technology in the nineteenth and early twentieth centuries when we focus on the representation of Hawai'i and Native Hawaiians? I will in later chapters be discussing the visual topoi of this othering in photographs of Native Hawaiians that illustrate "legends" at the turn of the twentieth century. But I will note here that these photographs already project the "soft" image of Hawaiians that Trask protests and that continues to support in a number of ways the development of the tourist industry in Hawai'i.[37]

What also matters is that these stereotypical images were accepted as "real." The wide circulation of colonial images and the excitement with which they met in the West depended not only on their novelty but their truth value: photographs "were widely believed to offer an accurate visual record of life in the colonies" (Maxwell 11).[38] Photographs of faraway places and peoples were thus seen to provide more powerful "evidence" than words, and their coded realism was read as mechanical or objective reproduction. The visible became a privileged source of information and representation in the new era of "visual culture" as pioneered by photography. Those who sought to promote Hawai'i to potential settlers and tourists immediately recognized the power of the image. While photographs of Hawai'i were displayed as early as in 1873 at the international exhibit in Vienna, in 1893—the year of the Hawaiian monarchy's overthrow—the World Colombian Exposition in Chicago featured a "Hawaii Exhibit" with a cyclorama, hula dancers, and picture postcards. The widely circulating magazine *Paradise of the Pacific* featured halftone reproductions starting in 1894 and so did even the earliest brochures and booklets produced by the Hawaii Promotion Committee in 1903. Since within printed texts, a certain "disjuncture between text and image" (Desmond 40) is not uncommon, I will be considering how the authority of photographic images played out in relation to the narrative text of these publications—whether and how it was articulated, what its effects in relation to the representation of Hawai'i and Hawaiians could be, and how it played a distinctive role in relation to "legends."

Lynn A. Davis has pointed out that the "politically tumultuous period" from the 1893 overthrow to 1900 when the powers of the interim republic were transferred to the annexed Territory of Hawai'i "coincided with a development of printing technology that, for the first time, made it possible to reproduce easily and cheaply continuous-tone photography by making halftone reproductions." Her bibliographic and analytical work has convincingly shown that, thanks to this technological development, "The campaign to persuade the American public to support annexation was promoted by photographically illustrated books and articles" ("Photographically Illustrated Books" 288). *Vistas of*

Hawaii: The Paradise of the Pacific and Inferno of the World; illustrated by photo-engravures from original photographs taken especially for this work, edited in 1891 by Lorrin Thurston, a chief orchestrator of the overthrow of the Hawaiian monarchy, provided a model for future promotional publications, and significantly Sanford Dole's reports to Washington, D.C., in 1900 and 1901 as the new governor of the Territory of Hawai'i were "lavishly illustrated" (Davis, "Photographically Illustrated Books" 297).[39] Davis's extensive bibliography includes photographically illustrated books about the United States' new possessions as well as Hawaii Promotion Committee publications, pictorial magazines such as *Paradise of the Pacific*, travel books, natural histories, and ethnographies (294–304). Having surveyed this massively large number of publications, Davis pointedly remarks, "the only photographically illustrated book written by a Native Hawaiian was *Hawaii: Its People, Their Legends* by Emma Metcalf Nakuina" (289).[40] I aim to foreground Nakuina's book as contesting the pro-annexation ideological campaign *and* also to identify the specific role that other photographically illustrated collections of Hawaiian "legends" in English play in that campaign.

Thus, while the dominant uses of colonial photography disempowered Native peoples, they were not simply or only objects of the camera. Photographs of Hawaiian royalty and studio portraits of Hawaiians projected alternative—though clearly exceptional—images of Native Hawaiians. English viewers were impressed with the stylishness of Kamehameha IV and Queen Emma when their cameo daguerreotypes were displayed at the London Exhibition in 1862. Clearly recognizing photography's power of representation, King Kalākaua, as Maxwell's and Tiffany Lani Ing's research has indicated, made an astute political use of it. In 1875, "he commissioned Max Eckhart, Honolulu's leading engraver, to produce a fold-out book of photographs and paintings of the royal family" and then had Andreas Montano produce carte-de-visite photographic portraits of the king and his queen, Kapi'olani (Maxwell 201–202). These two portraits in particular circulated widely, presented a "modern" and European-like image of the Hawaiian monarchs, and projected their individual personalities as well as their royal dignity. Photographic portraits of the king and queen were also strategically placed within Kalākaua's 1888 book *The Legends and Myths of Hawaii*, where they wordlessly asserted his authority and worked against primitivism (Ing). But Native agency about photography was not limited to royalty.[41] Studio portraits, Maxwell writes, were seen by Natives in various parts of the world as "mechanisms by which to recover pride and dignity" (13). Choosing to display themselves, many Hawaiians exercised their choice of clothing and pose in studio portraits, and some of these—not surprisingly—we find represented in Nakuina's 1904 book. Recognizing an albeit marginalized agency of Hawaiians in the history of photography matters not only to document their resistance in the past but to provide a genealogy for Hawaiian artists in the present, like Anne Kapulani Landgraf who strongly represents and advocates a photographic vision that emerges from Hawaiian values and views.

My Ethics of Location

Documenting the Hawai'i-specific dynamics of this triangulation—translation, photography, tourism—localizes my project to what I hope will be useful ends within the growing body of literature about Hawai'i's cultural production and colonialism. As the previous sections of this chapter have already signaled, I am deeply indebted to a number of individuals and their studies, the questions they pose as well as their perspectives on Hawai'i. Since I will be in conversation with their ideas throughout this book, I want to introduce the people and writings that have shaped my thinking about Hawai'i and made serious demands on it: the passionately anti-colonial political analysis and the poetry of Haunani-Kay Trask (1993/1999); the inspiring work that Vilsoni Hereniko and Rob Wilson (1999), Paul Lyons (2005), and Albert Wendt (1993) have done to reorient scholarship on cultural politics and literature in the Pacific; the indigenous history that Lilikalā Kame'eleihiwa (1992), Davianna Pōmaika'i McGregor (1995), Jonathan Osorio (2002), and Noenoe Silva (1998 and 2004) have recovered; the increasingly complex conceptualization of Hawai'i's literatures (Sumida 1991, Chock 1996, Fujikane 1994, 1997, and 2000; Ho'omanawanui 2005, Lum 1986 and 1998, Morales 1998, Nogelmeier 2003, Trask 1999 and 2000; Wood 1999); Lynn Davis's keen research on and through photography in Hawai'i (1980, 2001); David Forbes's formidable four volumes of *Hawaiian National Bibliography, 1780–1900*; the painstaking work on Hawaiian-language newspapers by Esther K. Mookini (1974) and Puakea Nogelmeier (2003); and, of course, studies of Hawaiian oral traditions and literature (Charlot, Ho'omanawanui, Johnson, Kame'eleihiwa, Kanahele, Kawaharada, Luomala, Mookini, Pukui, Silva [2006], Stillman). These scholars' projects and perspectives vary; in fact, there is open disagreement and debate in some cases; but I have learned from them and from the pull among them. It is thanks to the work of these scholars and to students, visual artists, writers, and storytellers who have affected my sensibility in transformative ways that I have found it possible to take on my own responsibilities as a scholar of narrative who, in addressing "traditional" and "literary" production, refuses to dismiss the history that brings Hawaiians to fight for sovereignty and self-determination today.

Not only for a "performer" or teller of traditional narratives, but also for me as scholar and teacher, then, responsibility or, better, a complex nexus of responsibilities goes hand in hand with knowledge and ambition.[42] As a non-Hawaiian professor teaching oral narratives in the English Department at the University of Hawai'i, it is to my students that I must answer not exclusively, but perhaps first and foremost. I have asked myself what this project can offer them. I think of this study as seeking to accomplish a goal that is also central to my classroom pedagogy: making a contribution to rethinking the roles that traditional narratives play in our lives and especially in our lives in Hawai'i. I see this re-viewing as a task for myself and for my students, but also as an invitation for us—each bringing distinctive knowledge and goals—to become more active and conscious participants in the reception and production of these narratives.

For me as a feminist scholar who has had a long-term and strong interest in fairy tales, rethinking the roles that traditional narratives play in our lives and especially in our lives in Hawai'i has definitely had an impact over the years. When I first taught a course on "Women and Storytelling" at the University of Hawai'i in the 1980s, Momiala Kamahele talked in class about how Pele and other strong Hawaiian female figures had had an important role in her upbringing: no fairy-tale princess could undo that. And when in the late 1980s our interdisciplinary faculty and graduate student reading group on "Feminist Theory" met with Haunani-Kay Trask, who had just published her *Eros and Politics: The Promise of Feminist Theory* (1986), I did not fully understand why or how, but I knew that focusing on gender in Hawai'i would have to mean something different for me from what it had in Italy or New York State. Since feminism is the perspective that foremost in my intellectual and emotional formation has led me to seek social change, learning about gender issues and dynamics in Hawai'i was homework I had to do. Reading and discussing Trask's next book, *From a Native Daughter: Colonialism and Sovereignty in Hawai'i*, was an unsettling and formative experience over several years; *Women in Hawaii: Sites, Identities, and Voices*, edited by Joyce N. Chinen, Kathleen O. Kane, and Ida M. Yoshinaga in 1997, also made a difference, and so has my exposure to poetry, hula, and visual art by women in Hawai'i—especially in their engagement with tradition. It is thus in light of a feminist perspective that requires attention to other social and political dynamics—especially colonialism in Hawai'i— that I approach a number of matters in this book: the feminization of Hawaiians and Hawaiian traditions through verbal and visual representations; the voice of Emma Nakuina countering the "authority" of a Thomas Thrum or a W. T. Brigham; the resistance strategies of colonial subjects *and* women as well as their creativity in the past and the present.

While gender is not a focus in this book, my changed feminist perspective certainly informs it.

To consider the value that rethinking the roles that traditional narratives play in our lives and especially in our lives in Hawai‘i may have for students in Hawai‘i involves seeking to be "attuned to the linguistic and cultural differences that comprise the local scene" (Venuti, *Scandals of Translation* 189) and to situate my position as teacher clearly within the uneven power relations of this local scene. Many of the English majors in my classes are women, but their relationship to larger-than-life or role-model females is not what, coming from a Euro-American framework, I had assumed it to be. Native Hawaiian students are a small minority in the classes I teach, with other Pacific Islanders being an even smaller minority; most students who are Hawai‘i-born-and-raised children of immigrants from China, Japan, Korea, the Philippines, and other Asian countries self-identify as "local." A few are "local *haole*" (that is, Caucasian) students who identify with growing up in Hawai‘i but also know that both class and ethnicity play an important role in "local" identity. Increasingly students from the continental United States also populate our University of Hawai‘i classrooms. When I first started teaching in Hawai‘i in the early 1980s, I assumed that my students would know Native Hawaiian things best of all: generally speaking I was wrong, and have had to rethink my pedagogy from the understanding that their common ground or the given was colonial education and immigrant acculturation. I still learned and learn a tremendous amount from Hawaiian and "local" students, but their lack of self-confidence within the academy brought another lesson home. At present—and this was not the case in the classroom twenty years ago—many of the Hawaiian students do know Hawaiian language and traditions thanks to the growing influence of Hawaiian Language and Hawaiian Studies programs, but this knowledge is often ghettoized in the larger academy.

Many faculty members at our university are aware of these problems and actively work to undo them in their classrooms. One of the small ways in which I intervene is to devise a course assignment for first-year writing students that pursues the same goal as this book: "rethinking the roles that traditional narratives play in our lives and especially in our lives in Hawai‘i." Students are to write an essay that seeks to understand how a place-centered "legend" or "myth" works within the contemporary culture of Hawai‘i. Some students select stories about "haunted" places; others focus on Hawaiian stories about the origin of an area's distinctive physical features. The students do research at the library, talk with family members, exchange stories with friends. They learn about the stories and history of a specific place that could be a cliff, a building, the dorm they are in. The focus of their inquiry, I explain, should not be simply what these stories say, but what they *do*. Pedagogically, my first objective is for students to become aware of how legends and myths do *not* simply belong to the past. This is not to deny that myths and legends come from the past, but to attend to what these stories do in the present. Telling and retelling these "belief narratives" in today's world takes on new or situational meanings and often involves, on the part of individuals and groups, addressing a problem metaphorically or projecting into a story a current fear or desire. My second objective is for the conflicted relation that these stories, in their various versions, have with one another to become apparent to the students whose often unquestioned assumption is that "stories bring us together in our shared humanity." This is not to deny that storytelling distinguishes us as human beings, but to attend to how we tell stories to make certain arguments or lay claims that are tied to a belief, history, or perspective, whether that is announced or not.

These two pedagogical objectives, I trust, are not uncommon among teachers of narrative and culture. I doubt the third one is uncommon, but it has distinctively localized implications for students in Hawai'i: to realize that a double standard is at work in the popular use of the label "myth" and by extension in our attitude toward related traditional narratives such as legends and folktales. This double standard has to do with the issue of belief. Nowadays, when "myth" is associated with belief it is usually the story that "others," the ancient Greeks or primitive aboriginals, believe(d) or told/tell; when "myth" belongs to one's own cultural repertoire it is either a hopelessly "untrue" fiction, as in "that is a myth!" or else, as Roland Barthes showed in *Mythologies* and Jack Zipes has argued in his research on the commodification of fairy tales, it is a story "naturalized" to the extent that at least apparently it does not concern beliefs, but tells us simply "how things are" as if we were not responsible for their representation (*Fairy Tales as Myth*). "We" have evolved beyond "myth" as a belief system, or this is what Western education has led us to assume; only less advanced or enlightened "others" pay reverence to "myth." We do not in everyday life reflect much on how one people's "myth" may be another people's religion or episteme. What "we" label as "myth" from other cultures then translates into the "that's *just* a myth!" formula that implicitly sustains the value of our own beliefs.

Thus trivialized—though in different ways—both outside and within Western culture, "myth" in common English-language usage today is the object of exoticizing amusement or dismissal; it is deprived of its associations with history, knowledge, and vision—what has made myth culturally valuable and has most fascinated scholars of myths and traditional narratives. As Haring states describing early twentieth-century

Western research on non-Western narrative, "myth had to be discredited as irrational, but it had also to be authenticated as an indigenous product" (194). While "we," as modern Western-educated thinkers easily distance ourselves from "myths" or apparently have no stake in them, when we encounter collections of ancient Greek or Hawaiian "myths and legends," it is "natural" for "us" as post-enlightenment individuals or non-Hawaiians to assume that "they" all believed, in the case of the Greeks and "traditional" Hawaiians, or still believe in the case of Hawaiians today in those backward and "primitive" tales. The result is that these tales become representative of "their" collectivity, which is implicitly othered, and that they—both the people and their tales—live somehow outside of historical time, as Johannes Fabian discussed in *Time and the Other*. This *discriminating* use of "myth" discounts not only the beliefs, but the knowledge and history of the "other."[43]

In the context of Hawai'i, it remains imperative to question this trivializing and discriminating understanding of "myth"—as it extends to all Hawaiian "tradition"—because it continues to affect Hawaiians and Hawaiian culture today in expropriating and demeaning ways. Because both the American education system and popular culture dismiss Hawaiian legendary traditions as "myth," Hawaiians have been discouraged from learning or valuing them, and Hawaiian culture is implicitly primitivized and conveniently confined to the past. If those of us who live in Hawai'i and learn about it do little to counter this repressive and ideologically pervasive function of "myth," we participate in reproducing a fiction that perpetuates discrimination. Unmaking the naturalized fiction that is a *legendary Hawai'i* constructed primarily for the interest of tourism is part of this necessarily questioning and demystifying project.

But attending to the ideological powers of myth or "traditional" narratives in our everyday lives means learning to re-cognize, in addition to the destructive uses to which we have put them, the constructive ones that narrative traditions have served and can serve. In Hawai'i, contemporary artists, like Solomon Enos, Anne Kapulani Landgraf, and Ipo Nihipali, and poets—among them Haunani-Kay Trask, 'Imaikalani Kalāhele, Ku'ualoha Ho'omanawanui, and Brandy Nālani McDougall—work with an understanding of cultural memory that emerges not from nostalgia but from the reappropriation of multiple, emplaced stories. The ongoing publication of *'Ōiwi: A Native Hawaiian Journal*—founded by the late D. Māhealani Dudoit with a *hui*, or group, of pioneering editors including Ku'ualoha Ho'omanawanui who has since become its editor in chief—has in recent years provided a new, politicized, and nurturing outlet for such Native Hawaiian verbal and graphic artists. Against the violent translation that Hawai'i has been subjected to, contemporary Hawaiian writers and storytellers in multiple media are translating tradition into the forms and contexts of the present for the sake of Hawaiian and Hawai'i's future. I suggest in the following chapters and in class that we learn from these storymakers' artistic eye to re-view Hawai'i's "storied places" in ways that their inscription into the paradigm of *legendary Hawai'i* occluded. My experience is that this is a potentially empowering move for Hawaiian and Pacific Island students, but can be a disturbing one for others.

As I see it, rethinking the roles that traditional narratives play in our lives and especially in our lives in Hawai'i means confronting how the asymmetrical "differences that comprise the local scene" shape our relation to Hawai'i as a place—specifically a place that was a sovereign kingdom before its forceful takeover by and unwilling annexation to the United States of America. Confronting these power differentials, as I seek to guide myself and my students through the process, need not be confrontational, but it is undeniably grounds for discomfort, as articulating the power dynamics in which we participate often is. It matters thus in this process that I also acknowledge my position, not to pursue a politics of identity but to mark the place from which I have the privilege of teaching and writing. As an Anglo-Indian Italian woman who grew up surrounded by very different markers of cultural history in Rome, was educated within literature departments in Europe and the United States, and has by now (2005) resided in the islands for only twenty-two years, I certainly do not pretend to be a spokesperson for Hawaiian culture, history, or "sense of place." But, as noted earlier, I mean to take to heart the responsibility of my expertise as a scholar of narrative traditions as well as to act on my passion for stories, my respect for what I have been able to understand and experience of Hawaiian culture and art, and my critique of what settlers—and I include myself in that category—have done to Hawaiians.[44] It matters that I self-identify as a settler and that I do so not in a disabling way. It is not guilt, but an invitation to taking responsibility for change that I want to communicate to those who, myself included, may feel unsettled by the realization that we are settlers.

Pursuing something akin to what Gayatri Spivak describes as the "uncoercive rearrangement of desire," I hope that accepting the invitation to dis-locate ourselves from *legendary Hawai'i* and to *learn* from its historicized and conflicted stories can be a small but enabling step in the process of supporting a sovereign Hawai'i where non-Native paradigms, whether they be scholarly or economic, are not the dominant ones.[45] During a "Conversation of Indigenous Issues and Settler Viewpoints" in April 2003, Lilikalā Kameʻeleihiwa, historian, scholar of oral traditions, and then director of the Center for Hawaiian Studies, urged: "Don't become us. Honor your own ancestors. But learn about the land and the language, for there is no Hawaiian sense of place without Hawaiians." Unmaking Western assumptions or fictions about Hawai'i is part of that learning process, unsettling as it may be for many of us. This is a story I feel responsible for telling.

Chapter 2

Hawai'i's Storied Places: Learning from Anne Kapulani Landgraf's "Hawaiian View"

All'origine di ogni storia che ho scritto c'è un'immagine
[There was a visual image at the source of all my stories]
—*Italo Calvino*

Anne Kapulani Landgraf's 1994 book, *Nā Wahi Pana O Ko'olau Poko: Legendary Places of Ko'olau Poko*, presents eighty-three black-and-white photographs of the southern windward district on the island of O'ahu, Hawai'i, that were first shown in loco at the beautiful Ho'omaluhia Park in Kāne'ohe (see Figure 1).[1] The photographs are displayed side by side with narrative text in both Hawaiian and English condensing traditional Hawaiian references that document the cultural and historical significance of each place.[2] In her introduction to *Nā Wahi Pana O Ko'olau Poko*, Haunani-Kay Trask, then director of the Center for Hawaiian Studies at the University of Hawai'i at Mānoa, states: "When I first saw the exhibit, I was determined to have it as the inaugural volume in the Hawaiian Studies publication series" because in Landgraf's photography "culture, political awareness, and a highly refined technical skill [combine] to reveal the Hawaiian view of our sacred places" (Landgraf, *Nā Wahi Pana* viii).

Landgraf's accomplishment was indeed something new in the photography of Hawai'i and deserves critical attention as an artistic and cultural landmark that engages Native Hawaiian tradition in the present. My goals in presenting Landgraf's "Hawaiian view" *first* in this volume are (a) to foreground a Native visual and narrative perspective on place that works in opposition to a tradition of landscape photography in Hawai'i; (b) to invite readers throughout the rest of this book to re-view *legendary Hawai'i* in light of this place-centered narrative and historicizing vision that entails a different epistemology and grapples with the history of land issues in Hawai'i;[3] (c) to foreground the value and creativity

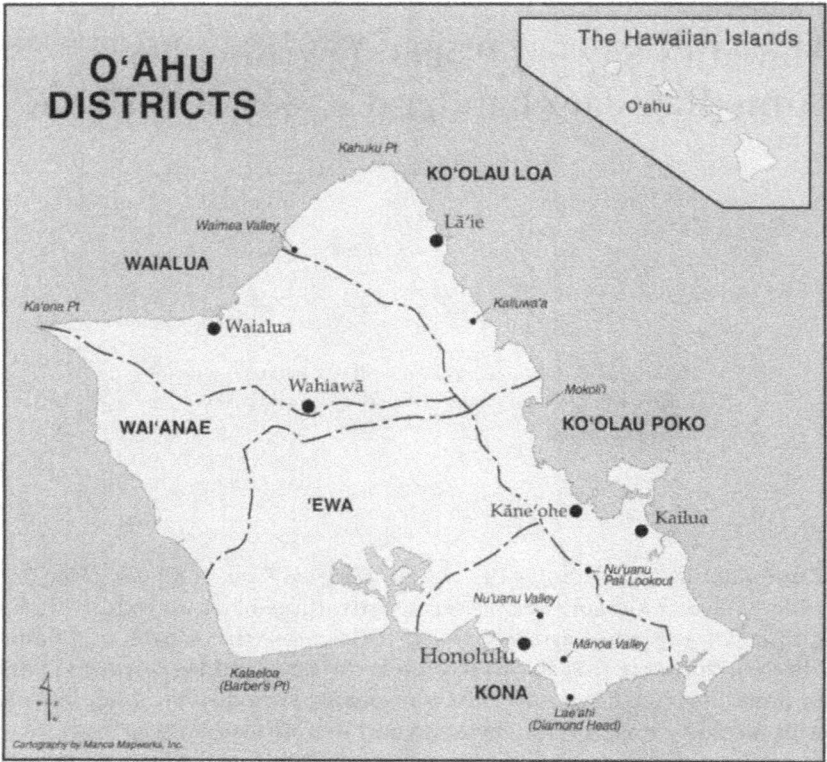

Figure 1. Oʻahu districts. Courtesy of Jane Eckelman, Manoa Mapworks.

of Hawaiian narrative traditions *today*; and (d) to show *how* Landgraf's photography contributed to my understanding of what Trask describes as "the Hawaiian view" of place. My readings of Landgraf's photographs are framed by my position as well as by the recognition that, whether Native Hawaiian or not, viewers/readers who unlike myself have grown up within these storied places will have other or differently layered insights to contribute.

Specifically, this chapter seeks to detail how Landgraf's articulation of place and narrative contributes to the visionary power of *Nā Wahi Pana O Koʻolau Poko*. In her preface, Landgraf writes: "I began this collection of photographs and texts to rediscover and perpetuate the significance of places in Koʻolau Poko" (v). As *Nā Wahi Pana*, or *Legendary Places*, already signals in the bilingual title, narrative or storytelling within a Hawaiian tradition informs such a re-vision. Working from this understanding,[4] I will be reading Landgraf's visual representation of "place" as grounded in Hawaiian storytelling. To this purpose, I analyze specific ways in which she uses legends to repopulate present-day Hawai'i for the many who have forgotten that it is an indigenous place. I also consider how not the photos alone, but the book, through its engaging dialogue of words and images, enacts a transformative recognition of place that involves a different understanding of "illustration"—again, one based on Hawaiian storytelling practices and one that is far from prevalent, as we shall see in Chapter 3, in photographically illustrated volumes of Hawaiian legends.

"Landscape" Photography and Hawai'i's "Storied Places"

Photographs of Hawai'i have been circulated and exchanged since the introduction of *nā pa'i ki'i*, literally "snap pictures" (Pukui and Elbert 302), to the islands in the mid-nineteenth century. Today photographic images of Hawai'i continue to play a familiar and primary role in the commodification of Hawai'i's beauty operated by the tourist industry. Landgraf's *Nā Wahi Pana O Ko'olau Poko* not only protests such commercialization; it distinctively talks back at "landscape" photography of Hawai'i in order to represent "place."

The word "landscape" was introduced into the English language specifically as a "technical term of painters" referring to a "picture representing natural inland scenery" or "the background of scenery in a portrait or figure-painting" and also to "a view or prospect of natural inland scenery such as can be taken in at a glance from one point of view" (*Oxford English Dictionary*). The position of the I/eye in relation to the scenery is of course responsible for how perspective works in a landscape painting; and within this genre, perspective was primarily achieved through a distancing of the eye from its object to ensure that the eye could take in some expanse of land in the process and organize it or frame it for the viewer's appreciation. While I cannot do justice to the large topic of eighteenth- and nineteenth-century landscape painting here, I should note the generic expansiveness of its vistas or views and its implicit assertion of human τεχνή as craft or art to capture nature as beautiful, sublime, or picturesque. Bird's-eye views and large panoramas were especially popular in nineteenth-century lithographs, watercolors, and oil paintings of Hawai'i.[5] This kind of prospect, as I will sketch in the next few paragraphs, found itself reproduced in early landscape photography as well. "Landscape" in this discussion, then, is nature as implicitly external to the viewer, painter, or photographer who perceives it as expanse and represents it as out there.[6] The human eye and its extended technologies—the paintbrush or the camera—produce or "create" (as the suffix "-ship" from which "scape" derives indicates)

Figure 2. Maunawili and Olomana in Koolau Poko. By Charles L. Weed.
Courtesy of Bishop Museum Archives.

the scenic object. Regardless of their diverse goals and techniques, early
photographers of Hawai'i landscapes establish and exemplify this
human-centered perspective from the outside.

From the first, in widely circulating photographs of Hawai'i, this
"landscape" vision was connected with and working in support of an
understanding of nature and an economy of desire that were not indigenous to the people of Hawai'i. For instance, Charles Leander Weed's
1865 panoramic images of Haleakalā or his monumental sugar mills on
Maui seek to capture the grandiosity of nature through human heroic
venture—be it the photographer's risk-taking expedition or the capital-
ist/colonizer's investment. Nature is an object of conquest or an opportunity for profit. More specifically, Weed's images—see the one of
Maunawili and Olomana in Ko'olau Poko (Figure 2)—are consistently
composition-ruled and grounded in a bottom-left human, but non-
Hawaiian, signifier (a person in this case, a road or fence in others). The
photographer's lens organizes and contains the natural world out there,
aiming for a larger-than-life or panoramic effect and at the same time
miniaturizing and objectifying nature.

This is not an isolated case, and neither is this representational approach to nature only a matter of artistic or technological import. As art historian Lew Andrews synthesizes "in the years following annexation, a number of photographers—mostly newcomers—adopted a panoramic approach, drawing on earlier landscape traditions and tailoring them to suit the rapidly changing circumstances in the islands" (226). Andrews discusses Melvin Vaniman's landscapes, especially the "Nuuanu Pali" (c. 1901) image that in the press "was heralded as the 'Best Photograph of the Pali Ever Made,'" to emphasize both Vaniman's "large, panoramic treatment" of the scene and the "physical risks" taken by the photographer (226). Like Vaniman's, Alonzo Gartley's images of "Diamond Head from Tantalus" (c. 1903) or of Kaua'i ("Looking Toward Wainiha Valley," c. 1904) were taken "from a rather distant *and* elevated position" (Andrews 238, my emphasis). One of the best and better-known "amateur" landscape photographers of the islands in the early twentieth century, Alonzo Gartley was also a successful business leader whose photographs were much reproduced in the magazine *Paradise of the Pacific,* and at least one of them was also used to promote Hawaiian Electric, the company he was managing at the time. Some of the first publications of the Hawaii Promotion Committee (*Beauty Spots* and *Hawaii* in 1903) featured Gartley's photographic "landscapes," and he himself was an active member of the Committee.[7] The beauty and even the "lyricism" (Andrews 226) of Gartley's panoramic images of Hawai'i went hand in hand with their post-annexation ideological and promotional uses.

The goal of ethnography pursued by photographers like William T. Brigham and, at times, Alonzo Gartley from the 1890s into the early 1900s meant not only adopting different techniques from Weed's but focusing on different objects of interest in the landscape, specifically temples or *heiau.* Nevertheless, the dimension of scope—of watching from the outside—pervades this "documentary" image-making as well. For instance, Gartley's "Alealea Temple and Kaahumanu Stone, Honaunau, Hawaii" (Figure 3) is an object of perusal for the camera's eye as well as for the visitors included in the picture whose stance clearly indicates they approach the *heiau* with curiosity rather than respect or worship; in contrast, the Hawaiian woman in the photo is, like the *heiau,* part of the "natural" landscape, seen but not actively a subject of seeing herself. "Ethnoscape," in Arjun Appadurai's terms, is thus again reduced to "landscape."

Serving for "Hawai'i as landscape" a function similar to that of photographic portraits for individuals, other images of Hawai'i also worked from the early days of tourism as introductions or "visiting cards." Stereo cards, whose "twin images created a three-dimensional effect" (Davis, *Nā Pa'i Ki'i* 31), for instance, promoted the idyllic, unspoiled

Figure 3. Alealea Temple and Kaahumanu Stone, Honaunau, Hawaii. By Alonzo Gartley. Courtesy of Bishop Museum Archives.

Hawai'i as well as the comfortable, modernized Hawai'i to lure visitors just as today's advertising does. By 1937, an Eastman Kodak Stores advertisement in *Paradise of the Pacific* declared "Hawaii is the World's Most 'Photogenic' Land": amateur photographers had multiplied, but objectification through "scoping" (as viewing a portion of territory from the outside) and "scaping" (as shaping that view from the outside) continued to be applied to the land and the people—the "photogenically" blossoming women especially—of Hawai'i.[8]

The Kodak Hula Show, which opened during that same year and ran—though not without interruptions—from 1937 to 2002,[9] enabled individual tourists to make the most of this scoping and scaping approach because the choreography staged dances and dancers specifically for the eye of the camera. A hula show during the daytime would ensure and increase sales of color film, and that's why the Kodak Hula Show emerged and thrived. I remember going in the 1980s with my Italian father, an avid amateur photographer himself. The Kodak hula dancers danced and danced well, but within the show every pause became a photo opportunity. The hula dancers were there to be photographed. They posed for group pictures, a great variety of them, with their green ti-leaf skirts, colorful lei, and instruments. Since the audience had to sit facing them and at a distance, the dancers could only be viewed as an ensemble and preferably from a camera lens; the dancers were positioned so that trees only—no buildings or cars—appeared in the background. Perhaps the most popular iconic moment was when the dancers stood gracefully holding the sign "HAWAII": click click click. The dancers were actually framed, even before the tourists clicked their cameras, ready-made for visual consumption.[10]

Against this archive of black-and-white and color-filled landscape images, Anne Kapulani Landgraf's photography asserts itself as *not*-landscape photography by actively conducting an exploration of "place." When I say "place," I mean not only a "lived-in landscape," a "specific location" that is known "from the inside" (Lippard 7)—rather than one observed from the outside as a landscape may be—the way cultural critic and art historian Lucy Lippard does. I also mean "place" as an emotionally, narratively, and historically layered experience.[11] "Place" is, as scholars Steven Feld and Keith H. Basso have remarked, "actively sensed" (7) through time and thus often narratively "voiced" (8); and "senses of place"—for there can hardly be only one—are "the experiential and expressive ways places are known, imagined, yearned for, held, remembered, voiced, lived, contested, and struggled over" (Feld & Basso 11).[12] For instance, in *Storied Landscapes*—the most extensive discussion to date (both scholarly and personal) of such an emplaced vision as it takes shape in Hawaiian literature and storytelling—Dennis Kawaharada writes out of wanting to "look again at the places of my childhood with a different set of eyes, a different vision, based on a knowledge of stories that people the landscapes with ancient spirits" (7). In reaching out to perceive these Hawaiian stories as part of the places in which he grew up, Kawaharada unsettles his own "sense" of place as a "local" Japanese and affirms the specificity and historical priority of the Hawaiian one. In her forthcoming essay " 'This Land Is Your Land, This Land Was My Land': Kanaka Maoli versus Settler Representations of 'Āina in Contemporary Literature of Hawai'i," Ku'ualoha Ho'omanawanui strongly reasserts on genealogical grounds this priority from a *kanaka maoli* (indigenous Hawaiian) position and articulates her sense of the distinctiveness of a Native "sense of place." [13] As I see it, it is the power dynamics among various "senses of place" that demands their definition and our attention.

Landgraf's *Nā Wahi Pana O Ko'olau Poko* seeks to expose its viewers/readers to a Hawaiian "sense of place" and to a Hawaiian re-vision of located history that rightfully demands sovereignty. Some may wonder how this can work given that photography is not a "traditional" Hawaiian art: on such grounds apparently Landgraf was denied a grant early on in her career.[14] But tradition is not static; "traditions are legitimated and authenticised by the processes of their use" (Siikala and Siikala 46), and the *wahi pana* tradition has found its articulation in a range of media, including photography, as other books also show (*Kahoʻolawe, nā Leo o Kanaloa: Chants and Stories of Kahoʻolawe* had, for instance, appeared in 1995). Leslie Marmon Silko's reflections on Pueblo stories as well as her own photography are relevant to understanding a Native American perspective *and* a Native Hawaiian one as well: "So long as the human consciousness remains *within* the hills, canyons, cliffs, and the plants, clouds, and sky, the term *landscape*, as it has entered the English language, is misleading. . . . Viewers are as much a part of the landscape as the boulders they stand on" (17).

From within a Hawaiian sense of place, landscape (meaning *external* landscape) was and is an oxymoron in that land, ocean, fire, humans, many-shaped ancestors, wind and all share the porous nature of lava rocks or the tender culture of *kalo* plants. The *kalo*, or taro, was the first sibling of human beings in Hawaiian legendary tradition. *Aloha ʻāina*, to love the land, includes taking care not abstractly of mother earth, but of one's ancestors and children, one's family members in the past, present, and future—extending to one's country. One etymological reading of *ʻāina* metonymically brings together feeding and parenting: "The term *ʻaina* represented a concept essentially belonging to an agricultural people, deriving as it did from the verb *ʻai*, to feed, with the substantive suffix *na* added, so that it signified 'that which feeds' or 'feeder'" (Handy and Pukui 3). Following Mary Kawena Pukui's gloss, Kuʻualoha Hoʻomanawanui cogently extrapolates that *ʻāina* "is the land that can nurture and sustain life by providing food, including the majority of environments from the ocean to the highest mountaintops; it is the land which provides food for all living things, not just humans" ("This Land"). Polynesian cosmogonies enact this familial relationship, and so do most Hawaiian *moʻolelo* as (hi)stories, songs and chants (*mele* and *oli*) in which, to recall folklorist Katharine Luomala's terse statement, "Nature is personal" ("Creative Processes" 244);[15] on the basis of Lilikalā Kameʻeleihiwa's scholarship in history and mythology (*Native Land; He Moʻolelo Kaʻao o Kamapuaʻa*), I would add, that within this conception of *ʻāina*, landmarks forge narrative links with ancestry through time.

It is therefore important to insist that animated and specific localization is the backbone—not the ornamentation—of much traditional Hawaiian narrative and to counter a Western reading of Hawaiians' insistence on place as description, that is, as pause or digression. *Nā wahi pana*—which I translate interchangeably as "storied places" and "legendary places" so as to avoid collapsing the Hawaiian into a Western genre that is nevertheless quite appropriate given its ties with belief and history—constitute a large body of narratives within Hawaiian storytelling.[16] To represent a Hawaiian "sense of place" *visually* in her photographs of Ko'olau Poko, Landgraf adopts and adapts—that is, she translates—specific Hawaiian *narrative* strategies. I will focus on two: the historic and metaphoric use of place names; and the animation or "peopling" of nature.

Place Names

Introducing each photograph in *Nā Wahi Pana O Ko'olau Poko* is its Hawaiian place name—the first ones in the book are Kualoa and Kalaeoka'ō'io—followed by a literal English-language translation ("Long Back" and "The Cape of the Bone Fish" respectively) and by narrative text in both Hawaiian and English that illuminates the name's relationship to cultural values and historical events that each place inscribes. For Kualoa, we read "I ke au kahiko, he pu'uhonua ia 'āina. A he kapu 'ihi'ihi kō Kualoa. . . . He 'āina kaulana 'o Kualoa i ka mahi wauke no ka hana kapa 'ana. . . . No kona 'ano kapu loa, he 'āina lanakoi nui 'ia 'o Kualoa e nā ali'i i ka wā noho ali'i 'ana o Kahahana i loko o nā makahiki o nā 1770"; or Kualoa "was a place of refuge, and was also under a special kapu. . . . Kualoa was a famous growing area for wauke, a tree whose bark was used to make kapa. . . . Because of its sacredness, Kualoa was coveted by the ali'i [chiefs] and played an important role in the politics of the reign of Kahahana in the 1770s" (2). The angle from which the photograph (*Nā Wahi Pana* 3; Figure 4) is taken emphasizes the majestic length of the ridge as well as its richness that in the past came from the cultivation of the land (*wauke*) and plentifulness of fish from the sea; the presence of a double-hulled canoe on the beach shows that it is still used as a canoe landing, and this may be a muffled allusion to the much celebrated launchings and landings that took place in Kualoa of the Hōkūle'a canoe starting in 1975, a venture that has been central in the revival and recognition of Polynesian star navigational traditions;[17] the presence of a small catamaran-like sailboat perhaps hints at how this is still a battleground. For the next legendary place, "'O Kalaeoka'ō'io ke kaupalena ma waena o nā moku 'o Ko'olau Poko me Ko'olau Loa. Ma muli o nā mo'olelo, aia ho'okahi o nā puka o ke ana awaloa 'o Pohukaina ma ke alo pali o Kalaeoka'ō'io ma ka 'ao'ao Ka'a'awa. 'O kekahi puka aia ma lalo ma ka punawai 'o Ka'ahu'ula, akā ua ho'opiha 'ōpala 'ia i ke kūkulu kahua pū ma loko o ke Kaua Honua II. Aia kekahi mau puka o Pohukaina ma Moanalua, Kalihi, Pū'iwa, Waipahu, a me Kahuku." The English reads: "Kalaeoka'ō'io is the boundary point dividing the districts of Ko'olau Poko and Ko'olau Loa. According to tradition, one of the entrances to the royal burial cave of Pohukaina was located in the

Figure 4. Kualoa. Long Back. By Anne Kapulani Landgraf. Courtesy of artist and University of Hawai'i Press.

cliffs of Kalaeoka'ō'io facing Ka'a'awa. The Ka'ahu'ula spring below the cave was another entrance, but it was filled with tons of rubble when a gun site was built above it during World War II. Other entrances to Pohukaina are said to be located at Moanalua, Kalihi, Pū'iwa, Waipahu, and Kahuku" (*Nā Wahi Pana* 4). The photograph of Kalaeoka'ō'io (5; Figure 5) offers a close view of the cliff that emphasizes on the one hand its role as outstanding landmark and on the other its protective cape-like quality. For both Kualoa and Kalaeoka'ō'io, while their place names are not fully explained by the verbal narratives accompanying the photos, their historical and metaphorical significance is made to emerge.

    As seen in the *mo'olelo* printed in nineteenth-century Hawaiian-language newspapers as well as in traditional and newly composed *mele* or Hawaiian songs today, the pervasive and multifunctional presence of place names is one of the most common localizing devices in Hawaiian prose and poetic narratives. In 1887, the Reverend Charles McEwen Hyde published a piece in the *Hawaiian Annual* in which he observed that "a prominent characteristic of Hawaiian poetry is the enumeration of names of places associated with the persons whose memory is perpet-

Figure 5. Kalaeoka'ō'io. The Cape of the Bonefish. By Anne Kapulani Landgraf. Courtesy of artist and University of Hawai'i Press.

uated in their songs" and the enumeration of epithets accompanying such names ("Hawaiian Poetical Names for Places" 79). While he praised the composers for their poetic skills, he also wrote: "It is natural that an uncultured race should give time and thought and appreciation to the observation of individual traits and striking physical characteristics, rather than to those reflections on abstract principles of conduct, and to that analysis of motives, which distinguish the master-pieces of modern *belles-lettres* in Europe and America" (79). I point our attention to this passage because it exemplifies a non-Native perspective on land as "physical" matter; and because its "othering" effect is very much in keeping with the Western "evolutionary" ideas of the turn of the century, ideas that are also inscribed in the collections of *legendary Hawai'i* assembled by Thomas G. Thrum and William D. Westervelt.

Working from a different perspective, a number of twentieth-century folklorists and linguists have also noted the importance of place names.[18] In the introduction to her 1918 translation of *Laieikawai*, the 1863 book that S. N. Hale'ole wrote gathering materials from oral traditions, folklorist Martha Beckwith noted as many as seventy-six place names in the narrative (Beckwith, "Introduction" 314). "The principal use of place names in a narrative is for their allusive interest, that is,

for their ability to recall to the audience familiar sayings and legends
associated with a locality and also to awaken the listeners' memories of
their own personal and group associations with it. The names evoke
emotion and give esthetic satisfaction," wrote Katharine Luomala in
1961 ("A Dynamic in Oceanic Maui Myths" 142), reporting on Martha
Beckwith's analysis of place names in *Laieikawai*.[19] In a later essay, Luomala focused on how a Hawaiian "composer selects place names for his
poems which express his emotion in regard to another individual to
whom he dedicates his chants" ("Creative Process" 238) and also on
place names as mnemonic devices, examples of animism, and opportunities for wordplay. In the appendix to the revised and expanded edition
of the invaluable *Place Names of Hawaii* by Mary Kawena Pukui, Samuel
H. Elbert, and Esther T. Mookini, Elbert commented on how "almost
all Hawaiian tales are filled with place names" and stated that *nā wahi*
(the places) are termed *pana* (celebrated) when "in their imaginations
people ally the place with amusement and affection for the wondrous
events of the past" ("Connotative Values" 272).[20] More recently, musi-
cologist and cultural critic Amy Kuʻuleialoha Stillman discussed the performance of *mele* about celebrated places in relation to specific historical
events ("Nā Lei o Hawaiʻi"); and Dennis Kawaharada took as one of his
starting points for *Storied Landscapes* (1999) that "the numerous place
names suggest a large population with a detailed knowledge of the
islands; nuances of the landscape were noticed" (9).

Places are indeed named frequently and to various effects in Hawaiian
narratives. But, with the exception of Kawaharada's examples in *Storied
Landscapes* and Stillman's analysis, the discussions I referred to above do
not foreground the connection of place names with story as history. Similarly, while they discuss the poetic uses of place names, they do not
underscore the relational and performative element of *wahi pana*.[21]
Landgraf's vision of *wahi pana* brings back into focus Hawaiian uses of
place names that have tended to be forgotten or marginalized. When
the narrated events take place in a Hawaiian narrative, when, that is,
they "emplace" or locate themselves, the place as such takes shape and
assumes its significance in historical and personal terms. And within this
context, the articulation of the place name itself has power in that, in
Amy Kuʻuleialoha Stillman's words, it works to "re-member cultural
memory":[22] it activates history in the present moment and location.

More specifically, place names may recall an event as in "Pueo," the
peak named after the chief who challenged Hiʻiakaikapoliopele, the
goddess Pele's favorite younger sister, and who was defeated there
(Landgraf, *Nā Wahi Pana* 24–25; Sterling and Summers 192); or they
may point to a feature of the place itself, a visible reminder of the event,
as in "Holoapeʻe," or "Run and Hide," where Kamapuaʻa, the pig god,

Figure 6. Holoape'e. Run and Hide. By Anne Kapulani Landgraf. Courtesy of artist and University of Hawai'i Press.

ran from the fiery goddess Pele by hiding in a hollow and digging through the ridge at Kualoa (Landgraf, *Nā Wahi Pana* 8–9; Sterling and Summers 182–83; Figure 6). Reactivated by the power of the place name itself, Landgraf's image of Holoape'e engages photographer and viewers in an exploration of "nuances" or specific configurations (where are the holes dug by the pig god? what or who may be hiding there? how to "see," find, or choose a hiding place) rather than a detached observation of composition. As Landgraf's notation suggests, "the ridge is also known as Kohoape'e," which loosely translates "choose and hide," perhaps a "choice" place for hiding. Displayed early in the book, "Pueo" signals an interpretive code: not only is this a "storied place" with specific connections with the ancient Hawaiian past, but the metaphoric power of place names informs the images themselves. Later in the book (134–135), "Ka'iwa," or "The Frigate Bird" (Figure 7), with its feathery slopes and its evocation of longing for an out-of-reach softness—like the longing of Ahiki for the chiefess Ka'iwa in the story that Landgraf summarizes—is another remarkable instance of Landgraf's figurative use of place names as condensation of experience.

The frequency and repetition of place names in Hawaiian narratives, then, as Landgraf's work shows, *perform* a reciprocal relationship between humans and nature, time and place, historical experience and present event.[23] Becoming aware of this relationship matters especially

Figure 7. Kaʻiwa. The Frigate Bird. By Anne Kapulani Landgraf. Courtesy of artist and University of Hawaiʻi Press.

to counter and move away from the lack of understanding and the negative feeling that often listeners, readers, students, and scholars have expressed toward such stylistic repetition: it makes things "difficult" or "boring." In 1965, Katharine Luomala explicitly stated that the "newcomer to this art [Hawaiian chant and poetry] often feels guilty if he does not find the traditional Hawaiian narrative style immediately attractive to his taste" and offered an explanation for this difficulty that is tied with problems of translation from Hawaiian to English, *oli* to poem, and performance to print: "when an alien narrative art is not only in an alien language but in forms that are alien to it the key to its appreciation is sometimes difficult to find" ("Creative Processes" 235).[24] Samuel Elbert, who studied place names with a passion, wrote in 1976 that "to the outsider, such detailed lists of places are boring, but not so to the narrator or his Hawaiian audience" ("Connotative Values" 124). Like Martha Beckwith years before him, Elbert also notes a "slighting of place names" in turn-of-the-century publications of Hawaiian (hi)stories, and not only in texts by non-Hawaiians. Elbert's example is that of Moses Nakuina, to whom the earlier "insistence on place must have seemed dull" when he translated the *mo'olelo* of Paka'a and the wind gourd for "the amusement and improvement of the youth in his Christian Endeavor Society"; Elbert speculates that Nakuina's 1902 "older" readers, especially if they "knew small places between Kaua'i and Hawai'i," would have been "disappointed at not hearing them in the narrative" ("Connotative Values" 126). Cutting down on the number of place names was common also in English-language translations. Beckwith in 1919 had quite strongly contrasted her translation of Hale'ole's *Laieikawai* "complete in all its dullness and unmodified to foreign taste" to the collections "gathered by Thrum, Remy, Daggett, Emerson, and Westervelt, . . . [and] Fornander" where "lengthy recitals" had been "cut down to summary narrative, . . . not picturing fully the way in which the image is formed in the mind of the native story-teller" ("Introduction" 295–96).

The awkwardness and ambivalence in these scholars' language, the diminished importance of place names in those translations of *mo'olelo* that are still most widely circulated today, even the self-censoring that Elbert detects in Moses Nakuina's English-language stories are signs not simply of change, but of colonization. So is, for many of us living in or visiting Hawai'i today, the ease with which Hawaiian place names are forgotten or never learned. In many cases, they have been replaced by names that tell or evoke a shorter version of history: Pūowaina has become known as Punchbowl, Pu'uloa has been turned into Pearl Harbor, Āliapa'akai has been converted to the generic Salt Lake.

Forgetting or never bothering to find out what the history, the longer story—better, the longer stories in the plural—behind a Hawaiian place name signals yet another effect of colonialism. The replacing of Hawaiian place names was more systematic starting in the early 1900s and imposed a new geographical ordering or mapping that not only ignored Hawaiian naming practices but also, as Houston Wood effectively points out in "The Violent Rhetoric of Names," asserted who had power over official naming (*Displacing Natives* 9–19). Because of this rupture, Hawaiians have suffered a number of losses that compound their loss of sovereignty over land and nation: specific knowledge of places, connections with them, sustenance from them, as well as opportunities for sustained public dialogue about their traditions. This is not to say that returning to a "traditional" name can per se restore knowledge of and relations with place, but that re-membering Hawaiian place names can help to challenge and shake settlers' hegemonic approach to land, place, and history in Hawai'i. That history, even when considering Hawaiian names, is not monolithic—how could it be if it is relational?—but it did and does matter. As Kame'eleihiwa and other scholars have observed, in response to the naming of specific places, it was common for other localized stories to emerge in dialogue with the narrative as told or printed: readers of nineteenth-century Hawaiian newspapers would write in with their own competing and corrective versions of the past, further corroborating that place-oriented knowledge mattered enough to be contested.[25] It still does. And Landgraf's historicizing and metaphorical use of Hawaiian place names today offers a way into the re-membering of *wahi pana.*

Repeopling the Land

Telling/visualizing the stories of Hawai'i from *within* a Hawaiian view comes from and works toward a different understanding of nature as well: a Hawaiian storied place is already alive, inhabited by gods and *kupua* (beings who can take many forms), not only humans, who transform and inform it. Following the traditional stories, or *mo'olelo,* specific places in Ko'olau Poko are represented in Landgraf's photographs as having been shaped, in the examples I have already mentioned, by the conflicted relationship of Pele and Kamapua'a or by Pele's younger sister, Hi'iaka, as she battles her way along the coast on her arduous journey to Kaua'i seeking the chief Lohi'au, Pele's lover. Admittedly, these black-and-white images are devoid of humans, possibly an absence that restates the decimation of Hawaiians since the late eighteenth century. They do, however, exhibit some relatively recent effects of human interactions with the *'āina* (paving, blasting, building, diverting water courses, not cultivating, over fishing, polluting, and so on). And, just as important, Landgraf's images are "peopled" or populated by living beings that, Hawaiian narrative tradition tells us, are related to humans. Nature not only has character but is character.

Mokoli'i, or "Little Mo'o," which is first seen on the book's cover (Figure 8), was as Landgraf's text summarizes (10–11), either a huge *mo'o,* or dragonlike lizard, or a huge rat (Sterling and Summers 181–82); in either case, Mokoli'i threatened and attacked travelers near Kualoa. Hi'iaka heroically slew Mokoli'i, whose body lies scattered along the coast, in places facilitating travelers' passage, his tail forming the tiny island off of Kualoa Point. Or, in another story, the demigod Ka'ulu tricked him to his death, and Mokoli'i's body fell to the ocean forming the island. In either case, Mokoli'i, the island, emerges as the outcome of a struggle, perhaps as a warning, certainly as a body.

Landgraf's photograph within the book ("Mokoli'i"/"Little Mo'o," Figure 9) meets the visual challenge of reclaiming the island as Mokoli'i, a being with a personality and story, especially when we think of how the island is more commonly viewed. Seeking to represent an animated or "peopled" land in Hawai'i *today* involves for many a process of reanima-

Figure 8. Cover of *Nā Wahi Pana O Ko'olau Poko*. By Anne Kapulani Landgraf. Courtesy of artist and University of Hawai'i Press.

tion, a process that requires defamiliarization. Landgraf's image actively struggles against the labeling of this storied place as "Chinaman's Hat," a reification of Mokoli'i that erases Hawaiian presence, center-stages the dynamics between Euro-American and Asian settlers, and works to confirm a stereotyping vision from the outside. When one is used to "Chinaman's Hat," an objectified place with some local color,[26] recognizing it as the dragonlike creature—or even as the remains of the creature—that terrified travelers may demand a close encounter. In Landgraf's photograph, "Chinaman's Hat" is not in sight; I see instead large and "here," the lizard/dragon's tail rising from the water, its scarred tissue where it has been torn from the body, the rush of the water through its cavities; perhaps the momentary stillness before a blow is delivered, and definitely the *mo'o*'s rage. Others may see someone else. But there is no simple going back to the picturesque hat.

This understanding of land and all elements as intimately related to living beings and their encounters is, of course, in accordance with the stories of origin of both the Hawaiian islands and the Hawaiian people. Wākea, the sky father, and Papa, the earth mother gave birth to

Figure 9. Mokoliʻi. Little Moʻo. By Anne Kapulani Landgraf. Courtesy of artist and University of Hawaiʻi Press.

islands—first the largest one, Hawaiʻi, and then Maui—and to a daughter, Hoʻohokukalani; the *kalo* plant that, as Kameʻeleihiwa reminds us in her history of land issues in Hawaiʻi, was the outcome of Wākea's union with his daughter or with Papa (depending on the version), provided not only "the main staple of the people of old," but "is also the elder brother of the Hawaiian race, and as such deserves great respect" (*Native Land and Foreign Desires* 24). Gods, land (as including ocean and sky, rain, winds, plants, animals), food from the land, *and* humans are

Figure 10. Makapu'u. Bulging Eye. By Anne Kapulani Landgraf. Courtesy of artist and University of Hawai'i Press.

all related in this story of origin that speaks to Hawaiian sexual, economic, social, and ethical values.

"Makapu'u," or "Bulging Eye" (162–63; Figure 10), at the other end of Ko'olau Poko, is also represented by Landgraf as a lived-in storied place, but here the emphasis is not on origin but on changes in more recent history. It is not only a matter of seeing anew—searching for the eight-eyed female Makapu'u—but more of noticing what cannot be seen or has changed and of asking why. Unlike the combative Pueo or Mokoli'i, Makapu'u, powerful being from Tahiti, was waiting to greet Hi'iaka and her companion Wahine'ōma'o with food when they approached O'ahu in their quest for Lohi'au (Sterling and Summers 257–58). But to the paddlers of their canoe, Makapu'u is a fearful sight, a landing to be avoided: her power is too much for them; she is even perceived as a hungry god herself (as the Keakuapōloli cave translates) and given the roughness of the waters pounding the cliff one can understand why. (A storied place does not hold the same meaning for all.)

The life and tale of another famed female rock and *kupua* who used to inhabit the area are embedded within the storied place of Makapuʻu. Malei, Landgraf's paraphrase of traditional Hawaiian sources tells, has a different cultural and social function: "It *attracted* fish to the shores of Makapuʻu, particularly the uhu, or parrot fish, of which it *was* the guardian." Landgraf's words foreground the Hawaiian people's worship of and gratitude toward Malei: "The people of Waimānalo *offered* her leis of līpoa [a prized seaweed], and prayers." And because the words in the past tense—"Malei *was* a stone *once located* on the ridge of Makapuʻu" (162, my emphasis)—point to what we cannot see in the photo itself, the juxtaposition of story and image invites us to enter Makapuʻu and Malei as altered *in* time, past and present, almost doubling the image via verbal evocation, as the words generate an alternate vision. This double vision can initiate further exploration, on the part of this viewer/reader at least, of the effects of change. The rocks appear bare: how much *līpoa* seaweed is there now? And what about the *uhu*, or parrot fish? I know that people fish there, but could fishing still sustain the people of the area? Whose rage do the foamy waters of what is now the most popular body-surfing spot on Oʻahu signify? From the superimposed images, questions of ecology, spirituality, economy, and cultural survival emerge. Landgraf's representation of the Malei story puts into focus the losses of the colonized present while re-imaging a reciprocally sustaining and intimate relationship among living forms.[27]

Landgraf's verbal and visual performance of *moʻolelo* signals that the genealogical and spiritually nurturing link of Hawaiian islands and people is not confined to the mythical past. Her artistic intervention to this effect is certainly not a solitary statement. For instance, if we move to another island, the most southern one, Hawaiʻi, where the volcano continues to erupt, Pele, the goddess of fire, continues to be active there destroying what's in her path but also giving birth to new land. Her resilient and healing sister Hiʻiaka continues to regenerate what Pele has dried up and covered in her path. And, independently of what has happened to the worship of the main gods of their pre-Christian religion, well-known shape-shifting gods, or *kupua*, like Pele and Kamapuaʻa as well as the many *ʻaumākua* (family protectors that take animal, plant, or mineral shapes including those of the *pueo* [owl], *manō* [shark], or *ʻiole* [rat]; Pukui, Haertig, and Lee 35–43), are for many Hawaiians today family relations. When renowned *kumu hula* Edith Kanakaʻole was interviewed for a Hawaiʻi public television channel in 1978 and asked about Pele and Kamapuaʻa stories, she began her telling by stating that she could "speak freely" of them because of where her parents came from (different parts of the island of Hawaiʻi) and where she was raised.[28] Her connection with the Pele family continues to be inscribed in the *hula* of her daughters' *hālau*.

Hālau o Kekuhi of *kumu hula* Pualani Kanaka'ole Kanahele and Nālani Kanaka'ole is perhaps best or most widely known for the production of *Holo Mai Pele*. This 1995 extended performance of Pele traditions—which had an energizing and transformative effect on contemporary experience of hula, theater, and narrative—has since been made into a successful television production as part of the *Great Performances* PBS series and also reached print in a richly chromatic assemblage of photographs (Carl Hefner's images of the performance and Franco Salmoiraghi's portraits of individuals and places on the island of Hawai'i), *oli* in Hawaiian and English, and words by *kumu hula* Pualani Kanaka'ole Kanahele.[29] Pacific Islanders in Communications (PIC), Hālau o Kekuhi, International Cultural Programming, and Thirteen/WNET New York partnered to produce the television adaptation; the Hawaiian writer and scholar D. Māhealani Dudoit was brought in to edit the book, and Ku'ulei Higashi provided translations for it. The ensemble production and multimedia dimension of *Holo Mai Pele* speak to both its contemporaneity and its traditionality; the participation of expert Hawaiians in every aspect of the production also speaks to the care with which these traditions are performed and offered to the public by this *hālau*. As its *kumu* writes: "At the core of *Holo Mai Pele* is a basic yet sophisticated understanding of the primary functions and powers of woman and the female Earth. The story involves numerous facets of plot, human entanglements, chaos of the creative forces, godly duties, and family responsibilities. *Holo Mai Pele* is an ancient myth that continues to evolve today. Kīlauea volcano continues to erupt, extending land and creating new islands. This mythical epic is not about volcano gods existing only in the past. It is about the volcano gods who have prolonged their lives from the past, to the present, to the future. . . . The creation of myth must continue as long as Kīlauea continues to erupt" (Kanahele xii).

Haunani-Kay Trask's poetry in the 2002 collection *Night Is a Sharkskin Drum* inscribes in contemporary Hawaiian literature the same message, the living presence and power of Pele's "traveling" and "devouring" ("Nāmakaokaha'i" 8) and Hi'iaka's "chanting / on the wind" ("Hi'iaka Chanting" 6), the value for Hawaiians of sensing spiritual and ancestral connections in everyday gestures and moments. "To hear the mornings" among the *hāpu'u* ferns and through indigenous bird songs, rains and winds is

To sense the ancients,
         ka wā mamua—from time before
      slumbering still
         amidst the forests
            of Ka'ū, within the bosom
               of Pele
("To Hear the Mornings" 40–41)

Figure 11. Kōnāhuanui. His Large Fruit. By Anne Kapulani Landgraf. Courtesy of artist and University of Hawai'i Press.

Trask's verses celebrate the world of the elements as a "generous, native Hawai'i" (41) that is both an ancestral and emergent source of nurturance to Hawaiians today.

Working from this relation to place and time that seeks to recognize Hawaiian traditions as *living* in the history of the land and the lives of its people, Landgraf's photography is an understated assertion of resilience and resistance. For instance, "Kōnāhuanui," or "His Large Fruit" (Landgraf, *Nā Wahi Pana* 100–101; Figure 11) is verbally introduced to viewers as "the tallest peak of the Ko'olau range, ris[ing] three thousand one hundred and fifty feet. Its name refers to the testicles of a giant, who threw them at a woman fleeing from him" (100). Landgraf cites *Place Names of Hawai'i* (Pukui, Elbert, and Mookini 117) as her source for the story of this place name and then Kamakau's *Ka Po'e Kahiko* as the source for the following: "Kōnāhuanui is said to form the roof, or high end, of the famous cave of Pohukaina. . . . The cave was used as a burial site for ali'i" (100). By establishing the connection of this place name with Kōnāhuanui's sexual act and with references to traditional social practices and history, Landgraf recognizes both the reproductive and regenerative quality of this storied place. In her image, the seminal power of the giant wordlessly asserts itself over the adjacent abandoned drive-in, the cemetery-like remnant of other desires and fantasies. While the screen is blank, Kōnāhuanui has more stories to tell.

"Visual Illustration" and "Storied Place"

Anne Kapulani Landgraf's images of Ko'olau Poko, then, take us— Native and non-Native viewers—to its storied places, urgently demanding that we do not simply observe, but that we relate to them—their birth and demise, conflicts and yearnings. I am not suggesting here that this relation would or could be the same for all: these storied places, I know, are not my ancestors; Native Hawaiians can instead claim, whether it is "immediate" or mediated through relearning, "the intimacy" of a genealogical relation and engagement with such places.[30] Rather I am suggesting that by bringing *wahi pana* into our "public sphere," here intended as the site for public discourse among heterogeneous social groups, Landgraf is extending the invitation to learn from these storied places to all who are willing to listen and see and experience them, however varied the depth and personal value of that learning may be.

This invitation has its own tradition in Hawaiian storytelling and culture. My focus here is on Landgraf's creative reconfiguration within the context of a *book* of another common Polynesian storytelling practice— that of "visual illustration"—as well as on her historicizing representation of sites emerging from conflicted dialogues of image and word. Thinking along these lines helped me to see how Landgraf's narrative texts *together with* the photographs contribute to the *whole* book's inspired representation of lived-in places.

"Visual illustration," as Katharine Luomala called it in her 1961 essay on Hawaiian localized myths, is the device by which "a narrator invites his listeners to look, with himself as the guide," at the storied place ("Dynamic" 137). Seeing and knowing (the Hawaiian word for both is *'ike*) come together in a telling display as speaker and listener engage the place itself as they visit it. According to scholar of Hawaiian religion John Charlot, Kaliuwa'a, the *wahi pana* in Ko'olau Loa on O'ahu most notably associated with Kamapua'a, was "a traditional location for Hawaiian sightseeing: sites would be visited, their famous names and related sayings explained, and the famous stories about them told" (*Kamapua'a Literature* 47). As documented, for instance, in an 1861 letter to the editor of a Hawaiian newspaper, this "sightseeing" of Kaliuwa'a applied to "chiefs" in the "olden times" as well as "visitors from foreign countries" in more recent times.[31] The Hawaiian historian Samuel Mānaiakalani Kamakau mimicked this practice in his 1865 newspaper articles translated as "Sightseeing Tour of Famous Places," a stranger's "imaginary visit to Hawai'i" that included going to famous sites and telling their stories (*Tales and Traditions of the People of Old*).[32] W. D. Westervelt, the already mentioned early twentieth-century translator of a great many Hawaiian stories, also provided an account of such visits to Kaliuwa'a: "One morning while the sunlight of May looked into the hidden recesses and crevices of these valleys, bringing into sharp relief of shadow and light the outcropping ledges, a little band of Hawaiians and their white friends lay in the shade of a great *kamani* tree and talked about the legends which were told of the rugged rock masses of each valley, and the quiet pools of each rivulet. Where the little party lay was one of the sporting-places of Kamapua'a the 'hog-child treated in the legends as a demi-god'" (*Hawaiian Legends of Old Honolulu* 248). Within the context of "visual illustration," spatial—rather than chronological—configuration, deictic markers (this and that from where we stand), and visibility would organize the telling.[33]

The layout of Landgraf's *Nā Wahi Pana O Ko'olau Poko: Legendary Places of Ko'olau Poko* reproduces the spatial organization of Polynesian storytelling, but within a book. By turning the pages, we move south from the most northern and sacred end of Ko'olau Poko in an appropriately clockwise direction: "The old Hawaiians had definite ideas on how one should travel. If one wanted to obtain and hold—fish, information, materials, etc.—one traveled about the islands with the right hand towards the mountains, i.e., on something solid" (1944 note by Mary Kawena Pukui).[34] And as we are introduced to the stories of the places there represented, we come to recognize and feel the weight of their historical markings. As we read linearly, there is a cumulative effect. Side by side, images and words draw viewers/readers in to visit and re-visit the storied places, explore the photos thinking of the stories, read the stories to hear what at first may not be visible. Landgraf's sustained practice of cross-referencing in the book (see, for example, "Makapu'u" [162] and "Waimānalo" [145]) also conveys the vital connection between places, very much in the mode of intertextuality or of story generating story. When, having first experienced the book, I closed it, the mirage-like image on the cover of *Nā Wahi Pana O Ko'olau Poko* had also changed for me. Since then I see how Mokoli'i—in what is a more common view of the islet from a distance—is part of a scattered body. I notice how gently Landgraf's eye approaches the contours of the district, how discreetly she greets from a distance those she knows and loves, how carefully she works to re-member the body of Ko'olau Poko.

Landgraf's book, however, does more than to spatially mimic the storytelling practice of "visual illustration." *Nā Wahi Pana O Ko'olau Poko* also reaffirms that, because storied places are shaped by history, the relationship between image and words is not a simple or one-way confirmation, a matter of corroboration where the image serves as example or proof ("seeing is believing") of what the words assert. In a 1997 paper, "Oral History and Landscape: Narratives in the Southern Cook Islands," folklorist Anna-Leena Siikala foregrounds the historicizing function of the space-oriented strategy of Polynesian "visual illustration." Having observed that narratives about landscapes are often performed in the location of the events, Siikala reaffirms that within a Polynesian framework the natural landscape is a "concrete testimony of history."[35] I find her conclusion that spatial markers guide the teller to recollect the markings of genealogy and history particularly helpful in order to foreground Landgraf's historicizing representation of storied places and her performative intervention in present political struggles by enacting a revisiting of familiar sites. This intervention, as with storytelling, actively involves the at times conflict-ridden dialogue between site and citation.[36]

A sacred site is now almost unrecognizable as such, and its destruction is symbolic of the status of Hawai'i as an exploited, colonized place. Another Kamapua'a *wahi pana* in Ko'olau Poko, "Kāwa'ewa'e," or "Coral or Stone Used to Rub Off Pig Bristles" (112–13; Figure 12; "Kawa'ewa'e" in Pukui, Elbert, and Mookini 97) represents the remains of a *heiau*, or temple, where, we are told, "'Olopana plotted to sacrifice Kamapua'a, the pig demigod, . . . but instead Kamapua'a killed 'Olopana." Based on her sources, Landgraf documents the size of the temple: "The walled enclosure measures one hundred and twenty feet by two hundred and fifty-three feet. . . . The walls were four to seven feet high and five feet wide." As the image from the past gains in stature and solidity, I refocus on the stones in the present-day picture, dwarfed and apparently suffocated by the vegetation. Landgraf's final verbal pointer refers to yet another time when "the heiau was used as cattle pen." Misuse and disuse, caused by the imposition of a Western economy and relationship to the land, seem to have killed this once sacred place.

And yet the story of Kamapua'a intervenes in this narrative of loss to illustrate how a desperate situation can be overturned. Kamapua'a— captive, wounded, and hungry, but strengthened by his grandmother's chant—is still able to defeat and, in fact, eat 'Olopana and all his people. The verbal evocation of Kamapua'a's victory, then, can bring about a reinterpretation of what we see: the lush vegetation can also be a sign of the pig god's vitality, his victory over the oppressive 'Olopana, the exuberance of Lono (the god of fertility with which Kamapua'a is associ-

Figure 12. Kāwaʻewaʻe. Coral or Stone Used To Rub Off Pig Bristle. By Anne Kapulani Landgraf. Courtesy of artist and University of Hawaiʻi Press.

ated) countering the bloodthirsty power of Kū (to whom a *heiau* for sacrifices would have been dedicated). Kamapuaʻa's story imbues the devastating image with hope. And the abundant presence of *lauaʻe* ferns within the place and image provides a dimension of comfort to the entanglement of these two jarringly opposed pictures—the desecration of the temple and the winning force of regeneration. Because *laua'e* are especially fragrant ferns that were used to perfume the *malo*, or loin-cloth, of chiefs (Krauss 70), their growth could be seen as protecting and reconsecrating the abandoned temple. Once again, what emerges from Landgraf's reframing of the *wahi pana* is its conflicted history as well as an urgency to act on the making of history in the present. Storied places are sites not only of colonization or loss, but also of resistance. This double vision, I believe, informs Landgraf's project. As she intends it, photography is "seeing history. It's discovering change in ways we cannot" (Landgraf in Burlingame, "From a Hawaiian Point of View" B6). And it is further a contribution to a decolonizing process in the present.

A scholar trained in Western disciplines, I believe that a decolonizing process must also involve questioning and denaturalizing our analytical tools. I have already argued that, in their reciprocally sustaining dialogue with stories, Landgraf's photographs are hardly a simple "illustration" of a point or even of the stories themselves. The relationship between image and text in *Nā Wahi Pana O Ko'olau Poko* is radically different from what we find in most twentieth-century collections of Hawaiian legends where photographs have an ancillary function to the tales, or in *Paradise of the Pacific* where photographs often function as phatic messages or mythic icons, seemingly detached from their ideological uses. When Landgraf's photographs enable viewers/readers to experience *nā wahi pana o Ko'olau Poko* anew, the phrase "visual illustration," which I adopted from Luomala, also becomes suspect: it retains the primacy of the word over the place itself and, while that is appropriate to other narratives or senses of place, it is problematized within Landgraf's photographic exploration of a Hawaiian relationship between place and memory, image and words, sight and citation.[37]

Let's look at the words in her book—the Hawaiian words especially, which are the translation of the English words (Figure 13). As I see it, if we do not know the Hawaiian language, the words are a graphic illustration of the process that revisiting the place itself enacts: the emergence of a forcibly silenced or buried culture.[38] The Hawaiian language was banned from public schools in 1896, and for several generations many Hawaiians grew up not speaking their own language and certainly not encouraged to speak it in public. In the last few decades, the resurgence of hula and Hawaiian music, the teaching of Hawaiian language at the University of Hawai'i, the Hawaiian-language radio progam *Ka Leo Hawai'i*,[39] the institution and growth of Hawaiian-immersion schools, and the recent publication of *'Ōiwi: A Native Hawaiian Journal* (starting in 1998) and the bilingual *Ka Ho'olina: The Legacy* (starting in 2002) have contributed to alter what was effectively a monolingual (English) situa-

Kāwaʻewaʻe

Aia ka heiau ʻo Kāwaʻewaʻe ma luna o ka lapa ma waena o Kāneʻohe (ma ka ʻaoʻao 92) a me Kailua (ma ka ʻaoʻao 118). Nā ʻOlopana i kauoha i ke kūkulu ʻana i ʻelima heiau: Kāwaʻewaʻe, Ahukini, Pahukini (ma ka ʻaoʻao 130), Holomakani, a me Puʻumakani. Na Kahikiʻula, kaikaina o ʻOlopana, i kūkulu i ka heiau ʻo Kāwaʻewaʻe i loko o ke kenekulia ʻumikūmālua. Ua hoʻolālā ʻo ʻOlopana e mōhai aku iā Kamapuaʻa ma Kāwaʻewaʻe, naʻe hoʻomake aku Kamapuaʻa iā ʻOlopana. ʻO Lonoaohi ke kahuna nui o Kāwaʻewaʻe.

Hoʻokahi haneli iwakālua kapuaʻi i ka lōkihi o hoʻokahi ʻaoʻao a ʻelua haneli kanalimakūmākolu kapuaʻi kō kekahi ʻaoʻao lōkihi o ia pā. Ua loaʻa he kīpapa iki ma ka ʻaoʻao ʻakau. ʻEhā ā ʻehiku kapuaʻi ke kiʻekiʻe a ʻelima kapuaʻi ka laulā o nā pā pōhaku. I kekahi manawa, hoʻohana ʻia ka heiau mehe pā pipi.

Coral or stone used to rub off pig bristles

The heiau of Kāwaʻewaʻe is found on the ridge dividing Kāneʻohe (see page 92) and Kailua (see page 118). ʻOlopana ordered the building of five heiau: Kāwaʻewaʻe, Ahukini, Pahukini (see page 130), Holomakani, and Puʻumakani. Kāwaʻewaʻe was built by ʻOlopanaʻs brother, Kahikiʻula, in the twelfth century. ʻOlopana plotted to sacrifice Kamapuaʻa, the pig demigod, at Kāwaʻewaʻe, but instead Kamapuaʻa killed ʻOlopana. The high priest of Kāwaʻewaʻe was Lonoaohi.

The walled enclosure measures one hundred and twenty feet by two hundred and fifty-three feet. A small terrace was found on the north side. The walls were four to seven feet high and five feet wide. At one time the heiau was used as a cattle pen.

Figure 13. Kāwaʻewaʻe text. *Nā Wahi Pana O Koʻolau Poko*. By Anne Kapulani Landgraf. Courtesy of artist and University of Hawaiʻi Press.

tion in a state that professes, however, to have two official state languages (Hawaiian and English). Hawaiian language and culture are reemerging, taking their place on the page and in our minds. Let's consider that place in Landgraf's book: in the layout, the Hawaiian precedes the English and is also placed above it. If we do know the language—and an increasing number of readers in Hawaiʻi are in that position or at least have rudimentary knowledge of Hawaiian—the Hawaiian can provide the very first means for recovering meaning in the photo, and the English text will no longer appear as a primary layer of mediation.

What connections can be drawn between these visual and cognitive dynamics and the recent history of Hawaiian language and textuality? While the stories were originally told in Hawaiian, many have been "preserved" through translation and are in print more readily accessible in English. Students of Hawaiian language and culture can now read Samuel M. Kamakau and Hawaiian-language newspapers in the original, but—as Landgraf's book confirms—documentation in, for instance, Martha Beckwith's *Hawaiian Mythology* or Elspeth P. Sterling and Catherine C. Summers's English-language *Sites of Oahu* is still a significant step in the process of returning to the source. The textual practice involved in the production of *Nā Wahi Pana O Koʻolau Poko: Legendary Places of Koʻolau Poko* mimics and extends this history. Fred Kalani Meinecke— teacher of Hawaiian language at Windward Community College, in Kāneʻohe, another storied place of Koʻolau Poko—translated into

Hawaiian Landgraf's condensation of these stories as retold in printed (often in English) traditional sources. And we can "see" in the words as graphs a story of erasure and recovery, loss and reappropriation. The layout of the words, having itself become an estranging form of "visual illustration," represents Hawai'i's layered storied places as well as the argument for reappropriation that runs through Landgraf's photographic essay. Visually, because the Hawaiian is placed before and above the English, the historical layering of languages and stories is transformed into both a statement of precedence as well as one of reemergence.

Living (with) Hawaiian Traditions

As my examples from the book show, the triadic relationship among bilingual place names, bilingual (hi)story, and black-and-white images throughout the book is, as we move from page to page, far from predictable; in fact, cumulatively, the variations within this compositional pattern mark specific points in Landgraf's argument about a Hawaiian view of the land, just as they mark nuances in the poetry of her images. Place names, stories, and images are not presented as explanations or illustrations of one another. One photographic image may point to a historical mark just as another may amplify its absence; some stories privilege the legendary past while others mention modern and contemporary structures or events; some place names herald the presence of life in a seemingly uninhabited space while others offer no key to read the image. The ways in which we put the pieces together, or make sense of this conversation and composition, have to do with Landgraf's arrangement or choreography *and* with our personal connections and experiences with the places she envisions. In this sense the book, in its varied dialogue of image and story, thrives on *kaona*, the hidden or multiple meaning of Hawaiian song and place, the mark of Hawaiian poetic oral/aural play.[40]

Kaona also inflects the graphic dimension of both verbal and visual elements of Landgraf's book. The black-and-white of the photos repeats the black-and-white of the words, and vice versa. The artistic choice of black-and-white photography definitely speaks to the need to defamiliarize Hawai'i, especially as represented in Kodak-colored brochures. But the lack of color, by indicating a turn to the past, could also encourage nostalgia. If we looked at only one or two of Landgraf's photos in isolation, they could be read simply as beautiful, mysterious landscapes. But her images' dialogue with the printed texts emphasizes indigenous sources without simply lamenting change and offers a perspective that steers us away from nostalgia, a relationship with the past that other black-and-white photography of Hawai'i has at times encouraged. In the

multiple dimensions of its layout—visual, verbal, spatial, and graphic—
and its various historicizing moves, Landgraf's book does not simply represent Hawaiian legendary traditions; rather it performs them and
recreates them *today*.

I came to Anne Kapulani Landgraf's photographs from a passion for
and scholarly interest in stories. I stayed with her work not only because
her politically grounded attention to "place" in Hawaiian culture refo-
cused my understanding that—as Italo Calvino has written—at the core
of each tale shines an image, but because her images have contributed
to changing my daily relationship to the place where I live, the land of
the Hawaiian people. To my Western-trained eyes, Anne Kapulani Landgraf's *Nā Wahi Pana O Koʻolau Poko* enacts a powerful transformation of
"landscape" into lived-in "place" via the re-imaging of Hawaiian legendary traditions in the present. In *ReViewing Paradise. Contemporary Photography from Hawaiʻi*, Landgraf has written that "landscapes" are
"environmental portraits of an altered place. At another time in Hawaiʻi
these places had names and significance. The land was cultivated and in
turn nurtured its people. . . . Today, subdivisions, golf courses, executive
homes, and public projects change the topography without regard for
Nature's power. . . . I am interested in rediscovering the significance of
a place" (Landgraf in Cashman et al. 9–10). How does this "rediscov-
ery" work? She engages in critical dialogueue with a tradition of landscape photography in Hawaiʻi; she actively employs Hawaiian narrative
strategies to represent today's Hawaiʻi as an indigenously peopled place;
she puts visual and verbal representations in a historicizing dialogue
with one another that questions "illustration"; she represents "storied
places" to generate a politicized double vision of contemporary Hawaiʻi.

The effects of these strategies in the quotidian are multiple and vary
in relation to our own histories, knowledge, ideological positions, and
interests. Some may see storied places for the first time, others recognize
them as living friends; mourning their violent near-death and celebrating their fluid vitality are also part of the emotional journey; and retelling versions of their stories inevitably plays some part in today's politics
of knowledge as well as the political future of the land. The struggle to
wrestle the island of Kahoʻolawe from the United States navy's use of it
for bombing practice was in the 1970s sustained by knowledge from
moʻolelo, of which the *wahi pana* are part; the struggle over Mākua, the
valley named "Parents" on the island of Oʻahu and also abused for military purposes, is ongoing as I write.[41] Conflicts that often tear communities apart continue to occur over tourist developments, golf courses, and
water distribution. Landgraf's re-visions have helped me acknowledge
that *wahi pana* are maybe shared but hardly common ground for today's
inhabitants and visitors of Hawaiʻi, myself included, and that all of us

need to realize that such "ground" has been living land, family, and history to Hawaiians. This is not to suggest that such "ground" holds the same meaning for all Hawaiians today or that its meaning has not changed; it is rather to orient us away from what Paul Lyons has called a "willed and stunning ignorance/ignoring of Oceanian priorities" that is often found in "U.S. cultural production about Oceania" (*American Pacificism* 2). Exposing layers of complexity, Landgraf's photography sustains the struggle to advance Hawaiian sovereignty and land repossession by artistically refiguring Hawaiian narratives of place in the present.

Chapter 3

The Production of *Legendary Hawai'i*:
Out of Place Stories I

> On the island of Oahu, where legends abound, the one most often spoken of
> is the Kahala Hilton. Legendary in its beauty, our grand resort is poised at
> the edge of the lazy lagoons of Maunalua Bay, against a backdrop of scenic
> mountains and a cascading waterfall. Legendary in its service, our gracious
> staff pride themselves in remembering your every preference from day to day
> and visit to visit. Legendary in its patronage, the Kahala Hilton is a favorite
> with dignitaries, celebrities, royalty and all of the world's most discerning
> travelers.
>
> —*Promotional video, 1989*

While the 1989 promotional video in the epigraph visually juxtaposes
the Kahala Hilton's modern comforts to otherwise seemingly uninhabited landscapes of Hawai'i—"Aloha! We invite you to step into a world
of timeless elegance and luxury set in a land of lush, tropical beauty"—it
unself-consciously publicizes the resort (since then replaced by the
Kahala Hotel Resort) as a "legendary place."[1] And yet, located at the
end of Kāhala Avenue and in the upper-class Kāhala neighborhood, this
"legendary place" is not shown to have any apparent connections with
its *ahupua'a* (the large Hawaiian land division of Waikīkī), its *'ili* (smaller
Hawaiian land divisions like Wai'alae Iki), or with any *mo'olelo* associated
with these areas.[2] Quite obviously, the video promotes a "legendary
place" taken out of its Native Hawaiian historical and cultural location,
even as the clause "where legends abound" makes a gesture toward
Hawaiian traditions that implicitly recognizes tourists' expectations of
Hawai'i as an exotic destination. Exploiting the image of Hawai'i's abundant traditions to legitimate its own use of the phrase "legendary place,"
the video nevertheless quickly relegates those traditions to a legendary
background out of which "the one [legend] most often spoken of"
turns out to be the Kahala Hilton tourist resort.

My overall concern in this chapter is to follow this kind of brazen displacement of Native Hawaiian storied places and *mo'olelo* traditions in the interest of corporate tourism back to the post-annexation produc-tion of *legendary Hawai'i* as a space constructed primarily for non-Hawaiians, and especially Americans, to experience Hawai'i as exotic and primitive while beautiful and welcoming. My argument is that the making of Hawai'i into a legendary space for the benefit of development and tourism was in part enabled by the translation of Hawaiian *mo'olelo* in the late nineteenth century and early twentieth century, and espe-cially by the appearance of narratives about Hawai'i's *wahi pana*, or "sto-ried places," in English-language magazine articles and printed collections. Visually enhanced by the novelty of photographic illustra-tions, this production of *legendary Hawai'i* was profoundly tied to the post-annexation promotion of Hawai'i as a tourist (and settler) destina-tion and translated "storied places" in several senses, including taking them "out of place."

How, and to what effect, did Hawaiian "legends" become important vehicles for Americans to imag(in)e Hawai'i at the very moment when Hawai'i was, against the will of so many Hawaiians, compelled to become part of America's economy and politics? How did the translation of "storied places" make the construction of a *legendary Hawai'i* for non-Hawaiians possible even as it took these stories out of the place they pur-ported to represent? How did photography construct a visual vocabulary that bolstered this visitor-friendly production of *legendary Hawai'i*? These questions structure the three sections of this chapter, in which I (a) map out the production and distribution of "legendary lore" to represent Hawai'i to American readers; (b) focus on the rhetorical and narrative strategies of two of Hawai'i's most prolific translators and popularizers; and (c) identify the visual vocabulary that represented and advertised *legendary Hawai'i* in the early twentieth century.

The Politics and Marketing of "Legendary Lore"

Three Hawaiian historians from the Lahainaluna School on Maui, Sam-uel Mānaiakalani Kamakau (1815–1876), Davida Malo (1795–1853), and S. N. Hale'ole (1819–1865) were steadily recording *mo'olelo* by the mid-nineteenth century, and printing *mo'olelo* for Hawaiians and non-Natives who could read the language was a common practice of the many Hawaiian-language newspapers in the century's second half (see Chapter 5).[3] Brief accounts of Hawaiian "legends" in English were also published quite early, beginning with the missionary William Ellis's *Nar-rative of a Tour Through Hawaii* (Boston and New York, 1825; London, 1826; Honolulu, 1917) and James J. Jarves's *History of the Hawaiian or Sandwich Islands Embracing Their Antiquities, Mythology, Legend* (London,

1843). And by 1885 in Honolulu, Abraham Fornander—a Swedish settler who married a Moloka'i chiefess and became a judge—had produced the foundational *Account of the Polynesian Race: Its Origin and
Migrations and the Ancient History of the Hawaiian People to the Times of
Kamehameha I*, which relied heavily on *mo'olelo*.[4]

But I submit that following the overthrow of the monarchy in 1893, in
the Republic, and even more so in the Territory of Hawai'i, a different
kind of cultural production emerged. The novelty and the abundance
of English-language translations of these stories in magazines and books
primarily intended for consumers outside Hawai'i signal that a *legendary
Hawai'i* was being produced for distinctly new audiences and with new
functions and urgency. Often accompanied by photographic illustrations, these English-language narratives were not for Native Hawaiians,
or even Hawai'i residents, but primarily for people with little knowledge
of Hawai'i—prospective tourists and settlers, Americans who wanted to
know more about "their" new Territory, and whose support for the
Americanization of the islands had to be won.

A case in point, Charles Montgomery Skinner's *Myths & Legends of Our
New Possessions & Protectorate*, was published by the J. B. Lippincott Company of Philadelphia and London in 1900. Skinner (1852–1907) had
already produced *Myths and Legends of Our Own Land* and *Myths and Legends Beyond Our Borders*, and in a movement paralleling the United
States' own late nineteenth-century politics of expansion, in the *New Possessions* volume he covered such Caribbean islands as Cuba and "Porto
Rico," and Hawai'i and the Philippines as well. Whetting the readers'
visual curiosity, the book also contained four small plates, two of
which—"Down the Valley Came Pouring a Flood of Lava" and "Avenue
of Palms, Hawaii"—prototypically illustrated Hawai'i's appeal as an
exotic, exciting land where orderly beauty and comfort could be sought.
"Our new territories have many legends, for among unbookish people
tradition takes the place of history, and myth of knowledge," writes Skinner in the introduction; he goes on to explain that Hawai'i was special in
comparison to Cuba, Puerto Rico, and the Philippines because Hawaiians
had a "class not unlike that of the ancient bards of European countries,
and of our new subjects—our brothers, let us rather say—the Hawaiians
are the only ones who have formulated these ancient stories" (9).

What this collation of legends from different "possessions" contains,
Skinner argues, is the poetry of a simpler life that primitive or "savage"
(11) peoples—ancient Greeks and nineteenth-century Hawaiians
alike—experience(d), a life that can tell us "truths of Nature and of
human nature" (14) through symbolic stories. "It cannot hurt us to live
in a fairy age a little longer," Skinner nostalgically pleads, "to keep away
from the screech of trains, the jar of factories, the bawling of hucksters,

the agonizing of mendacious journals, for a few still precious years" (11). How quickly he moves from associating tradition with history to identifying tradition as the core of humanism and universal symbols! Given the framework of progress that these "possessions" have fallen into, Skinner assumes the annihilation of the "fairy age" that the tales exemplify to be inevitable, while at the same time he invites his American readers to indulge in a temporary, holiday-like journey in the mindset of their "new subjects" as if they were long-lost "brothers."

Skinner presents thirty-two narratives from Hawai'i. Some feature divine beings like Pele, the Hawaiian volcano goddess, or Māui the trickster; others relate the adventures of Chief 'Umi or Captain Cook's death. The stories' titles often assert universality and brotherhood by relating the Hawaiian stories to ancient ones from another continent: "The Hawaiian Iliad," "The Hawaiian Orpheus and Eurydice," and "Hawaiian Ghosts." While he peppers his tales with dates that lend the accounts a historical dimension, Skinner also states that "Pele is the Venus of the islands" (235), or that for Kahikilani, "The Wronged Wife," "Lono built a yacht worthy of this Cleopatra" (257). The genres of fiction and romance are hard at work. His last Hawaiian tale, "The Lady of the Twilight" (285–86), exhorts his readers to recognize that in the Hawaiian stories fanciful "events are possible. Let us believe they are, at any rate, if thereby we enrich the imagination with a moment of romance" (14).

Ironically enough, one of Skinner's main sources for his compilation was *The Legends and Myths of Hawaii: The Fables and Folk-Lore of a Strange People*, published in 1888 by King David Kalākaua of these "unbookish" people.[5] Sharing Skinner's assumption that Hawaiians were not writers, the American press doubted Kalākaua's authorship from the start, with most of the credit going to his editor, Rollin Mallory Daggett, the American consul to Hawai'i who had orchestrated the volume's publication with the prestigious Charles L. Webster and Company of New York, and had written its introduction (Ing). Without going into the details of this authorship debate, my point here is dual. Kalākaua had the knowledge and the skill to write these stories—indeed, he had published *mo'olelo* and *mele* in Hawaiian-language newspapers and was well educated in the English language. As were other individuals. The preface acknowledges the following contributors to the volume: Kalākaua's sister Lili'uokalani; her husband, General John Owen Dominis; Walter M. Gibson, Kalākaua's premier and minister of foreign affairs; the Honolulu-born and Yale graduate Professor W. D. Alexander, who taught Greek, was in charge of the Bureau of Government Survey for many years, and published a Hawaiian history textbook; and "Mrs. E. Beckley, Government Librarian; Mr. W. James Smith, Secretary of the National Board of Education; and especially . . . Hon. Abram [*sic*] Fornander, the learned author of 'An Account of the Polynesian Race, in Origins and Migrations'" (6). Despite these attributions, not only was the Western concept of authorship applied to the king's compilation of knowledge from a range of oral and written sources, but the volume's clearly double-voiced diction (the "Introduction" reads quite differently from the stories) and ideology were ignored—and Daggett was assumed to be the ghostwriter or real author.[6]

Why would King Kalākaua enter in this publishing venture with Daggett? Tiffany Ing's ongoing research has already drawn one clear conclusion that reinforces Jonathan Osorio's and Noenoe Silva's assessment of the king's agenda: *Legends and Myths* was part of Kalākaua's multipronged project to keep "Hawai'i for Hawaiians," by reviving Hawaiian culture and securing his kingdom its rightful and respected place among other sovereign nations. Kalākaua's promotion of "the hula, the creation and funding of a Board of Genealogy by the legislature, the revival of the Hale Naua [*sic*], and the publication of Hawaiian mo'olelo as well as the epic mo'o kū'auhau (chiefly genealogy) known as the Kumulipo . . . were highly assertive of the glory and vitality of Hawaiian traditions and affirmed the cultural distinctions between Natives and foreigners" (Osorio 225).[7] Like the Brothers Grimm in early nineteenth-century Germany, Kalākaua had recognized the nation-building power of tradition or "folklore." Like Charles Montgomery Skinner, but with the opposite intent, Kalākaua saw the political currency of divulging the *mo'olelo* of Hawai'i beyond the shores of his kingdom.[8]

With *Legends and Myths*, Kalākaua sought recognition for his nation by presenting (hi)stories that recorded Hawaiian knowledge and beliefs yet at the same time tried to connect with non-Hawaiian readers. Though the Daggett "Introduction," and what are presumably his comments framing the stories, emphasize mystery and romance, most of the actual stories are presented as shedding light on the specific history and values of Hawaiians. Nevertheless, and responsibility cannot be clearly assigned here, a few of the tales' titles declare classical Greek connections ("Hina, the Helen of Hawaii," or more generically "Lohiau, the Lover of a Goddess"), and the collection proclaims the basic universal nature of human beings (67). It was this comparative and humanist frame that made it possible for Skinner to re-present Kalākaua's legends and myths as support for a political agenda directly counter to the king's, yet built on *some* of this volume's rhetorical strategies.

The Kalākaua and Skinner collections are only two indicators of the political currency and commercial potential of translated *mo'olelo* outside of Hawai'i at the end of the nineteenth century—especially within the context of international exhibitions featuring Hawai'i, Mark Twain's

"Our Fellow Savages in the Sandwich Islands" lecture tours, exotic post-cards, the heated debate over annexation, and the advertising of new business opportunities. Periodic publications in Hawai'i certainly recognized the attraction of such stories for non-Hawai'i readers and acted on this potential. Usually dubbed "legends," but also "myths" or "tales," translated *mo'olelo* began appearing regularly in the business-oriented *Hawaiian Annual*, published by Thomas G. Thrum, and in the English-language widely circulating magazine, *Paradise of the Pacific*.

The *Hawaiian Almanac and Annual*—subsequently referred to as the *Hawaiian Annual* or *Thrum's Annual*—first appeared in 1875 as "a hand book of valuable and statistical information relating to the Hawaiian Islands." Initially issued in December, and organized as a month-by-month presentation of news and events, and as a preview of the impending year, in time the *Annual* became less schematic. In 1901 the subtitle changed to "Reference Book of Information and Statistics Relating to the Territory of Hawaii, of Value to Merchants, Tourists and Others"; clearly this revision announces that the *Annual* is primarily aimed at businesses and tourists. This was not an attempt to reverse the publication's fortunes. Early issues had gone quickly out of print, and the 1899 "special anniversary issue" was "in more ways than one, a historic issue" (*Annual* 1898, Announcement 145), celebrating twenty-five years of publication and steady patronage with a detailed article on "Honolulu in 1853 with illustrations," but also with features on the "Joint Resolution of Annexation" and the "Flag-Raising Ceremonies in Honolulu"— events tied to Hawai'i's new status as a Territory of the United States of America.[9] Advertised at the turn of the century as selling at "75 cents each; foreign mail 85 cents," this successful *Annual* was published by Thomas G. Thrum until his death in 1932 (and it continued on for many more years after that). Each volume contained information ranging from "directory assistance," advertisements for businesses, and statistics (including demographic data) to articles about Hawai'i's weather, flora and fauna, history, "improvements," and sights. In 1923, the League of Nations in Geneva requested all forty-nine of the *Annual*'s issues published up till then for its reference library (*Paradise of the Pacific* 36.5 [1923]:13).[10] A 1954 article from the *Honolulu Star-Bulletin*, "Tom Thrum Knew All about Hawaii," notes the immediate and the long-term business value of the *Annual*: "Suppose you are a businessman with some capital and you want to invest that money in diversified agriculture," Clarice B. Taylor wrote, "Where would you start looking for details of the attempts other men have made to introduce new crops into Hawaii? . . . You would turn to Thrum's Hawaiian Annual and you would find that Thomas George Thrum had carefully documented attempts to diversify agriculture in his 1893 Annual and in many follow-up articles through 1932."

While articles such as "Hawaii Hospitality," "Mark Twain's Tribute on Hawaii," "Annexation of Hawaii to the United States," and "Hawaiian Pa-u Riders" profiled contemporary lifestyle and events, as early as 1879 Thrum was regularly publishing legends retold or translated by such settlers as the Reverend A. O. Forbes, the Emerson brothers, William D. Westervelt, and of course himself, given his own keen interest in "antiquities."[11] Joseph M. Poepoe (1892), Moke Manu (1901), and Emma M. Nakuina (1893 and 1897) were among the few Hawaiians he also published. Under "Folklore" in the *Annual*'s 1875–1923 cumulative index, there are forty-three entries for translations of *moʻolelo* or commentary on them, an average of one translation per volume, confirming the feature's stable place in the publication. The first entries are about Māui ("Origins of Fire" and "Maui Snaring the Sun, Legend") and Pele ("Pele and the Deluge, Tradition"), all "by" the Reverend A. O. Forbes (1833–1888), a second-generation settler and preacher.[12] From 1900 up to his death, though, Thrum produced half of the "Folklore" articles and translations himself (Figure 14). In the *Annual*'s 1924 cumulative index, "Folklore" items are classified separately from "Historical" articles; with very few exceptions, the latter featured such topics of modern history as the post office, fire department, postal savings bank, steam coasters, land titles, and changes in government. As early as 1879, then, *moʻolelo* presented a salient and distinctive feature of Hawaiʻi in the *Annual*; not as historical accounts, however, but as colorful and appealing stories of ethnographic interest.[13]

English-language magazines also helped to create this turn-of-the-century currency of Hawaiian "legends" for Americans. The chief contributor was a monthly, *The Paradise of the Pacific*, produced in Hawaiʻi, but not primarily for Hawaiians. Perhaps not surprisingly, Thomas G. Thrum was the editor when it first appeared in January 1888. First issued as a *pro bono publico* free publication, devoted to "Hawaiian Tourist Travel Interests" (1.1 [1888]:1) and more generally, to "the business interests of the Hawaiian Islands" (3.10 [1890]:1), *Paradise of the Pacific* was dedicated to "diffusing abroad for the benefit of tourists and others, reliable information on all points relating to climate, natural scenery and volcanic wonders, tropic life and travel, agricultural and commercial interests, together with occasional papers on current events; though politics and personalities will be carefully avoided" (1.1 [1888]:1). Reliability was a guiding principle. In "Misstatements Corrected," an 1889 article, the author notes that: "There is much to be said and written before intelligent people in the United States and elsewhere will come to understand about Hawaii," and that *Paradise of the Pacific*, very much

Figure 14. 1900 cover of the *Hawaiian Annual*. Courtesy of Hamilton Library, Hawaiian/Pacific Collection, University of Hawai'i-Mānoa.

in the spirit of the *Annual*, was working to correct such "ridiculous" but popular views of Hawai'i as Mark Twain's passing on in public lecture in San Francisco the "mistaken information that cannibalism had been a Hawaiian practice.[14] And yet, while the twentieth-anniversary issue could proclaim that the magazine had "conscientiously" fulfilled its original goal "to hold the Islands up to the world as a resort for those who seek the most pleasant conditions and surroundings of recreation or a new sphere of agricultural activity," its original promise that this business goal would be achieved without "politics and personalities" was not exactly kept. A May 1893 editorial announced that "there is no hesitancy in saying that the *Paradise of the Pacific* being, as it is, 'devoted to the interests of the Hawaiian Islands,' is most *positively in favor of annexation.*" In 1897, an editorial directed toward "Tourists and Investors" rewrote the magazine's goals somewhat: "It is the aim of this journal to disseminate information concerning the advantages of the Hawaiian Islands as a place of rest and pleasure for tourists, health and change for convalescents, profit for those who have money to invest in new and growing industries, and lastly a good living for those who are willing and anxious to work and are not afraid to go into the primeval forest if necessary to gain their livelihood."[15]

By 1900 *Paradise of the Pacific* had a declared circulation of 5,000 copies, at $1.50 for a one-year subscription. Only 500 subscribers lived in the Islands.[16] Even before annexation, distant readers could learn that Hawaiians were "a race of great possibilities" ("Happy Hawaii"), and Hawai'i itself had the "progressive spirit" in trade that would make it an attractive "field for enterprise."[17] The magazine printed testimonials from visitors like the Reverend John W. Sellwood and his wife of Portland, Oregon, that "The natives of the city of Honolulu are pleasant, hospitable and intelligent"; other pieces detailed the comforts of Honolulu as "The Metropolis of Hawaii," or presented "Inducements to Settlers" by assuring readers that "Though Honolulu is a tropical town in every respect, it is impossible for one to be ashore five minutes without realizing that, after all, the energy and propelling power of this wonderful land are not tropical, but Anglo-Saxon. Wherever there is directing energy, or organizing power, or enterprise, or action, there one will find the American."[18] In 1898, the year of Hawai'i's annexation to the United States, *Paradise of the Pacific* subscribers would therefore not have been surprised to read Sereno E. Bishop's proud assertion that "even fifty, years ago, little to remind one of America was to be found in the Hawaiian islands. . . . Now Hawaii has grown to be substantially American in its institutions. The gentle natives have dwindled in numbers from 100,000 to 30,000, with 8,000 part-whites. . . . The atmosphere is American, socially and politically" ("Americanism of Hawaii"). And of course,

Paradise of the Pacific was itself an example of such "progress": by 1895, it had a new quarto format, halftone illustrations, and distribution "to every principal city in the United States and Canada, as well as to England and Europe."[19]

Paradise of the Pacific variously but consistently promised that the "stranger in Hawaii is sure to meet with a cordial welcome" and to enjoy a certain standard of modernity and comfort; however, to be distinctively attractive, Hawai'i's image also had to celebrate "its picturesque isle[s]." Articles and illustrations recording journeys to the Mauna Kea volcano, the majestic Nu'uanu Pali (*pali*, cliff), or the "uncultivated gardens" on Moloka'i supplied the necessary exotic touch to make Hawai'i a unique tourist destination, still supported by "soft primitivism." The publication of *mo'olelo* provided just that. These stories of "superstitious natives" offered an entertaining but safe glimpse into the fascinating "strangeness" of Hawai'i.[20]

Although "A Legend of Waikiki as Told by the Late R. S. Smith," the first text to bear that generic label, appeared in September 1888, it was a *Punch*-like parody about Mr. Da Diva, his wife on the phone, and his host Alcyoneus.[21] Apparently the potential value of *legendary Hawai'i* did not occur to the editors of *Paradise of the Pacific* until a few months later—perhaps in response to the 1888 publication of King Kalākaua's *The Legends and Myths of Hawaii* (which had the subtitle of *The Fables and Folk-Lore of a Strange People*); the magazine would positively review it in October 1889 (2.10:4). The first summary of a Hawaiian *mo'olelo* appeared in May 1889, in an anonymous recounting of the story of Waiānuenue, or "Rainbow Falls, Hilo," that featured the trickster Māui—the "Hawaiian Superman," in Israel Kamakawiwo'ole popular modern song—saving his mother Hina by opening up "the present channel for the pent up water" (2.5:6). A June 1889 article, "Where Tourists Can Go," however, describes in detail the magazine's understanding of the value of *mo'olelo*:

The antiquarian will find matter of great interest in legends famed in Hawaiian song and story, which he will meet with on the very soil where the incidents occurred. At Laieikawai, for example, will be found the pond where dwelt the maiden who could be approached only by diving under the water, although we cannot guarantee him an interview on the same terms. The famous water-fall and valley of Kaliuwaa will be pointed out as the scene of the life and the exploits of Kamapuaa, and the various spots traveled by Hiiaka-i-ka-poli-o-Pele in quest of her sister Pele's lover. There are many curious fragments of Hawaiian history still current in Kailua and Koolauloa. The English-speaking tourist need have no fear of traveling among people of an unknown tongue, for, thanks to the labors of the Board of Education, many of the Hawaiian are acquainted with the English language, and he will be pretty sure of having all proper questions answered to his satisfaction; and wherever he goes, he may count on being treated with a measure of civility fully up to the standards of his own practice. (2.6:5)

This mix of exoticism and safety promised potential tourists on their journeys in search of Hawaiian lore also characterized a number of narratives that began to appear in 1890. At this time, *Paradise of the Pacific* introduces a new series, "Legendary Lore," that would continue for the next decade.

At least four distinct types of translations or representations of Hawaiian *mo'olelo* were published in *Paradise of the Pacific* between 1890 and 1900. First, summaries of legends were embedded in ethnographic or scholarly pieces. The Reverend M. R. Forbes tucked Pele's and Kahawali's *holua* challenge (sled sliding down grassy slopes) into his "Hawaiian Antiquities"; later instances include the publication of the first two papers of the Hawaiian Historical Society in 1892, and a June 1893 piece on "Hawaiian Sharks" by Emma M. B. Nakuina. Second, excerpts from travel books (Ellis and Jarves), the *Annual*, or reports were reprinted under the heading "Legendary Lore." In November 1890, "A Legend of Pearl River" appeared; this was a reprint of Professor W. D. Alexander's story about why sharks are believed to be harmless in the district of 'Ewa, "now opened out to the tourist by the Oahu Railway," where the days when Natives "lived an easy unambitious life . . . are gone and now there is little to recall them to memory, but remnants of long deserted homes and the legends, still afloat, which the following is one" (3.11 [1890]:1). Third, anonymous texts, like "An Hawaiian Ogre" (4.3 [1891]:), or "Origin of Fire" (5.3 [1892]:1), also appeared under the "Legendary Lore" umbrella. A December 1890 piece, "A Story of Holua (Sliding Down Hill)" is an early example. This was a story that had already been published in Forbes's summary earlier in February, but the *Paradise of the Pacific* version is anonymous and includes some dialogue in both Hawaiian and English.[22] And fourth, certain authored texts simply invented Hawaiian traditions or cast them in a familiar Euro-American narrative frame and rhetoric. For example, Lilian Lyman's story in the March 1890 issue begins "In the olden times, long, long ago, before the algaroba trees in the yard were even seeds, there dwelt on the snowy summit of Mauna Kea a beautiful, happy race of little people, with childlike forms and silken locks, and voices like the tinkling bells, which were never raised in angry strife" ("The Fairies of Mauna Kea"). Whether cast in the mold of ethnography, travel literature, anonymous tale, or fiction, then, this "legendary lore" was always either safely in the past—that lifestyle, those people, their language were no longer—or had always been a childlike fantasy.[23]

These various re-framings of *mo'olelo* crystallized in the numerous contributions of William D. Westervelt to *Paradise of the Pacific* starting in 1900. His own brand of "Legendary Lore" became the norm for readers of the magazine. In 1905, Westervelt explained his assumptions as a guide to both story and culture in this way: "A myth is a purely imaginative story. A legend is a story with some foundation in fact. A fable tacks on a moral. A tradition is a myth, or legend, or fact, handed down from generation to generation. The old Hawaiians were frequently myth-makers. They imagined many a fairy story for the different localities of the islands, and these are very interesting" (18.2:12). After recognizing a relationship between "legend" and "fact," if not history, Westervelt then zooms in on Hawaiian *mo'olelo* as having stronger ties to a "purely imaginative story," or metonymically, with the "fairy story." His own career follows this pattern. His first contribution to *Paradise of the Pacific* was "A Hawaiian Historical Tale: The Law of the Splintered Paddle," which concludes that this law "marked the awakening of a pagan conscience to a sense of just dealing between the powerful and the weak" (13.5 [1900]:9). More commonly though, in his retelling of legends, phrases such as "fairy stories" or "delightful little story" point to the generic and ideological horizon of expectations Westervelt acknowledges in his Euro-American readers.[24] A short article in the December 1920 issue of *Paradise of the Pacific* about the "legends and stories written and published by the well-known authority, W. D. Westervelt" makes this strategy explicit: "All of the legends are fresh and charming and help to give glimpses into the workings of the thought and imagination of the simple dwellers in the Isles of the South Seas. Most persons never outgrow *fairy tales* and these have a glamour that makes them well worthy of preservation as companion pieces with the better known myths of Europe and Asia" ("Some Notable Hawaiian Books" 33.12:63, my emphasis). In addition to his books discussed in the next section and his articles published in other serialized publications, from 1900 through 1920 Westervelt contributed at least sixty-seven "myths" and "legends" to the *Paradise of the Pacific* alone.[25] Together, they display a style of retelling that skillfully combines the ethnographic, travel, and fictional modes of other *Paradise of the Pacific* contributors into a "signature" Westervelt, not unlike a Foucauldian "author function."

Translation: Popularizers, Rhetorical Frames, and Readership

In his 1949 *Hawaiian Legends in English: An Annotated Bibliography*, Amos P. Leib notes that a "great resurgence of interest in Hawaiian folklore began in the early twentieth century," concluding that "At least part of the interest was caused by Hawaii's annexation to the United States, for people on the mainland wanted to know more about their new island possessions." Leib credits these political dynamics and new money sources—"The funds of the Bureau of American Ethnology were made available for Hawaiian studies"—with contributing to the increase in commercial and scholarly publications in English about Hawaiians and their stories after 1900 (Leib and Day 14).[26] In his introduction, however, Leib himself seems to share this post-annexation (and later post-statehood) perspective that naturalizes the continental United States as the "mainland." Leib's focus was not on how annexation affected the politics of translation and publication, but on how successfully the "important" translators had met their "mainland" readers' interests. In his discussion of seven twentieth-century collectors and translators, Leib identifies three as holding center stage during what is implicitly a heroic period. These three men disseminated knowledge about Hawaiian culture in distinctive ways, linked closely to their vocations. Nathaniel B. Emerson was a man of medical science, Thomas G. Thrum, a man of commerce and publishing, and William D. Westervelt, a man of the church. We all know that empirical science, capitalism, and religious proselytism have helped to spread colonialism, but to narrow our focus to the production of knowledge most relevant here, they have all played a part in the emergence of folklore as a scholarly discipline.

Who were these translators who contributed to the production of *legendary Hawai'i*, and therefore, to the dissemination of popular notions about Hawai'i for Euro-American readers? Though all three are significant, because of my focus on photography's contribution as a new technology in producing an image of Hawaiians and Hawai'i, especially for non-Hawaiian readerships, in the early twentieth century, I will deal at length with Thomas G. Thrum and William D. Westervelt, not only because their books were photographically illustrated but because their English-language legends were also widely available in *Hawaiian Annual* (Thrum) and the *Paradise of the Pacific* (Westervelt), allowing me to discuss their books within this wider context of publication.

THE TRANSLATORS

Born in Australia, Thomas George Thrum (1842–1932) arrived in Hawai'i as a young boy in 1853. Though his formal education ended at age fourteen, he became an influential businessman, printer, and publisher. At first, he worked as a clerk in the Waterhouse and other Honolulu stores; he was also involved in the whaling and sugarcane businesses. But apparently he'd become fascinated with "printer's ink" at the age of twelve, when he met Abraham Fornander in his print shop, and while Thrum certainly did not otherwise share Fornander's views, he did start a stationery and news business in 1870, and then expanded to printing (Kuykendall 45; Chapin 79).The first issue of the *Annual* appeared in 1875. From 1880 to 1885, his *Saturday Press* paper, supported by the advertisements of Honolulu merchants, contributed to weakening King Kalākaua's legitimacy (Chapin 79–80). For a few months in 1888, he served as the first editor of *Paradise of the Pacific*, but between 1888 and 1904, he left the management of his business to his sons while he worked as registrar of conveyances, "serving under four governments, Kingdom, Provisional Government, Republic, and Territory." In 1913 his stationery and book business was incorporated as Thrum's Limited (Kuykendall 46); a 1915 profile of "Thomas G. Thrum, Researcher" in *Paradise of the Pacific*, reports that, after resigning the registrar position, he "devoted his time and energies to his business interests and to that research work which means so much toward the enrichment of his *Annual* and the general knowledge of the Hawaiian islands" (28.9: 9). In addition to several collections of legends, he produced a number of publications on Hawaiian *heiau* (temples) based on surveys he conducted on the various islands. A charter member of the Hawaiian Historical Society, he was further recognized as an authority in things Hawaiian when the Bishop Museum asked him to complete the editing of the *Fornander Collection of Hawaiian Antiquities and Folklore* (1916–1920).[27] In 1921, he became part of the museum staff as an "associate in Hawaiian folklore" (*Builders of Hawaii*, vol. 3 of *Men of Hawaii* 808); in 1931 the University of Hawai'i awarded him "the honorary degree of Master of Arts" (Taylor, "Tom Thrum").

Thrum was greatly respected for his *Annual*, which was not only a commercially successful enterprise, but a treasure trove of stories and information. He selected some of these texts for publication in two photographically illustrated volumes, *Hawaiian Folk Tales: A Collection of Native Legends* (1907) and *More Hawaiian Folk Tales: A Collection of Native Legends and Traditions* (1923). Both were published by A. C. McClurg and Company in Chicago. The first collection, *Hawaiian Folk Tales*, has gone through a number of editions (1912, 1917, 1921, 1976, and, with no photographic illustrations, 1998). He reprinted a few stories from *Hawaiian Folk Tales* in *Hawaiian Traditions: Stories of the Menehunes*, also issued by A. C. McClurg & Co. in 1910; in 1920, Thrum also published *Tributes of Hawaiian Traditions: The Pali and Battle of Nuuanu; Kaliuwaa Falls and Kamapuaa, the Demigod*, versions of tales from the *Hawaiian Annual* and *Hawaiian Folk Tales*. While the 1907 collection seemed more like an anthology, identifying a number of different redactors or authors, only Thrum's name appeared in the later books, paralleling the trend I noted earlier in the "legends" feature of his *Annual.* In 1954, Taylor would write that: "Thrum has been dead 22 years, yet luster is constantly added to his name as more librarians, scientists, economists, historians and students of the many phases of Hawaii's changing life rely on Thrum for information." Clearly, he had become a recognized author(ity) about Hawai'i and Hawaiian lore.[28]

Though of Thrum's generation and also a settler, the Reverend William Drake Westervelt (1849–1939) had a college education and did not move permanently to Hawai'i until after its annexation to the United States. Originally from Ohio, Westervelt received a B.A. from Oberlin College in 1871, "attended Yale from 1872 to 1873," and then served as a pastor in Ohio, New York State, Colorado, and Michigan. First coming to Hawai'i for two years "to make a study of mission work" in 1889 (*Men of Hawaii* 3:858–60), he returned in 1899, after some years in Chicago, to live in Honolulu, where he studied the Hawaiian language with a native Hawaiian (Leib and Day 22) and married his second wife, Caroline D. Castle, of the influential missionary Hawai'i family. "This country fascinated me," he was quoted to have proclaimed (*Men of Hawaii* 3:858). Affiliated with the Kalihi Union Church and the Anti-Saloon League, he was "a foremost worker of all the benevolences of Honolulu" (860), translating religious works into Hawaiian and printing articles about temperance in *The Friend*.[29] A member of the Polynesian Society of New Zealand, the National Geographic Association, and the Hawaiian Historical Society, where he presented several reports on Hawaiian history, he was also "One of the world's first stamp collectors" ("Westervelt, Veteran Isle Figure" 6) and belonged to the Pan-Pacific Union, Hawaiian Board of Missions, and Chamber of Commerce.

Having published a great many individual Hawaiian tales, first in the Chicago-based *Cram's Magazine* (1899–1901), and then in English-language magazines in Hawai'i—most notably in *Paradise of the Pacific*—Westervelt eventually collected a number of these translated tales in a series of volumes. *Legends of Ma-ui* (1910) and *Around the Poi Bowl* (1913) were both published in Hawai'i; his most widely known books were *Legends of Old Honolulu* (1915 and 1916),[30] *Legends of Gods and Ghosts* (1915), *Hawaiian Legends of Volcanoes* (1916), all published by the Boston-based Press of Geo. H. Ellis Company, and *Hawaiian Historical Legends* (1923), published by the Fleming H. Revell Company (New York and Chicago). All contained photographic illustrations, often with no attribution, though some were reprinted from *Paradise of the Pacific* and some were possibly Westervelt's own amateurish takes (Davis, personal communication, 2003). With slightly different titles in two cases (*Hawaiian Legends of Old Honolulu* and *Hawaiian Legends of Ghosts and Ghost-Gods*), Westervelt's books were reprinted by Tuttle in the 1960s and 1970s, testifying to his success as a popularizer. Recent paperback editions are numerous (1981, 1987, 1998, 1999, 2003); like the latest Thrum reprint, the most recent paperback editions of Westervelt do not contain photographic illustrations. All are readily available today in Waikīkī stores, usually shelved with Hawai'i postcards and souvenirs.

THE FRAMES FOR THEIR TRANSLATIONS

"I should state my right" to present the myths and legends of Polynesia, Fornander admits at the beginning of his preface to *An Account of the Polynesian Race*, "how I came about them, and also the lights that guided me and the aids that assisted me on the journey" (iii). Departing from Gérard Genette, Mieke Bal's cultural analysis has shown that the verbal and the visual world of story comes to us filtered through liminal devices that frame it and set the parameters for readers' access and expectations. The verbal and visual apparatus of a text in print can include its preface, introduction, notes, genre denomination, illustrations, cover, graphics, and self-representation of the author/translator/editor. This often multifaceted paratext, which accompanies and comments on the text, becomes even more complicated when the printed text is the product of translation—from oral to written, from the Hawaiian language to the English, from one genre system to another—or even more specifically from colonized peoples to colonizing ones in the form of folklore (Naithani, "Prefaced Space"). When examining Thrum's and Westervelt's volumes of translations, I have found that taking note of their paratextual framing devices foregrounds the rhetorical construction of their subject matter and their authority, which in turn shapes how Thrum's and Westervelt's translations enact "visual illustration."

Though minimal compared to Westervelt's, the verbal paratext of Thrum's volumes is nevertheless telling. His 1907 *Hawaiian Folk Tales: A Collection of Native Legends* (*HFT*) contains twenty-five tales or chapters by different contributors—five by Emma Nakuina, four by the Reverend A. O. Forbes, three by Moses Nakuina (Emma's second husband), and individual tales by other "recognized authorities" (Thrum *HFT* vii). Four are explicitly by Thrum. Several of these "legends" had already been published in Thrum's *Hawaiian Annual.* Preceded by King David Kalākaua's *The Legends and Myths of Hawaii* (1888) and by Emma Nakuina's own *Hawaii: Its People, Their Legends* (1904), Thrum's was certainly not the first volume devoted entirely to Hawaiian legends to be published in English. But, even if we take into account Daggett's editorial intervention in King Kalākaua's collection, Thrum's was the first book produced by a settler focused exclusively on Hawai'i tales. The volume also includes a preface by Thrum, a glossary of Hawaiian terms, and advertisements for Dr. Henry M. Lyman's *Hawaiian Yesterdays*, a memoir also published by McClurg.

Thrum's focus too seems to be on "Hawaiian Yesterdays." Dated January 1, 1907, his two-page preface opens with an expression of "regret that a larger amount of systematic effort was not established in early years for the gathering and preservation of the folk-lore of the Hawaiians" (*HFT* v). Though he names a number of "devoted" scholars, Judge Abraham Fornander foremost, he unequivocally states that "the *haku meles* (bards) of Hawaii are gone" and that it is now up to scholars and institutions such as the new Bishop Museum and the Hawaiian Historical Society "to give us further insight into the legendary folk-lore of this interesting race" (vi). This book, therefore, not only answers the "repeated requests" of readers of the *Annual* but also responds to an urgent need to "rescue the ancient traditions that are gradually slipping away." In the very brief foreword dated July 1, 1922, to *More Hawaiian Folk Tales: A Collection of Native Legends and Traditions* (1923, *MHFT*), Thrum notes the "very favorable reception" of the first volume, and acknowledges his debt to the *Annual* for providing "choice gleanings in the field of Hawaiian folklore" (*MHFT* n.p.)—a phrase that strongly echoes Englishman William John Thoms's devolutionary rhetoric of nostalgia for a Saxon rural past when in 1846 he first proposed the introduction of the word "folk-lore" into the English language.[31]

As for Westervelt, given his prodigious production as a translator of Hawaiian *mo'olelo*, I will refer here primarily to his best-known collections: *Legends of Old Honolulu* (*LOH*), *Legends of Gods and Ghosts* (*LGG*; also reprinted as *Hawaiian Legends of Ghosts and Ghost-Gods* [*HLGG*]), *Hawaiian Legends of Volcanoes* (*HLV*), and *Hawaiian Historical Legends* (*HHL*). Each collection is framed by a foreword, an introduction by the translator, and an appendix, which includes a note on Polynesian language (reprinting W. D. Alexander's 1865 preface to Lorrin Andrews's first *Dictionary of Hawaiian Language*), and a partial list of Hawaiian names.

Still the best-known popularizer of Hawaiian legends in English, Westervelt built a reputation in the first quarter of the twentieth century as the translator whose production of legends "surpasse[d], in quantity at least, the output of any other author on the subject" (Leib and Day 21). As in Thrum's volumes, Hawaiian "antiquities" are Westervelt's subject matter, but the paratextual apparatus of his books and his own narrative style indicate that his construction of legendary Hawai'i far more explicitly puts "yesteryear" nostalgia in the service of a religious and political narrative of "development." In the foreword to *Legends of Old Honolulu*, George H. Barton of the Teachers' School of Science in Boston declares that this collection confers "a great favor upon all those residents of Hawaii and of [*sic*] those visitors to its shores who may take an interest in its original inhabitants, once an exceedingly numerous people, but now a scattering remnant only" (*LOH* iii–iv). In a foreword (dated 1916) to *Hawaiian Legends of Ghosts and Ghost-Gods*, J. W. Gilmore, professor of agronomy at the University of California at Berkeley, writes that "no doubt none will appreciate this volume more than the people of Hawaii themselves. May it serve them as a light showing the path they have trod in passing through the valley of superstition to the high lands of truth and understanding" (*HLGG* x). Though the preservation of fragments from the past is important, these scholars from well-known institutions of American education, and presumably Westervelt himself, agree that making a lesson out of the contrast between precontact Hawai'i and Christianized territorial Hawai'i should be the primary task.

The familiar folktale or fairy-tale narrative that moves from lack to transformation and redemption—or, in the anthropological framework of the time, the developmental narrative that moves from primitivism to civilization—therefore also structures Westervelt's volumes. Though "imaginative," he writes, "the ancient Hawaiians were not inventive" (*LOH* vii), but thanks to the American missionaries, they were "rapidly" "taught to read and write their histories and ancient stories." Or, as Gilmore puts it, the Hawaiians' "capacity for rapid intellectual development" accounts for how "rapid" "their transformation under organized government and institutions" has been (*HLGG* x). In the later volume *Hawaiian Historical Legends*, Westervelt gets to the point: "From mist to sunshine—from fabled gods to a constitution and legislature as a Territory of the United States—this is the outline of the stories told in the present volume" (n.p.). Caught in the sunlight metaphor of revelation and progress, and unfolded chronologically in the pages of the book itself, this developmental narrative finds approval from Sanford Dole— Supreme Court judge, president of the Interim Republic of Hawai'i, and first governor after annexation—who states in his introduction that "The Hawaiian legends are not mere stories. They are tremendously interesting and valuable in that they contain real characters, they bring out the characteristics of the people" (n.p.)—people who have apparently emerged "from the fogs of the imagination" (Westervelt, *HHL* n.p.).

Representing the "other" as primitive is hardly uncommon in early folklore studies. What I find instructive in these volumes and in *Paradise of the Pacific* is the development of "safe" exoticism or "soft primitivism" (Desmond 4, based on Bernard Smith's locution) in the representation of Hawaiianness, and the speed with which this "scholarly" narrative merges with a political and economic post-annexation agenda. As the cover of the January 1892 *Paradise of the Pacific* visually demonstrates (Figure 15), in this manifestation of American Pacificism (Paul Lyons), the imaginative, nonthreatening, and eager-to-learn Hawaiians can have

Figure 15. *Paradise of the Pacific* cover 1892. Courtesy of Hamilton Library, Hawaiian/Pacific Collection, University of Hawai'i-Mānoa.

"legendary" or "mythic" allure, *and* welcome progress, development, and tourism enthusiastically:[32]

> The "Paradise of the Pacific" presented to its readers a work of art, in the cover, from the artistic lithographing establishment of the well known Crocker Co. of San Francisco. The subject was allegorical and represented the Hawaiian islands shown in the female form divine' [*sic*] advancing to partake of imbibition in the waters of the "well of progress" and advancement; the lamp of enlightenment diffused its light and disclosed the volumes of history and knowledge. This main picture is truly representative of the present transitory state of the Hawaiians and has received very favorable comment. (5.1 [1892]:4)

Graceful and classically garbed female figures move willingly toward the "Well of Progress," displaying all the visual appeal of those "divine" or "legendary" beings of classical mythology that Euro-American translators often compare them to. Truly, though, these Hawaiian figures are on the way to the world of enlightenment, where "history and knowledge," even about themselves, will largely come from books that Natives have not written.

Westervelt's "from mist to sunshine" frame therefore also raises issues of authority. Introduced and vouched for by "important" American men,[33] the "author" is commended for his "patience and persistence" (*HLGG*). Westervelt himself declares that *Legends of Old Honolulu* is the product of "careful research" through newspapers and magazines published from 1850 to 1870, and of "several years' worth of notetaking and compilation" (xi). While Native historian Samuel Kamakau, Hawaiian-language newspapers, and "old Hawaiians," some "still living" (*LOH* vii) have "been of great assistance in searching for these 'fragments of Hawaiian history'" (*HHL* n.p.), just as the "development" of Hawaiians "is the result of the labors of American missionaries" (*LOH* viii), so does the praise belong to Westervelt and his project. As Sadhana Naithani notes of British translators of Indian legends, the amateur—and colonizing—folklorist stands forth as the authority and real hero of this kind of colonial translation and enterprise.

THEIR RE-FRAMING OF GENRE AND READERSHIP

Along with claiming authorship through translation and signature—a phenomenon that scholars of folklore and literature both will recognize—comes the authority of granting meaning to stories by classifying them. Though Thrum calls his collections *Folk Tales*, in the subtitles he is already labeling the stories as "legends." In 1907, at least, classification was loose and not of primary interest to him in a collection containing a range of identified translators and views. Westervelt's books and articles in *Paradise of the Pacific* also refer to "fairy stories," "myths," and "legends" as interchangeable Western genres within which to read Hawaiian (hi)stories. But he also explicitly seeks to categorize Hawaiian *mo'olelo* anew. As I have already pointed out, the "fairy story" is the dominant framework for his *Paradise of the Pacific* translations of *mo'olelo*. In his books, though, Westervelt suggests other frames that also do violence to Hawaiian epistemology and narrative. While granting that Hawaiian stories are "diverse" (*LGG* xii), his titles nevertheless group them as religious (*Legends of Gods and Ghosts*), geographical (*Legends of Old Honolulu*), and historical (*Hawaiian Historical Legends*). These types of legends are Western classifications; the deeply located, spiritual, and historical dimensions of "storied places," which *together* inform the Hawaiians' articulation of *mo'olelo*, are thus separated and re-sorted into a foreign framework. While it is common practice to search for a link with what we know in order to understand something "foreign," this classification results in appropriation. Now authoritatively arranged, these legends tell stories of religious, social, and political "development" from a settler perspective.

This Western comparative lens re-frames Hawaiian narratives by obscuring the emplaced significance of the *wahi pana*, instead aligning *mo'olelo* with "the laws upon which all myths are constructed" (*LGG* v). Comparative analyses suggesting parallels with biblical texts or other Oceanic narratives were of course neither new, nor are they per se unproductive. I do, however, want to suggest that Westervelt's adoption of a comparative frame worked primarily to further the commercial potential of his retellings. In the "Introduction" to *Legends of Gods and Ghosts*, for example, Westervelt states that the "Islanders have developed some beautiful nature-myths"—stories that paradoxically follow the laws of all mythology and yet are "entirely distinct in form and thought from the fairy-tales which excite the interest and wonder of the English and German children." Even after noting how the Hawaiian "imagination has fitted the story" to particular phenomena, such as the formation of rainbows or the color of fish, he re-places the results, declaring that: "Such nature-myths as these are well worthy of preservation by the side of any European fairy-tale" (*LGG* v and vii). Hawaiian epistemology, or the relationship of Hawaiians to Mānoa Valley, the materials providing the basis for the rainbow example, go out of focus, as the comparative frame moves Westervelt's books into Euro-American libraries. Fairy tales function as the strongest association for "nature-myths"; when Westervelt turns to stories about chiefs, he reminds his readers of "the days of the Nibelungen Lied" and "the voyages of the Vikings" (*LGG* x). These associations are often only that: hooks to make the reader both comfortable and curious. By providing them, though, Westervelt's own authority

and the appeal of *his* mediated retellings increase. Not surprisingly perhaps, salient sections of this "Introduction" were reprinted in *Paradise
of the Pacific* in 1923 as "'Myths Are Phenomena Plus Imagination' by
W. D. Westervelt, author of 'Legends of Honolulu,'" a piece that under
the guise of a short article was more of a glorified advertisement for his
oeuvre (36.11:4).

To and for whom were Thrum and Westervelt writing and translating?
In his foreword to *Hawaiian Legends of Old Honolulu*, Barton claims that
"The legends of a people are of interest to the scholar, the thinker, and
the poet" (vii), feeding Westervelt's scholarly pretensions and also allud-
ing to those disciplines closest to Western folklore studies: history and
anthropology, philosophy and psychology, linguistics and literature.
Thanks to the work of folklorists like Roger D. Abrahams, Richard Bauman, Regina Bendix, Simon Bronner, Domenico Paredes, and Jennifer
Schacker, it is now clear that while early folkloristic endeavors were generally understood to be disinterested at the time, they served nation-
building and other politicized agendas in Europe and in the United
States. A more pointed question therefore emerges for us in retrospect:
for whose *benefit* were these books of Hawaiian legends translated and
published in post-annexation Hawai'i? In the Kalākaua period, Abraham
Fornander dedicated *The Polynesian Race* to his daughter Catherine Ka-
onohiulaokalani Fornander, "as a reminder of her mother's ancestors
and as a token of her father's love." In his preface, he unequivocally
stated that: "I submit this work without hesitation to the favourable
regard of the Hawaiians and the Polynesians," whose past, "in the busy
hum of a new era and civilization," has been "derided by some, disputed
by others, unheeded by all" (ix). When introducing his *Legends of Old
Honolulu* in 1915, however, Westervelt writes that: "These legends
belong of course to Honolulu people, and will be chiefly of interest to
them" (viii). Native Hawaiians are not mentioned, and "Honolulu people" certainly makes sense from a marketing perspective for a book of
"Old Honolulu" legends. But Westervelt also hopes that "those who are
acquainted with the city and the island of Oahu" would appreciate the
tales. And perhaps most important, "folk-lore lovers the world over will
also enjoy comparing these tales with those of other lands" (viii). Read
in the context of the stories' presentation in the English-language
medium and the Western rhetorical frames I have been limning, this
statement further confirms that the beneficiaries of Westervelt's volumes
were not Native Hawaiians.

Though newcomers, visitors, and prospective visitors were the likely
target, as the marketing of *Paradise of the Pacific*, or the *Annual*, and the
numerous other books about Hawai'i circulating around annexation has
already suggested, for Westervelt, researchers and collectors of folklore

were also a specific and explicit audience outside of Hawai'i. Reviews of Thrum's and Westervelt's books appeared not only in publications like *Dial* or the *Times Literary Supplement*, but also in more scholarly journals such as *Journal of the Polynesian Society*, the British *Folklore*, or the *Journal of American Folklore*. In fact, when we consider the range of their publications, it becomes clear that Thrum and especially Westervelt were with their "translations" seeking to interest *both* the general and the scholarly Euro-American reader.

Sometimes the authors altered the format of publication in response to the assumed audience. In Thrum's 1907 volume of *Hawaiian Folk Tales*, the section "Stories of the Menehunes: Hawaii the Original Home of the Brownies" gathered together five narratives "from various native sources." He explained that "this adventurous nomadic tribe were known to the Hawaiians long before Swift's satirical mind conceived his Lilliputians" (107), and assured readers that while some Hawaiians "treat the subject with gravity and respect," certainly "the more intelligent and better educated look upon the Menehunes as a mythical class of gnomes or dwarfs, and the account of their exploits as having been handed down by tradition for social entertainment, as other peoples relate fairy stories" (108). Reprinted in 1910 by McClurg as *Hawaiian Traditions: Stories of the Menehunes*, this version had more photographs and, typical of the period's Hawaiiana, a lovely *koa*-leaf design framed its pages. The text was the same, but the first story's title was changed from "Moke Manu's Account" (*HFT* 109), an acknowledgment of Thrum's source, to "Character of the Menehune"; no longer mediated by the Hawaiian writer, Thrum's words respond to the readers' implied curiosity by foregrounding it (Figure 16). In a prefiguring of later translations of Hawaiian legends into children's literature, this booklet is visually attractive and appears to be fairly light reading in the spirit of "social entertainment," only one of the modes enacted in the 1907 volume. In 1920, however, Thrum published the "Story of the Race of People Called the Menehunes, of Kauai (A Hawaiian Tradition)" in the *Journal of the Polynesian Society*; this time, he provides "a somewhat free translation to lessen the tautology of the original" of an accompanying Hawaiian-language text and some ethnographic commentary in brackets. The translation presents a first-person account of stories that the narrator heard from his grandparents, but the source for the Hawaiian text remains anonymous. The pictures and mention of "social entertainment" are gone, but two footnotes have appeared.

That there could be different versions of and attitudes toward the *menehune* stories is not the issue. What interests me is how the stories—even when presented in the exact same words—were inflected differently to suit different markets, a strategy that Thrum, as a publisher

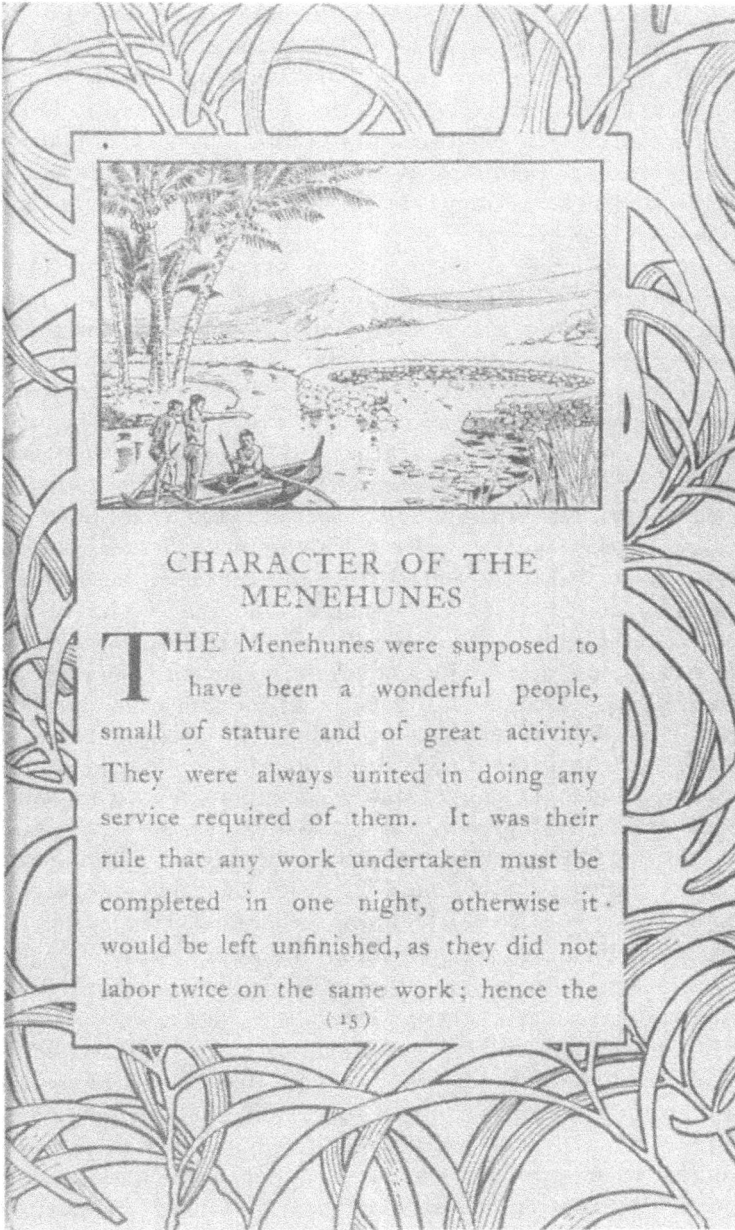

CHARACTER OF THE MENEHUNES

THE Menehunes were supposed to have been a wonderful people, small of stature and of great activity. They were always united in doing any service required of them. It was their rule that any work undertaken must be completed in one night, otherwise it would be left unfinished, as they did not labor twice on the same work; hence the

(15)

Figure 16. Thomas G. Thrum, "Character of the Menehunes" 1910. Courtesy of Hamilton Library, Hawaiian/Pacific Collection, University of Hawai'i-Mānoa.

himself, would have known well. Whether the 1910 book was his idea or not, Thrum knew how to write for different audiences. As early as 1882, his *Tributes of Hawaiian Verse* showed that he recognized the appeal of books as a "holiday souvenir" ("Preface"). In my view, while he followed his own agenda as a researcher in ways that did eventually bring him recognition at the Bishop Museum, in most of his publications this scholarly tendency was framed by the demands of commerce, and his skills in negotiating them.

In contrast, whether they appeared in his books or in *Paradise of the Pacific*, Westervelt's "translations" were consistent in style and manner, complete with photos, lots of interpolated commentary, and no notes. In keeping with his profession as a pastor, "his" story was the same wherever it was delivered—though always framed by his enlightened authority *and* an attractive packaging. National reviews of both Thrum's and Westervelt's volumes generally appreciated their rescuing Hawaiian traditions from oblivion and also their effort to produce interesting books that the general reader could enjoy. Specialized journals, however, did not always approve of Westervelt's style or ambition. Though the *Journal of the Polynesian Society* did remark that "Mr. Westervelt has a vivid style and an unerring sense of the dramatic, and no one who has begun the book [*Hawaiian Historical Legends*] will easily lay it down" (Skinner 141), *Folklore* would note that "unfortunately the collection [*Legends of Ma-ui*] is by way of republication of popular magazine articles, and is, in most cases, without definite references to authorities" (Wright 521), and the *Journal of American Folklore* levels accusations: "Mr. Westervelt does not refer his readers to his sources, and he sometimes takes what seem like personal liberties with his material" (Beckwith, "Review" 325). And yet, while a trained folklorist like Martha Beckwith might question his claims to scholarly activity, in that same 1925 review she acknowledges that "It is mainly through Mr. Westervelt's four earlier books of tales that Hawaiian legendary material has been known in Europe" (325).[34]

I have two points here. First, that not only general readers and prospective visitors, but folklorists and anthropologists as well were paying attention to Thrum's and Westervelt's books in the early twentieth century. Second, that marketing, whether it affected the graphics, the style, or both, strongly influenced how successful these books were with their different audiences outside of Hawai'i and also how these two men negotiated their reputations as "experts" on *and* "popularizers" of Hawaiian legends at a time when, in Beckwith's words, "Hawaiian story" was understood to be "in its more genuine shape difficult of assimilation to the European imagination" ("Review" 327).

Whether it was under the umbrella of Western scholarship, or of development and tourism, the re-framing process of translation and marketing instituted several kinds of transformations that drastically reduced the say that Hawaiians could exercise in print over their own traditions. Anonymous informants but not interlocutors, Hawaiians in these volumes were, in the eyes of Euro-American readers, objects of interest rather than the subjects of their own *mo'olelo*. Abraham Fornander openly acknowledged his "obligations" to Kalākaua and Kamakau, to the "intelligent and educated Hawaiians" he had hired, as well as to the "old natives" from whom they had collected and transcribed legends, prayers, and history methodology (*Polynesian Race* iv–v). Thrum's and Westervelt's methodology was mysterious. Thrum went from anthologizing stories recorded or translated by others—whom he acknowledged—to publishing stories under his own name with vaguely generic or no credit at all given to sources. Reviewers of Westervelt might claim his sources were both oral and published, but for the most part he himself did not acknowledge them. In both cases, though, the complex negotiations of collecting, interpreting, and translating became largely subsumed into the enterprise of publishing and "authoring."

And yet, these appropriations somehow did not require Thrum or Westervelt to acknowledge their roles as "producers" or fiction-makers. In the preface to his 1923 volume, Thrum cautioned readers that "The growing interest in all that relates to the past of the Hawaiian race, makes the temptation strong for story-writers to provide legendary tales on hearsay fragments to meet the demand" (n.p.). That Thrum and Westervelt explicitly or implicitly could claim to be providing "unvarnished tales" (*MHFT* n.p.) meant that questions of translation could not be raised. This silence is particularly striking if we read an 1898 letter about his own translation of Davida Malo's *Moolelo Hawaii* by N. B. Emerson:

> The accomplishment of this work would have been impossible without the aid of a few elderly Hawaiians, well versed in the lore of their own people, whom I have consulted, and to whose opinions I have given such weight as my judgment approved. For though I consider myself fairly well equipped as to the knowledge of the Hawaiian language and the traditions, history, mythology and literature of the people, still when it comes to getting at the inner meaning of passages, the key to which is to be found in some *local allusion*, or that is veiled in obsolete, or highly poetical language, such words as are not found in the dictionary, I have found it necessary to resort to some Hawaiian, one who was *acquainted with the locality*, or to whom the legend, poetry or myth was familiar. (Institutional Records, Bernice Pauahi Bishop Museum, Letters in Bk II, 1897–1898; my emphasis)

This was not the *legendary Hawai'i* that Thrum and Westervelt create. Whatever unacknowledged assistance they received, their productions promote their own authority on Hawaiian traditions and rely on the fiction of translation's transparency.

Their Translations of "Visual Illustration"

To further unmake this fiction, I will now examine how what Luomala called "visual illustration"—a narrative strategy that often informs the telling of *wahi pana* stories, as we saw in Chapter 2—became integrated into Thrum's and Westervelt's frameworks.[35] What interests me is that these recontextualized and entextualized (Briggs) narratives do seek to reproduce the spatial organization and localized experience of Hawaiian storytelling, but in ways that uproot storied places and violently reconfigure their articulation of narrative, place, and history. My point here is not that all translation is invariably violent; rather I will contrast the performative aspects and historicizing effects of Thrum's and Westervelt's translations to those of Anne Kapulani Landgraf's—whose use of "visual narrative" was at the heart of Chapter 2.

Kaliuwa'a is the place on the island of O'ahu most associated with the tricksterlike pig god Kamapua'a, his birth, and his first successful tricks. This place name recalls an event and points to a feature of the location that is itself a visible reminder of that event. When, after being robbed of their chickens, King 'Olopana and his men attacked Kamapua'a, the pig god grew in size and, then, leaning against the hard rock of the very high cliff of Kaliuwa'a, he saved his family by letting them climb up his body to safety on the other side. Kamapua'a's body either created the falls, or "created the uniquely grooved cliff face, which today looks like a dugout canoe" (James 66). Literally "the canoe leak" or "the canoe hold" (Pukui, Elbert & Mookini 77), Kaliuwa'a itself, therefore, comes into being as a place marked by Kamapua'a's body and power (Figure 17).[36]

Thomas G. Thrum must have regarded Kaliuwa'a as a significant "legendary place" since he took his readers to it more than once. In his 1907 *Hawaiian Folk Tales*, he reprinted a nineteenth-century piece from the *Hawaiian Spectator* to introduce Kaliuwa'a, "one of the most beautiful and romantic spots of the island, and famed in tradition as possessing more than local interest" (*HFT* 193). The "traveller" (193) in this piece is both "one" and "we," thus functioning as focalizer in the detailed description of the valley, the narrator, and the implied reader as future visitor. His attention, after leaving his horse and following "up the stream for about a quarter of a mile, . . . is directed by the guide to a curiosity called by the natives a *waa* (canoe)" (193–194). The traveler therefore has a guide, implicitly a Native guide, whose words point out a place that "one" would otherwise not see, because from the traveler's

FALLS IN THE VALLEY OF KALIUWAA

Figure 17. Falls in the Valley of Kaliuwaa. By Dr. J. S.B. Pratt. Emma Nakuina's *Hawaii, Its People, Their Legends*. Courtesy of Bishop Museum.

perspective, other features stand out: the "luxuriant verdure" (195), the beauty of the stream and fall, and the shadow of the *kukui* (candlenut) tree on the water appear in spatial sequence that traces the steps of the visitor, and these sights all contribute to the traveler's gratification of mind and soul. Step by step, the anonymous narrator takes us through what in his guide's eyes must have been a lived-in place, a *storied place*, marked by the visible signs of Kamapua'a's powerful presence and actions. For the guide, the lush vegetation, water, and *kukui* nuts would be the body shapes, or *kino lau*, of the pig god, and the "furrow" or "leak" of the canoe would be significant story triggers. "Popular books by early settlers, travellers, government officials, missionaries, and journalists often contain anecdotes about visits to inspect legendary sites," writes Katharine Luomala: "There the native guides may or may not have told the associated myths. The narrating depends on their ability to communicate with their guests by other means than pointing and demonstrating" ("Dynamic" 138). Whether the storytelling in loco occurred or not, though, the stories would have been part of the Hawaiian guide's "invisible luggage" (Carter xiv), in a sense guiding him and his perceptions of Kaliuwa'a.

But the narrator only reports these stories in summary, as a coda to his own self-gratifying narrative of landscape. Kamapua'a's exploits are summarized simply to "assist the reader to understand the character of the native mind and throw some light also on the history of the Hawaiians" (*HFT* 197). The telling does not offer a way to know the place in its intimate details, but instead supplies a general explanation for "why there are no more islands formed" (following the "happy ending" marriage of Kamapua'a and the volcano goddess Pele) and provides evidence of "the superstitious awe" that "even to this day" would account for the offerings visitors see (199). The stories, therefore, separate the "traveller," for whom Kaliuwa'a is "a spot [of] natural scenic attraction" (197), from the naïve Native. While this indexically or geographically grounded telling may mimic the Hawaiian place-based storytelling performance, the Western narrator's double-voiced narrative conforms to his own culturally marked nature versus history dichotomy, silencing the Hawaiian "storied place" in the process and displacing the Native as the authoritative guide to it. Even the scene itself gets displaced. The photo accompanying the "Kaliuwaa" chapter features a completely different water and verdure scene, with the caption "Kuumana the Rain God of Kau."

In his 1920 *Tributes of Hawaiian Traditions*, Thrum's own narrative "Kaliuwaa Falls or Sacred Valley" retells the story differently, and supplies a photo, "Kaliuwaa Falls," taken by his son (Figure 18). Thrum begins by promising a "descriptive account of a recent summer outing" that "may serve as an aid to others to do likewise" (19). As "a delver into myths and traditions of the land," he decides to "visit the scene of Kamapuaa's alleged marvellous exploits" with "a young native familiar with the historic valley" to serve as "guide, informant, and helper" (22). The narration then carries us into stories and places simultaneously, lin-

KALIUWAA FALLS   D. F. Thrum, Photo

Figure 18. Kaliuwaa Falls. By D. F. Thrum. *Tributes.* Courtesy of Bishop Museum.

king natural and cultural geography, without describing either in great detail but maintaining a certain distance from the "alleged" history of the place (22–23). Native offerings "to propitiate the deities of the glen for a safe and successful valley trip" are in evidence, "and the custom was duly observed by my factotum at the first rude altar," leading Thrum to suggest that this is "why it is frequently called the "sacred valley" (23). When they get to the famous falls and "grooved cliff," Thrum's language exudes skepticism: "This fall is but 87 feet high, and the clear, inviting pool at its base is said to be bottomless, though I have never known this to deter any of the many valley trampers from a refreshing bath in its cool waters" (23). At this point, Thrum appends to this personal account the more detailed "guided tour" offered by the *Hawaiian Spectator* "early writer" he had ventriloquized in 1907 (24–29).

In interesting ways, Thrum's multivoiced 1920 descriptive account (his own, the early writer's, and the summarized native stories) draws attention to competing senses of place in a less ideologically rigid and evolutionary stance than he did as the "early writer." Even in this layered frame, however, Thrum's narrative relegates the "storied place" to the past in a number of ways. The guide's own storytelling on location remains unreported; the early writer's description is the most detailed and thus seemingly authoritative; and the final words assure readers that, since "extensive eruptions" are over, there is no "new" land, no growth—and implicitly, no future "storied place" (29).[37]

Tributes of Hawaiian Traditions was a photographically illustrated booklet that Thrum published through the Hawaiian Gazette Company as "a souvenir of notable scenes of O'ahu, and historic traditions and myths connected therewith" (3). It included only two pieces: a reprint of "The Pali and Battle of Nuuanu" from the *Hawaiian Annual* and the expanded "Kaliuwaa." When introducing the latter, Thrum notes that its "remarkable geological formation" and the Kamapua'a legends have "made the locality a Mecca for sight-seeing tourists and others in undiminished annual numbers" (19), and it is easy to surmise that this "souvenir" book is meant for such visitors.[38]

Westervelt's tour-guide approach to "legendary places" informs his re-framing of "visual illustration" in even more consistent and obvious ways. "Kamapuaa Legends: Legends of the Hog-God" is the last chapter of *Hawaiian Legends of Old Honolulu*. Westervelt takes his readers to the "the sporting places of Kamapuaa," on a May sunlit morning, when "a little band of Hawaiians and their white friends lay in the shade of a great kamani tree and talked about the legends which were told of the rugged rock masses of each valley, and the quiet pools of each rivulet" (248). Kamapua'a's adventures follow in summarized form, and geographical markers do get mentioned: "Several large stones on the edges

of the valleys were pointed out as monuments of various adventures."
But which valleys? Which stones? Here is how he identifies Kaliuwa'a:
"An exquisitely formed little valley ran deep into the mountain almost
in front of the legend-tellers" (248). The storytelling tour here takes
place "virtually," with its description cast in a generic mode: "steep cliffs
. . . black rocks . . . beautiful stream . . . deep gorge" (254). The valley
and the falls are painted in the broad strokes of an imaginary landscape,
which like the dark forest of the German fairy tale, does not require
detail to be vivid. The scene of storytelling stays in focus, while the legendary places remain covered in "mist"—a recurring image in this
book—that reinterprets the erotic and poetic metaphor of Hawaiian
song within the Western developmental narrative I outlined earlier.

But if "storied place" becomes mythic landscape in Westervelt's storytelling, the landscape itself is given meaning by modernity in at least two
ways. First, by offering a safe tour of exotic places, *Legends of Old Honolulu*
functions like a Baedeker of early cultural tourism. The map at the back
provides visitors with information about modern ways of transporta-
tion—roads and the railroad—to places outside of the city. Especially in
the chapter entitled "Legendary Places in Honolulu," we also find fre-
quent references to buildings and streets. These are the "bread crumbs"
or "pebbles" that allow Westervelt's readers in Hansel-and-Gretel fashion to find their way in *legendary Hawai'i*. The farmland of what used to
be known as "Honolulu" (*LOH* 14) has been replaced by "the junction
of Liliha and School Streets." "Ula-kua, the place where idols were
made, was near the lumber-yards at the foot of the present Richards
Street" (16), Westervelt notes, and the "Bank of Hawaii along the sea-
ward side of Merchant Street" marks the gathering place of chiefs (17).
As for "Waolani," "the wilderness home of the gods," it is now the
"home of the Honolulu Country Club" (19). Modern landmarks appear
in other chapters (*LOH* 9, 28, 40–41, 62, 91). Westervelt's readers would
know of, and even be able to tell about, if they'd done their homework
ahead of time, the *mo'o* or the story of "The canoe of the dragon god"
"in the heart of modern Honolulu back of the old Kaumakapili church
site" (104). Within this urban deictic system, some new legendary figures can emerge: "This place [Puuhonua Temple] is now the site of the
Castle Home" (131).

Second, the camera lens also frames the view Westervelt offers of these
"legendary places." It is no accident that one of his early pieces in *Paradise of the Pacific* was entitled "Snap Shots of Legendary Places in Hawaii"
(18.12 [1905]:68–71), and it is not surprising that it went through various reprints (Leib and Day 114). Despite Westervelt's great "narrative
effort" to include description (Denevi), he maintains a great distance.
The panorama is his favorite. Mānoa Valley, the home of Kahalaopuna,

appears framed by "the highest peaks of the island of Oahu," rising "near the head of the valley." Here, "the sun, which, looking on the luxuriant verdure and clinging mist, sends its abundant blessing of penetrating light," while rainbows "chase each other in matchless symmetry of quiet, graceful motion" (*LOH* 127–28). Hawaiian writer Emma Nakuina zoomed in to identify and name "a spur of the Koolau mountains at the head of Manoa Valley" and the "lehua bushes on the brow of the ridge" that are Kahalaopuna's grandparents (in Thrum's *HFT* 118). Westervelt invites readers to enjoy a spectacle: a place worthy of a picture, the caption to which could be "one of the most beautiful rainbow valleys in the world" (*LOH* 127). "Visual narrative" has turned into tourist slogan.

Photography: Storying the Illustration

The visual paratext of Thrum's and Westervelt's collections played a crucially important role in the translation of *wahi pana* into *legendary Hawai'i*, and in the post-annexation promotion of Hawai'i as a desirable tourist and settler destination. The announcement on the title page of Thrum's *Hawaiian Folk Tales* that sixteen photographic illustrations appeared within is a signal of how in 1907 photographic illustrations were an attractive, relatively new, and marketable feature of publication. His later volume, *More Hawaiian Folk Tales*, included eighteen such illustrations. Westervelt's 1915 *Legends of Gods and Ghosts* featured sixteen illustrations from photographs plus a sketch and several drawings of Hawaiian fish; almost doubling the images in its 1915 edition, the 1916 *Legends of Old Honolulu* contained twenty illustrations—some "from the author's own snapshots" (n.p.)—and a map. The 1923 *Hawaiian Historical Legends* had fewer pictures—eight, including the title page—and all were "courtesy of" *Paradise of the Pacific*. Reviews often mentioned these photos as "pleasing" and "useful," or as adding "to the value of the book for the tourist or resident in Hawaii."[39]

Initially published by photographer James J. Williams, and introducing itself as the only "illustrated" journal in Hawai'i, *Paradise of the Pacific* was featuring "half-tone pictures" as early as July 1894. Photographic illustration, the technological innovation of the time, was clearly intended to enhance the appeal of the publication and of Hawai'i as a product. The December issues in particular were richly illustrated, contrasting the lushness of the tropics with the wintry bareness of many American readers' surroundings. Two different pieces in the May 1901 issue also spoke to the "objective" advantage of photography over verbal narrative. "The camera has done more to present the beauties of Hawaii to the world than the most flowery effusions of the most imaginative story writers" declares the first piece, "While one invariably tells the truth—and the truth is what the public wants—the others practice deceptions on their readers that work harm to the Islands" (14.5:8). The second sees photography as a transforming force in publication: "A well executed picture tells more than a column of type, sometimes, and in this age of rapid metal reproduction of the photograph the counterfeit presentment of everyday scenes can be given in the morning or evening papers at a small cost. The halftone is crowding much of the letterpress out of the page, and the public appreciates the change. . . . The order of new things is apt to be: story the illustration, not illustrate the story" (14.5:18).

Certainly, photographic images were being marketed and read as "reliable" introductions to Hawai'i. As Lynn A. Davis documents, this campaign had political and economic motives, and extended into all kinds of publications. The 1891 *Vistas of Hawaii* by Lorrin A. Thurston, soon to become one of the engineers of the Hawaiian monarchy's overthrow, "was to provide the model for the use of photographs to promote the islands as a tourist destination" (Davis, "Photographically Illustrated Books" 289). Its photos juxtapose images of powerful steamers to Native canoes, and beautifully landscaped "private" yards to "glimpses of the great volcano, Kilauea." Thurston illustrates the binaries of his subtitle, *Paradise of the Pacific and Inferno of the World*, by displaying Native Hawaiians as part of the "infernal" scenes—these representing the desolate volcano and that dark world before civilization brought trains and hotels to the islands. (The book was produced for the Oahu Railroad and Land Company and the Kilauea Volcano House Company.) After examining numerous early travel books like *Picturesque Hawaii: A Charming Description of Her Unique History, Strange People, Exquisite Climate, Wondrous Volcanoes, Luxurious Productions, Beautiful Cities, Corrupt Monarchy, Recent Revolution and Provisional Government* (1894) and *Picturesque Cuba, Porto Rico, Hawaii and the Philippines: A Photographic Panorama of Our New Possessions* (1899), Heather Diamond convincingly concludes: "The visual capture/captivity of the Native Hawaiian in illustrated promotional texts initially coincided with the capture/captivity of Hawaiian land by American imperialist expansion. . . . According to these texts and subtexts, Hawaiians are Hawai'i's past, museumized in photographs." *Hawaiian America*, an 1899 book with over seventy photographic illustrations, explicitly states that "the native Hawaiian is passing" (Caspar Whitney 69) and visually supports the claim by contrasting images of the busy and modern streets of Honolulu with those of the clearly outmoded customs of Hawaiians.

Legends, as we have seen, had much to offer to this project of transforming a living culture into artifact. It is telling that even early collec-

tions of legends like Skinner's *Myths & Legends of Our New Possessions &
Protectorate* had featured photographs—four to be precise, two of which
were of Hawai'i. Halftones regularly accompanied the publication of
Hawaiian legends in *Paradise of the Pacific*, and some of those pictures,
like ones in Thrum's *Annual*, were circulating on postcards and being
reproduced in the later compiled volumes of legends. Extending Diamond's argument that "the photographs in early travel literature on
Hawai'i are unreliable as ethnographic documents but can be read as
socio-political contact zones that form potent sub-texts to the literature
they also support," I propose to consider the photographic illustration
of *legendary Hawai'i* in Thrum's and Westervelt's volumes against this
backdrop of the extensive visual promotion of Hawai'i, and especially as
enacted by the photos accompanying "legendary lore" in *Paradise of the
Pacific*. Extrapolating from the vigorous post-annexation campaign to
promote Hawai'i that was conducted both verbally and visually in *Paradise of the Pacific*, I want to look at this magazine, and at Thrum's and
Westervelt's photographically illustrated publications of legends, to
reveal the emergence of a legendary topology, a visual vocabulary
employed to "story" Hawai'i as both a "legendary" and appealing place
for Americans in the early twentieth century.

Photographs in Thrum's and Westervelt's volumes featured (a)
Hawaiian people and (b) Hawaiian places. In these books, whether they
were taken by established photographers (J. J. Williams, Ray Jerome
Baker, Alonzo Gartley), or by amateurs, as in Westervelt's volumes, the
photos of Hawaiians represented "Hawaiian types"—the caption for two
photos in Thrum's 1923 volume stated this explicitly. This "sampling"
of people was very much in the mode. Visitors could find such Hawaiian
"types" in magazines, photography shops, and international exhibitions. Predictably, the most common iconic images are young women
wearing lei ("Hawaiian Girl of the Old Regime," *HFT*; "Wearing the
Lei" by J. Baker, *LOH*), hula performers ("Dancing the Hula," *HFT*),
surfers (Bonine's "Surf-Riding Contest," *MHFT*), and individuals identified by their Native work, especially fishermen ("Hawaiian Fisherman
Using a Throw Net," *HFT*; J. J. Williams's "Hukilau Fishing Scene,"
MHFT; and Baker's "A Trusty Fisherman," *LGG*), but also a "Poi
Pounder" (*LOH*), and a "Hat and Mat Maker" (both in Westervelt's
LOH and in Thrum's *MHFT*). In photos that had a clearly ethnographic
function, the caption erased the presence of the Hawaiian people in the
picture ("Hawaiian Grass House; Exterior and Interior View" *MHFT*,
Figure 19), or mentioned them not by name ("Hawaiian Family Group
at Shelter Hut" *MHFT*). In the case of hula, the ethnographic documentation of Eduard Arning's photos (*HFT*) gave way in time to a posed
image, "Dancing the Hula," a postcard of young girls that appeared in

Figure 19. Hawaiian Grass House; Exterior and Interior View. *More Hawaiian Folk Tales.* Courtesy of Bishop Museum.

Westervelt's *Legends of Gods and Ghosts.* Again the caption identifies the activity, rather than the human subjects of representation.

As my sampling is intended to suggest, these "Hawaiian types" were not only denied individuality, but were confined to what Johannes Fabian has called the "ethnographic present tense," and therefore lack a history, or a capacity for change. Though the fisherman's *malo* (loin-cloth) is the most obvious example of the "old regime" dress code, it's unlikely that any of these "types" would have been comfortable in the bustling post-annexation and business-oriented Honolulu downtown of the early 1900s. A different visual form of this ahistorical present tense is a photo like the "Landing of a Canoe Fleet," which records twentieth-century reconstructions of historical events without mentioning this in the caption (*MHFT*; Lynn Davis, personal communication). Not only is *legendary Hawai'i* safely in the past, but so are the Hawaiians. Such presentation of Hawaiians through this untouched-by-progress-and-thus-doomed iconography can be illustrated with just two photos: the image of a "Hawaiian Arrayed in Feather Cloak and Helmet" in *Hawaiian Folk Tales*, actually a photo of John Tamatoa Baker posing for the statue of Kamehameha I (Figure 20); and "Young Honolulu and Leahi" (*LOH*), the photograph of two silhouettes against an ocean-beach-and-sky background: a small naked child standing in the water and the profile of Lē'ahi (from the older Lae'ahi) or Diamond Head.

As Anne Maxwell has shown, these ahistorical "reductive tropes" are common in the early representation of people of the Pacific. I am interested, however, in what this imagery specifically foregrounds to promote post-annexation Hawai'i. One of the "misstatements" that *Paradise of the Pacific* editors recognized as needing to be corrected in 1889 was that

The natives are such an ill-natured, blood-thirsty set, always around with bow and arrows looking for the fairest and fattest of the missionarys' [*sic*] children to slay and roast or stew or boil for dinner. We should never have thought of this absurdity if a letter had not lately come from NY to a gentleman here, gravely asking if cannibalism still existed here. . . . Seriously, we repeat what has often been stated before, that cannibalism has never existed in any of these islands (we mean the Hawaiian group). The natives are a good-natured, easy-going people, not inclined to any violent exertion of either the physical or mental powers to be sure, and yet they have made the most rapid progress in all that distinguishes civilized men of any of the uncultivated races that have been discovered. (2.5:4)

Similar articles, countering the misconception that Hawaiians were dangerous and inhospitable, were still appearing in *Paradise of the Pacific* after annexation—and so were photos. In Thrum's and Westervelt's volumes as well, instead of appearing as violent, even cannibalistic, the photographs portrayed Hawaiians as primitive, but with no dangerous edge. The message was unspoken, but clear. See, these simple good-natured people can now be civilized because even in legendary times they were devoted to beauty and entertainment (surfing, dancing, feasting). As for their current economy and supposed subsistence activities (fishing and weaving), these will not interfere with the businesses (sugar and trans-

Figures 20. Hawaiian Arrayed in Feather Cloak and Helmet. *More Hawaiian Folk Tales*. John Tamatoa Baker modeling for the Kamehameha I statue. C. J. Hedemann's Collection. Courtesy of Bishop Museum Archives.

portation) that most interested investors at the time. Hawaiians posed
no threat, and in any case "the native, pure and simple, is passing"
(Caspar Whitney 61).[40]

Primarily visualized through its natural beauty and often represented
as devoid of its people, *legendary Hawai'i* appears as landscape in most
photographic illustrations in Thrum's and Westervelt's collections.
Coconut trees (usually "with reflection"), waterfalls, valleys, and peaks,
hardened lava flows of the *'a'ā* type—these icons were repeated again
and again in the books of legends and on the pages of *Paradise of the
Pacific.* These pictures appealed to the non-Hawaiian imagination by
presenting Hawai'i as an attractively other and mysterious space, an
inviting land whose stories these publications recorded. Because of their
recurrence, these images helped to construct the figurative/visual
vocabulary that came to image and advertise Hawai'i at the start of the
twentieth century.

This visual vocabulary foregrounded and promoted specific tourist
destinations and landmarks. The Nu'uanu Pali figures foremost, appearing in both of Thrum's books and in Westervelt's 1915 books: "Scene
from the Road over Nuuanu Pali"; "Nuuanu Pali" (*LOH*); "The Misty
Pali" (possibly from a painting; *LGG*); and "Oahu Pali Scene" (by J. J.
Williams, *MHFT*). The Nu'uanu Pali was *the* primary tourist attraction
for the time. But while it was and is a storied place, publications did not
always feature its legends or history. Under "What to See, and Where to
Go," the first *Hawaiian Guide Book* in 1875 simply notes: "We say, go to
the 'pali,' for a view that cannot be surpassed in California even" (Henry
Whitney 22). And in 1888, *Paradise of the Pacific* reports: "Every new
arrival in Honolulu goes to the Pali, at the top of Nuuanu valley, as soon
as the excursion can be arranged: even the through passengers by the
Australian boats, who are but six hours in port, secure carriages or
horses, and at once set forth rejoicing, for the prospect from the Pali—
the precipice—is superb, and the round trip can be made for a few dollars, and leisurely enough in three or four hours" (1.8:4). But other
articles and photos in *Paradise of the Pacific* did register a two-sided fasci-
nation with the Nu'uanu Pali, even dubbing it " 'A Dark and Bloody
Ground' in Hawaiian History" (6.8 [1893]:113) because of the bloody
battle fought there in 1795, while still declaring that "like the Yosem-
ite," it was "one of the twenty wonders of the world" (5.10 [1892]:1).
Lofty and dreadful, mysterious and beautiful, this misty peak offered a
peek at Hawai'i's bloody past, and a majestic view of its bucolic present[41]
in a landscape that could alternately remind tourists of the "Vesuvian
bay"[42] or of the Alps:

The fame of the wonderful scenic beauty of Nuuanu Pali, Honolulu, the precipice over which Kamehameha the Great drove the brave followers of Kalaniku-

pule and Kaiana ere he conquered Oahu and proclaimed himself monarch of all Hawaii—is known to many outside of readers of Hawaiian history. Few tourists that come to Honolulu [do not take] the opportunity to make a visit to this picturesque spot, which equals in scenic grandeur, the most famed of alpine views. (*Paradise of the Pacific* 4.12 [1891]:3)

What did this legendary place offer to the tourist or newcomer? Stunning beauty, with a historical significance that reinforced the understanding that "old" Hawai'i was, and should be, in the past. In this battle scene, the Hawaiians are only "ghosts," and one can admire the scenery. While photographs of Native Americans at exhibitions during this time period highlighted "stereotyped images showing the re-enactment of famous battles such as Little Bighorn" (Maxwell 105), no warriors in Nu'uanu threatened the potential visitor or investor. The Pali metonymically stood in for a heroism safely confined to the imagination.

Though a few specific tourist destinations were featured prominently in the early visual representation of *legendary Hawai'i*, most images of Hawai'i remained unmarked in Thrum's and Westervelt's collections and in *Paradise of the Pacific*. Readers of legends could view "Coconuts and Pandanus Grove with Reflection" (by J. J. Williams, *MHFT*, Figure 21), more "Coconuts" (*LGG*), "Misty Falls" (*LOH*), and a "Coast Surf Scene" (*HFT*). But the locations were not disclosed. This generic labeling ignored, and even worked against the Hawaiian grounding of *mo'olelo* in "storied places"—constituting another example of the displacement referred to in the subtitle of this chapter. And in any case, within the books' layouts, the relationship between stories and images was so haphazard that images often echoed the themes in the stories only faintly. Like Westervelt's denotative ("black rocks") and panoramic verbal illustrations, photographs constructed a generic imaginary, where water, palm trees, and scenic beauty offered a welcome and exotic respite to modern Euro-American readers.

Legendary Hawai'i

The visual apparatus of these volumes of Hawaiian legends in translation tells a tale that confirms or naturalizes the introductory words and other verbal frames, and in the process does violence to Hawaiian narratives. "Hawaiian story," Martha Beckwith incisively observed in 1925, is

in its more genuine shape difficult of assimilation to the European imagination, although a Hawaiian audience enters into the spirit of an Arabian Nights' tale as breathing native air. Hence the tendency is . . . to lose the meaning of old customs, to incorporate European material and impose European motives. Thus

COCONUT AND PANDANUS GROVE, WITH REFLECTION

Figure 21. Coconuts and Pandanus Grove with Reflection by J. J. Williams, *More Hawaiian Folk Tales*. Courtesy of Bishop Museum.

any collection of Hawaiian folk-tale must be accepted at its present value as a mere reconstruction of the art of the past, however useful it is as an expression of the folk art of to-day. ("Review" 327)

Unfortunately, few outsiders understood, let alone "accepted" this fact. Rather, from the beginning of the twentieth century, that mere "reconstruction" came to represent Hawaiian *mo'olelo*, doing violence to it and producing a *legendary Hawai'i* for non-Native popular consumption that would nevertheless affect Hawaiians.

Both Thrum's and Westervelt's prefaces adopt a devolutionary rhetoric of nostalgia for Hawaiian folklore, and especially for "the *haku meles* (bards) of Hawaii [who] are gone" (*HFT* vi). Westervelt—to this day the best-known divulger of Hawaiian legends in English—enlists this nostalgia in the service of a religious and political narrative of development: "From mist to sunshine—from fabled gods to a constitution and legislature as a Territory of the United States—this is the outline of the stories told in the present volume" (*Hawaiian Historical Legends* n.p.). According to this narrative, the Hawaiian people can emerge "from the fogs of the imagination" (*HHL* n.p.) because they "have shown capacity for rapid intellectual development" (which accounts for how "rapid" "their transformation under organized government and institutions" has been, *HLGG* x). But they can emerge only into a non-Hawaiian imaginary, where the Natives belong to the past, and Hawai'i's beauty is taken "out of place"—dislocated, that is, and for the taking.

Chapter 4

Emma Nakuina's *Hawaii: Its People, Their Legends*: Out of Place Stories II

> *Show the tourists something they have never seen before and they will remember the Islands and tell of their charms as long as they live. . . . A large number of tourists . . . look for a few relics of the life of the early Hawaiians. Native color . . . is what the pleasure seeker likes to have imbued in his entertainment.*
>
> —*"Give the Tourists More Variety," March 1905*

In her 1905 *Paradise of the Pacific* article "Give the Tourists More Variety," Elinor A. Langton suggested that while "Climate and scenery are well enough for the visitor at first," many tourists coming to Hawai'i harbored the desire to get "an insight into the wild life of the Polynesians," as an Oregon lady had told her (18.3:15). Just how to satisfy this desire while still promoting Hawai'i as a safe and modern American destination was one of the challenges the post-annexation tourist development industry faced.

In Chapter 3, I outlined the historical production of *legendary Hawai'i*, and examined its verbal and visual apparatus of translation in relation to the post-annexation marketing of Hawai'i in books and magazines, the dominantly antiquarian and colonial project of folklore studies at the time, and the violent dis-placement on which the rhetorical re-framing of authority, genre, readership, and geosymbols implicitly operated. But neither the promotion of Hawai'i as a settler and tourist destination, nor the role of *legendary Hawai'i* within this campaign could be absolutely uniform in its ideology or successful in its effects. This should come as no surprise for, contrary to pro-annexation rhetoric, Hawaiians were—and are—not a people or a culture of the past, and their agency did matter in ways that were not fully controllable, predictable, or homogeneous.

In this chapter I focus on Emma Kaili Metcalf Beckley Nakuina's 1904

Hawaii: Its People, Their Legends as a complex, autoethnographic intervention by a Hawaiian author into the preservation of Hawaiian knowledge
and stories in a post-annexation and tourist-oriented cultural economy.
First, I consider the agenda and promotional strategies of the Hawaii
Promotion Committee as a backdrop for Nakuina's collection. I then
examine *Hawaii: Its People, Their Legends* in relation to the production
of *legendary Hawai'i*, asking the same questions about rhetorical frames,
authority, audience, representation of place, genre ideology, and translation that I raised about Thrum's and Westervelt's publications. Finally,
to begin to set Nakuina within an alternative context, and to gain a better understanding of her as a cultural translator during politically trau-
matic times, I discuss two other English-language *mo'olelo* that did not fit
the *legendary Hawai'i* model around the time of annexation.

As a woman of knowledge and authority, and a Hawaiian closely tied
to the monarchy, and then, through her husband and son, to the territorial legislature, Emma Nakuina faced numerous challenges, which she
met at personal and professional cost. While her *Hawaii: Its People, Their
Legends* was never reprinted, she deserves recognition as an important
link in the Native Hawaiian genealogy of tellers and translators of Hawaiian *mo'olelo* into English for, engaging with dominant discourses, her
writings affirmed the value and values of her people. She practiced
autoethnography and translation in clever ways that—epistemologically
and rhetorically—countered the violence of *legendary Hawai'i* and defied
the tourism industry's agenda.

Promotional Literature

Between the overthrow of the monarchy (1893) and the annexation of
Hawai'i (1898), leading newspapers in the United States reported on
the political debate over Hawai'i. Regardless of positions taken, this cov-
erage resulted in a tremendous amount of publicity for the islands.[1] During that same period, Lorrin Andrew Thurston, a chief orchestrator of
the overthrow, and the editor of the 1891 *Vistas of Hawaii*, was in the
United States promoting annexation—and the Volcano House, the
hotel he owned, where the number of registered guests went from 452
in 1893 to 1,010 in 1900, reaching 3,076 in 1909 (Crampon 323). Starting in 1892, Thurston and Benjamin F. Dillingham of the Oahu Railway
and Land Company helped to develop a Hawaiian Bureau of Information to encourage tourist travel to the islands, often by offering information about Hawai'i at fairs, including the World Colombian Exposition
(Chicago, 1893) and the Midwinter Fair (San Francisco, 1894).[2]

The experiences of those American soldiers who stopped in Honolulu
on their way to and from the Philippines for the Spanish-American War

in 1898 also made Hawai'i more real and attractive on the continent. In 1901, the first Moana Hotel was built; by then, electric streetcars and railroad service were available on O'ahu, and telegraphic cable was operating from 1903. In 1902, the Honolulu Chamber of Commerce and the Merchants' Association funded W. C. Weedon to give a six-month series of lectures illustrated with stereopticon views, which drew packed houses on the West Coast (Hodge and Ferris 60). All of these initiatives contributed to the development of tourism in territorial Hawai'i. "Those who had long thought of Hawaii as a South Sea sister of Bora Bora and Tahiti, an almost mythical paradise, were awakened to the fact that Hawaii was real, that it was much nearer to the California coast than other islands, that English was spoken by many of its inhabitants, that Hawaii was possibly a place that they could visit, and thanks to Thurston's promotion, that Hawaii had a real live volcano that everyone should see" (Crampon 221).

The first *Hawaiian Guide Book, for Travelers* had been published by Henry M. Whitney in 1875; and Thrum's *Annual*, the *Paradise of the Pacific*, and a number of photographically illustrated books were distributing information that would lure tourists and settlers to Hawai'i. But when reporting the success of his California lectures, Weedon lamented "the lack of advertising materials to follow up on our talks." He wrote, "Good literature or pamphlets would surely be a great aid," but the Chamber of Commerce replied that there was "nothing to send" (quoted in Hodge and Ferris 60).

In 1903, the Territory of Hawaii, the Chamber of Commerce, and the Merchants' Association created the Hawaii Promotion Committee with a $15,000 legislative appropriation and an office in the Alexander Young building. "The preparation of copy for booklets, and for use in the magazines and newspapers which had been selected as advertising mediums was undertaken with vigor," Edward M. Boyd, its first secretary, reported. Mandated to provide better publicity to induce tourism in Hawai'i, between 1902 and 1904 alone, the Hawaii Promotion Committee produced and printed "a general folder in edition of 250,000," and a number of other pamphlets or "folders," giving "the committee a total of about 500,000 pieces of printed matter" (quoted in Crampon 228). In addition to placing ads in the leading American magazines and reissuing *Hawaii*, the "general folder" several times over the years, the Committee published the pocket-size *Honolulu, What to See and How to See It* as well as *Beauty Spots: Hawaii* (also titled *Scenery in Hawaii*) by Dr. Sereno E. Bishop in 1903; *Hawaii: Its People, Their Legends* by Emma Nakuina in 1904; and *Hawaii, a Primer: Being a Series of Answers to Queries* and *Letters from Hawaii* in 1905 and in later editions. Other pamphlets give information about game fishing and what to wear in Honolulu. Captions in the

1903 *Hawaii* promised "No Fogs," "No Malaria," "No Hurricanes," "No Sunstrokes," "No Reptiles," "No Tidal Waves," blurring fact and fiction in ways that are reminiscent of Mark Twain, whose poetically nostalgic praise of Hawai'i prominently featured in Thurston's *Vistas* was often reprinted in the Promotion Committee publications.[3] As George T. Armitage, executive secretary of the Hawaii Tourist Bureau, wrote in the 1923 *Hawaiian Annual*, through advertising, and steamship and railway agencies, "the Hawaii Promotion Committee was launched with flying colors" (78).

Novelty and visual lure are the hooks of advertisement, so most Hawaii Promotion Committee publications were photographically illustrated. An announcement entitled "A New Brochure" in the March 1904 issue of *Paradise of the Pacific* read:

Hawaii: Its People—Their Legends is the name of a handsome brochure that has just come from the press of the Hawaii Gazette Co. Its author is Mrs. Emma Metcalf Nakuina, whose talents as a descriptive writer long ago placed her in the first rank of Island literary women. The publishers are the Hawaii Promotion Committee. The work takes up a novel line of tourist promotion endeavor, presenting in its 64 pages of pictures and narratives a good deal of Island folk lore that appeals to that class of tourists who always take an interest in the people of the strange places they visit. As the history of all unlettered nations is derived from their legends so are the deeds of the forefathers of the present Hawaiians brought to our knowledge by the old tales that have come down through the centuries of verbal recital. Mrs. Nakuina has a pleasing way of telling these things. The appearance of the brochure alone will attract notice. The front cover has the royal Hawaiian arms, in gold, and the title in embossed gold letters. The printing and presswork eclipse anything previously turned out by the Committee, and the quality of the paper and the 40 or more halftones is of the best. The Hawaii Promotion Committee are to be congratulated on their success. (17.3:16)

To understand how Emma Nakuina's collection fit within this "novel line of tourist promotion," it helps to consider how the Hawaii Promotion Committee represented Hawai'i in its other publications, and how its rhetoric echoed developing American tourism at large.

"That the Hawaiian Islands are rich in scenery is not the thing to be said of them," begins Sereno E. Bishop's *Beauty Spots of Hawaii*. "The truth is that they are all scenery, and that of the grandest, most varied kinds, rivalling any other spots on the Earth's surface" (3). Richly illustrated, this booklet featured panoramic views and idyllic scenes, for the most part devoid of humans. The effects of modernity—rice fields and railroad—are present only in a few images, while "Grass Houses on the Seashore" (17) and "Surf Boats" at Diamond Head (23) are the only signs of the Native. Twenty years later, in "Capitalizing Hawaii's Climate," a report on the activities of the Hawaii Promotion Committee and Hawaii Tourist Bureau, George T. Armitage would boast that Hawai'i "has been favored with the finest climate in the world" and that "her whole popularity has been and must be built largely on this." This exceptional climate was not only responsible for the islands' beauty and fertility: "it is her climate that produces daytime and moonlight rainbows, liquid sunshine, soft-toned singers, winsome women and stalwart men; it is her climate that has won for Hawaiians an enviable reputation for hospitality" (76).[4] Climate set the hospitable scene; Natives add color.

By focusing on Hawai'i as "scenery" or landscape, this promotional literature fell into an American national trend, and in the process encouraged readers to annex Hawai'i ideologically into the American nation. In her work on the emergence of the American tourist industry, and its role in the development of a national culture, Marguerite S. Shaffer has argued that between 1880 and 1940, this industry "manufactured and marketed America as 'nature nation,' defining a shared history and tradition that manifested an indigenous national identity sanctioned by God and inscribed across the national landscape" (5).[5] Building on the mythology of nature as a refuge from both modernity and corruption, elite tourism in particular

adopted notions of the sublime, the beautiful, and the picturesque. . . . This aesthetic classification of nature, first articulated in the eighteenth and early nineteenth centuries, helped transform wilderness into scenery: the sublime scene embodied by dramatic natural landscapes—mountains, waterfalls, cliffs, and canyons—conveyed the power of God through its infinite, rugged, and overwhelming character and provoked a more expansive vision; the beautiful landscape, with its gentle curves and inspiring vistas, along with the picturesque landscape, with its romantic ruins and pastoral character, evoked literary and artistic conventions, connecting the viewer to a long tradition of refined genteel culture. (Shaffer 277)

Though Shaffer does not mention Hawai'i, tourism promotion in the newly annexed Territory extended these same notions to what was called "greater America."

For instance, verbally and visually, *Beauty Spots* depicted Hawai'i— definitely an elite tourist destination at the time—as offering that national landscape of mountains ("vast mountain masses stand forth out of the ocean in a sublime simplicity, crowned with fleckings of perpetual snow" on the island of Hawai'i [Bishop 6]), waterfalls ("a chief attraction of Hilo town is the beautiful Rainbow Falls, about a mile inland" [24]), cliffs ("a continuous perpendicular wall of precipice falls boldly down from the great summit line of pinnacles to a wild confusion of lowland hills reaching to the sea. . . . It is this vast precipice, twenty miles long and over 2,000 feet high, with its picturesque green foothills which form the chief elements in the marvelous view presented at the sudden overlook over the celebrated Nuuanu Pali" [14–15]), and canyons ("the southwest side [of Maui] as seen from passing steamers presents an impressive aspect of huge broken pyramids with pinnacled ridges in the interior of their separating gorges. Immediately back of Lahaina is a group of some of the grandest of canyons of enormous depth" [10]). The frontispiece image is "Falls of Hanapepe on the islands of Kauai," and most of the photographs open the viewer's imagination to grand vistas.[6]

Such sublime and picturesque landscapes invited middle- and upper-class Euro-American tourists to escape and "temporarily reimagine themselves as heroic or authentic figures" discovering the true nature of America (Shaffer 5). In the American territory of Hawai'i, tourist adventures took on especially novel features. "To stand on the very edge of the great chimney of Halemaumau and look down 1000 feet to the living fires, secure in the knowledge of public safety, is a new experience," noted the folder *Hawaii* (4); and Sereno Bishop declared that "The summit ridge of Haleakala crater is quite accessible on the northwest side, and the view from it is considered perhaps the grandest piece of scenery in the group" (9). Hawaiian volcanoes added to the heroic dimensions of these American-tourist escapes, where excitement comes with the assurance of safety and accessibility. Furthermore, whether with one's eyes or one's camera, seeing and viewing were the actions of tourist privilege, a contemplative leisure that reflected their social status, and imaginatively appropriated these lands as souvenir-like scenery.

Shaffer argues that as white and middle- or upper-class tourists ritually came to recognize themselves as "Americans" by appreciating a certain natural landscape, they also "distinguished themselves by commenting on the work, culture, and behavior of others they encountered on their journeys, most notably Native Americans, African Americans, Mexican Americans, Chinese Americans, and Mormons. From the perspective of elite tourists, these social others became an extension of the tourist spectacle, further allowing tourists to define and distinguish their social status" (280). Native Americans—or, more accurately, the touristic, imagined memory of Native cultures—held a special attraction, since, as we know, notions of "primitive" and "natural" overlapped.[7] Without oversimplifying, though Native Americans were not imag(in)ed in the same ways as Hawaiians were, both groups evoked nostalgia for a simpler way of life, but a nostalgia that confirmed the superiority of American progress as development. The interest in legends and folklore that promotional literature about the United States and, more specifically, about Hawai'i tried to encourage in the tourist industry from the start can therefore be read as the assertion of a national cultural identity that relied on a voyeuristic appreciating or consuming of the "natural," as scenic landscape and "primitive" life. Not all tourists would care about legends or local lore, but those who wanted to assert their cultivation (and worldliness) did; and, as seen in Chapter 3, the tourist industry's infrastructure played to this interest by constructing a *legendary Hawai'i*.[8]

Hawaii: Its People, Their Legends was very much a product of its time: a slick "promotional endeavor" featuring a large number of photographic illustrations that took on more fully than any other Hawaii Promotion Committee publication the "cultural tourism" approach that Langton had suggested. And yet, though the Hawaii Promotion Committee's secretary Boyd described Emma Nakuina's collection as "a most important contribution to the literature of the country" (in Crampon 229), it was never reprinted. Why? I suggest that Emma Nakuina made a remarkably complex intervention in the discourse of tourism and the production of *legendary Hawai'i*, and while it made sense to be producing a publication like *Hawaii: Its People, Their Legends*, this book exceeded, and even defied, the Hawaii Promotion Committee's agenda—even if the Promotion Committee couldn't exactly say how.

The Writer

The number of public and professional arenas in which Emma Kaili Metcalf Beckley Nakuina (1847–1929) performed tells us something about her versatility and commitments. A young lady of the court who was well-educated about Hawaiian law and history, she became a teacher and translator,[9] museum curator and librarian, researcher, judge and commissioner of water rights, literary writer, and well-known authority on Hawaiian culture and customs. Her genealogy, education, marriages, talent, and character made her a widely influential Hawaiian at a time when women were becoming less common in high government positions, and this influence continued over a long time, from the last decades of the Hawaiian kingdom into the turbulent times of the republic and territory.

Born in Mānoa Valley, O'ahu, she was the daughter of Theophilus Metcalf—a Harvard graduate, civil engineer, and the first photographer in Hawai'i (Schmitt and Ronck 209)—and the Hawaiian chiefess Kailikapuolono of Kūkaniloko, descendant of a proud Hawai'i and O'ahu lineage. In Honolulu, Emma Kaili Metcalf was educated at Sacred Hearts Academy and Punahou School, where she was one of the school's first Hawaiian graduates; she also attended Mills Seminary in California (Figure 22).[10] Her father, who had published articles on Hawai'i's agricultural resources and "was an excellent French scholar," took much interest in her education.[11] She is reported to have been fluent in

Figure 22. Emma Beckley, by Charles L. Weed, 1865. Courtesy of Bishop Museum Archives.

Figure 23. Kalihi Valley, Mrs. Emma Beckley's house, by Eduard Arning, 1884.
Courtesy of Bishop Museum Archives.

English, Hawaiian, French, and German. While it is important—and the
preface to her book will remind us of that—to keep in mind that her
education was bicultural, and her social standing high in both Euro-
American and Hawaiian society, I will be referring to her as Hawaiian
because her life and work so strongly identify with that side of her background.

Emma Kaili Metcalf married twice, in 1867 and 1887, and information
about the men in her life tells us more about her social stature, commitments, and fortunes as the times changed. Her first husband, Frederick
William Beckley (1846–1881), was the grandson of George Beckley, an
"English sea captain" who in the early nineteenth century had been
close to Kamehameha I and married a Hawaiian chiefess; the ancestors
of Frederick's mother, the chiefess Kahinu, were also tightly connected
with Kamehameha I.[12] Frederick William Beckley served as Kamehameha V's and King Kalākaua's chamberlain; he was governor of Kaua'i
when he died prematurely. A widow with children, Emma was appointed
head of the Hawaiian National Library and Museum—her first official
position as a professional woman, and a sign of the respect she com-
manded during the monarchy period (see Figure 23, "Kalihi Valley,
Mrs. Emma Beckley's House," 1884).

Moses Kuaea Nakuina (1867–1911), her second husband, came from a chiefly Moloka'i family, attended Royal School in Honolulu, and was Emma's second cousin. During Kalākaua's reign, he worked in the Government Records Office and library—where he met his future wife—and he later served as Deputy Registrar of Conveyances under Thomas Thrum. He later became President of the Territorial Christian Endeavor Society, campaigned for prohibition, and was appointed "traveling evangelist" (quoted by Charlot, *Nākuina* 13); in 1905, he was an active member of the territorial House of Representatives. The editor of the Hawaiian-language newspaper *Ka Hoaloha* (1907), Moses Nakuina also published *mo'olelo* in Hawaiian—most important, *Moolelo Hawaii o Pakaa a me Ku-a-Pakaa, na Kahu Iwikuamoo o Keawenuiaumi, ke Alii o Hawaii, a o na Moopuna hoi o Laamaomao* and the incomplete *Moolelo Hawaii no Kalapana, Ke Keiki Hoopa-pa o Puna* (1902 for both; see Charlot, *Nākuina* 2005)—as well as in English (Thrum's *Annual*). His obituary in the 1911 *Pacific Commercial Advertiser* notes that "he was one of the Hawaiians who threw in his lot with those who overthrew the monarchy."[13] After his death, the twice-widowed Emma lived eighteen more years.

She had six children from her first marriage, and two more from her second. At least two of the Beckley children died as infants; a daughter from Nakuina lived for many years in the leper colony of Kalaupapa, Moloka'i. Educated in both languages, her oldest son, Frederick William Kahapula Beckley (1874–1943) was "the last official Hawaiian interpreter in the Supreme Court under the Monarchy," and was often consulted in court cases involving translation during the territorial period. A clerk at the Registry of Conveyances in the 1890s—presumably supervised by his stepfather and Thrum—in 1902 he was also the editor of the short-lived bilingual newspaper *Ke Kiai* (*The Sentinel*). A Home Rule candidate, he was elected to the first and third territorial legislatures, serving as Speaker of the House of Representatives in 1903. Only later did he become, like his stepfather, a Republican. Beckley taught Hawaiian history and language at McKinley High School, and in 1922 he became the first teacher of Hawaiian language at the University of Hawai'i. Also in 1922, with his sister Sabina Hutchinson and his mother Emma Nakuina, Professor Beckley played a prominent role in the ceremonial funeral of his friend, Jonah Kalaniana'ole Kūhiō, the Hawaiian prince who had been a Republican delegate from Hawai'i to the United States Congress for twenty years. A member of the influential Sons and Daughters of Hawaiian Warriors, he was also an accomplished musician and music expert. His Hawaiian opera based on the story of Pele and Lohi'au was performed in 1925; a few years later, he published "Voice Culture in Ancient Hawaiian" in *Paradise of the Pacific* where he discussed Hawaiian language and voice training, and lamented that the introduction of jazz was corrupting the "plaintive and harmonious music of the Hawaiian."[14]

As for herself, Emma Kaili Metcalf Beckley Nakuina had learned much about Hawaiian government and the Kamehamehas' laws at the court of Kamehameha V. In 1882, Emma Beckley was appointed by Kalā-kaua's premier, Walter Murray Gibson, as curator ("curatrix" as she signs herself) of the Hawaiian National Museum at Aliʻiolani Hall; during the following five years, she was also the government librarian. When the Bayonet Constitution of 1887 forced Gibson to flee the islands, she was dismissed. According to a recent assessment, she and Gibson had "pursued the interests of the museum with enthusiasm as well as imagination" (Roger Rose, *A Museum* 4), and indeed, her reports to the legislature record her efforts to expand the holdings and functions of both museum and library. Her museum catalog, her fieldwork, and her reports display her expertise as ethnologist and folklorist, and her sensitivity in dealing with Hawaiians who gave her their "old family possessions" for the museum ("Mrs. Beckley's Report on Her Visit to Molokai," 1886).

In 1892, Emma Nakuina became a commissioner, or judge, of the water court, adjudicating water disputes on Oʻahu for the next eighteen years. Her essay, "Ancient Hawaiian Water Rights and Some of the Customs Pertaining to Them" (*Hawaiian Annual*, 1894), continues to be an important historical document on how Hawaiians had regulated and shared vital water resources.[15] But she never lost interest in the museum and what it represented for Hawaiians and Hawaiian knowledge preservation. Her Hawaiian National Museum was soon incorporated into the Bishop Museum, instituted in memory of Princess Bernice Pauahi Bishop, and in 1890 this museum came under the direction of Emma's former Punahou teacher and lifelong antagonist, Dr. William Tufts Brigham. Symptomatic of the racial and gender prejudices of the time, the feud between Emma Nakuina and Brigham was informed by power struggles over ethnographic authority. In 1897, Emma formally protested to the Bishop trustees Brigham's offensive behavior to her and other Hawaiians on the museum's grounds. Just before that, he had been in the news as telling "lies" about Hawaiians. In "Brigham Bellows: Nauseating Rubbish from the Ethnologist," the *Independent* reported that when asked in Boston about "the feeling among Hawaiians in regard to annexation to the United States" Brigham had claimed:

I think the majority would like it. . . . But to tell the truth, I think it is scarcely worth while to consider the natives as an important factor in the politics of the islands anymore than the Indians are regarded as a political factor in the States of the Union. . . . Speaking from the standpoint of an ethnologist, I feel sure that ten years from now there will scarcely be a full-blooded Hawaiian on the islands. . . . Even the ex-Queen Liliuokalani['s] father, and the father of her brother, Kalakaua, the late King, was a Portuguese negro. (April 13, 1897, 3)

These two incidents led Brigham to resign from the museum, but he was reinstated shortly thereafter. In 1917, Brigham was again charged for treating Emma Nakuina disrespectfully in the museum, when as a guest she had contradicted his assertions about Hawaiian feather cloaks. Trustee Charles R. Bishop thought Emma Nakuina was "a person of rather hot temper and free speech," but he acknowledged that she knew "a great deal about the old habits and customs and the antiquities of Hawaii." Brigham called her an "old hag" and "thief," a "physical or moral leper," and a "vile woman."[16]

Brigham remained curator until 1920. In the meantime, Emma Nakuina had become "the first woman judge" in territorial Hawai'i and remained a formidable intellectual and public figure. Though only as "corresponding members," she and Teuira Henry of Tahiti were the first women admitted to the Hawaiian Historical Society in 1894. This society focused on the ethnology, archaeology, and history of the Hawaiian Islands; among its early leaders were several men associated with the queen's overthrow and pro-annexation activities. In this learned, dominantly Euro-American circle and elsewhere, Emma Nakuina was recognized as knowledgeable—but in a subordinate way. When for instance, the Census Bureau superintendent in 1896 wanted to collect information from "an old lady in Honolulu who claimed to be 124 years of age," even though Emma Nakuina, "a Hawaiian lady of high cultivation . . . and very thorough knowledge of the history of the country" actually conducted (and translated) the interviews, she is presented as assisting Professor W. D. Alexander (*Annual* [1897]: 118–24). A brief 1907 article, "Manuscripts of Great Value," in the *Pacific Commercial Advertiser* announced that the work of translation of Fornander's manuscripts had been assigned to "Mrs. Nakuina, well known as a judge of water rights and an authority on all Hawaiian matters" but again under the supervision of Professor Alexander. And when the *Fornander Collection of Hawaiian Antiquities and Folklore* (1916–1920) was completed by Thomas G. Thrum, her name was on the list of Alexander's collaborators.[17]

Emma Kaili Metcalf Beckley Nakuina died in her son's house on April 27, 1929, at the age of eighty-two. The main English-language newspapers in Honolulu remembered her as the "First Hawaii Woman Judge." Of the very few Hawaiian-language newspapers circulating by then, two recorded her passing. One described her as a "woman renowned in the days of the chiefs," poetically intoning "Aloha no ia makuahine kama-aina o ka aina" (Beloved indeed was this well-known mother of the land). The other foregrounded her closeness to the *ali'i* and her learning, concluding: "He nui na kulana oihana a Mrs. Nakuina i paa ai me ka ewaewa ole o na hana ame ke kuokoa pu o na lawelawe ana a maka'u ole i kekahi mea" (There were many professional positions that Mrs. Nakuina held, carrying them out without bias and independently, fearing no one).[18]

I have provided a fairly detailed sketch of Emma Nakuina's life to suggest the close and complex dynamics of the personal and the political, and because all of the *mo'olelo* she published are somehow tied to her life, embodying a knowledge that comes from personal and professional experience. She wrote about the places where she grew up (Mānoa Valley) and went to school (Punahou Spring); and about places bearing family connections (Kūkaniloko; Nu'uanu). She gave the stories of fishing implements she had collected for the museum (Na-iwi-o-Pae; Nanaue, the shark-man). She made decisions in court about water, the life source; and the waters of Punahou Spring, Kaliuwa'a waterfall, the Wai'anae coast, and the 'Īao River flow through her stories. As we approach Emma Nakuina the writer, it may also help to keep in mind that she stood by her professional responsibilities in the face of turmoil, political upheaval, and personal loss, and that she was judged, at least by some, to be independent and intrepid. Though her interventions in the establishment print may not seem transparent, or even entirely coherent in their motivation, I see them as marks of intellectual commitment and resilience during times of strife, a refusal to be "put in her place," a belief that "autoethnographic expression"—when "colonized subjects undertake to represent themselves in ways that *engage with* the colonizer's own terms" and discourse (Pratt, *Imperial Eyes* 7) but do not succumb to them—mattered intensely. Thanks to this indomitable devotion to knowledge, even when writing for the Hawaii Promotion Committee, Emma Nakuina contested or stood against the production of *legendary Hawai'i* and left her mark as a Hawaiian writer of traditions and as a distinctly different kind of translator.

While fluent in Hawaiian, she was a prolific writer in English, which was increasingly the language of government, education, and law.[19] As curator of the Hawaiian National Museum, she published *Hawaiian Fisheries and Methods of Fishing* (1883), meant to be "an interesting and useful adjunct to the Collection of Fish and Fishing Implements forwarded by the Hawaiian Government to the Great International Fisheries Exhibition of London" (preface). From 1884 to 1886, her reports to the legislature about the museum and the library were also printed. As "Mrs. E. Beckley," she is acknowledged in King Kalākaua's 1888 collection, most probably for the "Kahalaopuna" tale. In the years before annexation, she contributed a handful of *mo'olelo* to the *Saturday Press* (1883), *Paradise of the Pacific* (1893), and Thrum's *Annual* (1884, 1893, 1897)—all mainstream publications, with two of them primarily addressing audiences outside of Hawai'i. As commissioner of private ways and water rights for the district of Kona, O'ahu, she wrote her article on "Ancient Hawaiian Water Rights" for the *Annual* in 1894; two years later, her "Legend of the Shark-Man, Nanaue" was read at the meeting of the Hawaiian Historical Society, and approved for publication. In territorial times, a few of her stories were reprinted in *Paradise of the Pacific* and *Hawaii's Young People*, and five of them appeared in Thrum's *Hawaiian Folk Tales* (1907); the Christian publication *Friend* published her "Legend of Kawaiahao Stone" in 1919. During her lifetime, though her stories appeared in publications appealing to widely different audiences, the contents and style remained consistent; only in the case of "Kahalaopuna," did she publish three different versions under her own name (1883, 1904, and 1907). After her death, her work continued to be reprinted in English-language magazines—sometimes with added commentary, other times with no credit. One Hawaiian-language newspaper, the *Kuokoa*, summarized her version of the Punahou Spring *mo'olelo* in 1915 ("Kahi'i Loaa Mai Ai Ka Inoa Kapunahou" November 26, 1915, 3). Though the 1904 Hawaii Promotion Committee book was her most substantial literary endeavor, and also the only photographically illustrated volume produced by a Hawaiian during that time, it is currently her most obscure publication.

In 1961, in her *Honolulu Star-Bulletin* series "Tales About Hawaii," Clarice B. Taylor would remember Emma with that belittling praise women and representatives of other nondominant groups so often receive: "Mrs. Nakuina scribbled incessantly. She was the Kawena Pukui of her day. She knew much of the old Hawaiian culture and she knew English well enough to be able to express herself." While Emma Nakuina was featured in "Native Chiefs of Honolulu," the lead article in the 1907 *Picturesque Hawaii*, as a Hawaiian woman of "high birth" who "has been well educated and has considerable ability, taking much interest in all that pertains to her native land and to the Hawaiian people," she was not sufficiently esteemed as author to be in the following article on "Honolulu Literature and Authors." Nor is she part of the select group of "Important Translators" profiled in the editors' introductory essay for *Hawaiian Legends in English: An Annotated Bibliography* (Leib and Day). One could argue, I suppose, that as a Hawaiian fluent in both languages who does not cite a Hawaiian source for her English-language text, Nakuina was not technically translating. But Leib and Day do include a brief entry for Emma Nakuina's book (87).[20] Though one of the few Hawaiians included in mainstream English-language publications, Emma Nakuina's contributions have therefore been neglected even by those who have valued English-language representations of Hawaiian narrative.

Verbal and Visual Frames

Designed by A. R. Gurrey, the front cover of the 1904 *Hawaii: Its People, Their Legends* is simply and elegantly black (Figure 24), bearing "the royal Hawaiian arms, in gold, and the title in embossed gold letters," as *Paradise of the Pacific* described it. Opening the slim volume—which I will call a "book," rather than "pamphlet," "brochure," or "folder," so as to assert its intellectual accomplishment—readers first encounter an appropriately formal photograph of the writer and a facing preface. Turning the page, a map of the Hawaiian Islands appears with an added insert of the "Hawaii at the crossroads of the Pacific" map that commonly accompanied advertisements for travel to Hawai'i in early-twentieth-century publications; this map traces out the connections that steamers, railroads, and cables made between the islands, and the shores of various continents bordering on the Pacific. On the same page, a chart of "Honolulu Temperature for 1903," a standard feature of Thrum's *Annual*, reassures prospective tourists that they can indeed look forward to Hawai'i's climate. Eleven chapters then deliver on the subtitle's promise by presenting "The Hawaiian People" and a selection of their stories. Photographic illustrations throughout bring to life the attractions anticipated in the beginning by the dry but effective geographical and statistical synthesis. At the end of the volume is a list of illustrations, crediting photographers, designers, the cover artist, and Thomas Sharp for the fanciful initials that graphically embellish the beginning of each chapter. This pocket-size book was presumably distributed to other chambers of commerce (Morais), and—possibly without its cover (Davis, personal communication)—offered to those elite tourists with a special interest in Hawaiian lore.

Genealogy as Preface

Hawaii: Its People, Their Legends opens with the unqualified statement that "The Hawaiian Race is universally recognized as foremost among those of the Pacific archipelagoes, and there is much in its history to arouse interest." Found in the one-page preface, this "universal" declaration does not reject the outsiders' perspective of Western scholars, but does not depend on it either, for as the next few sentences explain, Hawaiian superiority is based on their history and stories, found in an "unwritten record extending back 1,000 years" that cannot be reduced to peaks and

Figure 24. Cover of Emma Nakuina's *Hawaii: Its People, Their Legends.* Courtesy of Bancroft Library, University of California at Berkeley.

traces of developmental capacities, as defined by European-centered theories of race.

The preface also praises Hawaiians as verbal historians and artists: "Gifted with an imaginative faculty well developed, a capacity to clothe thought in ornate language, and adorn recital with word picture, as well as a vocabulary that lends itself to poetic expression, the meles, or historical songs, are virile and have the swing of the trade wind." Of course, Westervelt also called Hawaiians "imaginative"—though "not inventive." But rather than being described in terms of what they lack, Hawaiian *mele* and *moʻolelo* are praised for their many adornments. Further, these (hi)stories are represented as indistinguishable not only from the people who compose, sing, recite, and dance them, but from the winds that animate Hawaiian places. Though newcomers to Hawaiʻi might perceive the title as simply a list of topics—*Hawaii: Its People, Their Legends*—Nakuina stresses their familial relations. Finally, this collection of legends is in fact a restatement of Hawaiian values, since each legend "points a moral." These stories then are not valuable because they extract from the past some "ethnographic present tense" of Hawaiian essence, but because they point to "a moral"—an imperative, a course of action—and therefore speak to Hawaiians and others about the present and future of Hawaiʻi and its people.

Who is the author of the preface? Though unsigned, it is quite possible that Emma Metcalf Nakuina wrote it, since the style and referring to herself as "the writer" are consistent throughout the book. What legitimizes her as a writer? Neither academic titles nor scholarly endeavors authorize Emma Nakuina, but—synthesized in a paragraph—her genealogy does. By placing side by side, rather than sequentially, the preface's statements about her ancestry, I will highlight their rhetorical variation:

Mrs. Emma Metcalf Nakuina springs from blood lines which touch Plymouth Rock, as well as midseas islands. High priests, statesmen and warriors join hands in their descendants with pilgrims, lawmakers and jurists.

Broadly and liberally educated under the immediate care of her father, a Harvard man, nephew of the late Chief Justice Metcalf of Massachusetts, Mrs. Nakuina is fitted to present legends which bring out strongly characteristics of her people.

She "springs" from "blood lines" which like the ocean "touch" different lands and "join" their people. Very much within the tradition of Hawaiian poetry, the figurative language of the first sentence represents Nakuina as intimately connected with "the living earth": she owes her being to the oceanlike wetness thanks to which promontory and island otherwise distant from one another touch and know each other. The second sentence recognizes in her the union of people who in their different traditions have assumed high social roles and responsibilities: high priests and pilgrims, statesmen and lawmakers, and warriors and jurists are recognized as participating in different social orders—but neither is subordinated to the other. The common Hawaiian trope of the child as the flower of this union is implicit, but what also emerges figuratively is a parade of impressive authoritative figures who have preceded and lend stature to their descendant, thus affirming the shaping force of genealogy and history. In this way, while stating that she is not all Hawaiian, this first introduction is informed by Hawaiian style and values. Shifting to the right, we read that the writer's father comes from a powerful East Coast American family, attended Harvard, and was responsible for her education. This statement—were it not for the genealogical connection and the reference to a "broad" education—would seem to invoke that patriarchal, institutionally sanctioned form of knowledge that would give Westervelt an American stamp of approval.

The double-voiced rhetoric of this passage marks how the identification of Emma Nakuina's status as "author" rests on more than one authority. But should we interpret this rhetorical mix as signaling a historical progress? Though the long view of her lineage privileges a Hawaiian perspective, by 1904 American institutions and mental habits were becoming more prominent. Or does the rhetorical shift point to a violent change of perspective and power? At that time, her father's American name and actions would hold most weight with Euro-American readers. Or is this complex paragraph celebrating a wholesome joining of the two, not unlike one version of the annexation of Hawai'i? Today's readers may reach for varying interpretations—and tentative ones, since this is after all only the preface. But because we have already been invited to recognize the Hawaiians' "capacity to clothe thought in ornate language," I think this rhetorical duality is the first significant marker of the importance of Nakuina's fluency in different cultures and language uses and of her intention to use it. This author's privileged access to both worlds enables her to write these stories in English—*and* to foreground in them Hawaiian devotion to family, land, and justice.

This reading suggests another possibility, corroborated by the stylistic difference between the two registers. While the components of the education Emma Nakuina received from her father are simply listed, vitality surges through her multigenerational, multilocated genealogy. The point is not racial purity, but the knowledge and education she has received and will use to "bring out strongly characteristics of her people." Though the collection comes with the Hawaii Promotion Committee's stamp of approval—"Mrs. Nakuina is fitted to present legends"—I read the preface as encouraging readers to look for *kaona*, to assume, that is, that a different, hidden source of authority is present, that the "ornate" language is often possessed of more than one meaning.

Working backward, then the front cover of *Hawaii: Its People, Their Legends* can also be read for *kaona*. In territorial Hawai'i, the Hawaiian coat of arms was no longer in official use, but—fashioned as a pin or pendant—it had become a precious souvenir, its fetishlike, nostalgic aura making it an appropriate promotional image.[21] But the gold grants it added depth and value, reminding us that the imprimatur comes from Hawaiian royalty, and that the writer was well-connected to the monarchy and possessed privileged knowledge about the chiefs' history. In 1914, Emma Nakuina would write about the "Royal Arms of Hawaii" for the *Pacific Commercial Advertiser*. The occasion was the commemoration of the birth of Kauikeaouli, Kamehameha III, during whose reign the coat of arms had originally been designed.[22] Here, Nakuina stresses the Hawaiian symbolism of the design, quoting from an 1845 letter to identify the two men on the coat of arms as the royal twins, Kame'eiamoku and Kamanawa, Kona chiefs who were steadfast supporters of Kamehameha I, Kauikeaouli's father. She continues to write from personal experience about this "royal standard" during the Kalākaua times.[23] Though within the framework of the 1904 promotion of Hawai'i this symbol is a commodity, on the cover of *Hawaii: Its People, Their Legends* it also suggests Emma Nakuina's intimate and authoritative knowledge, and it displays her loyalty to a sovereign Hawai'i. After all, the coat of arms had first come into wide use after the kingdom was restored to Kamehameha III, following its first brief "provisional cession" of sovereignty to the United Kingdom in 1843. Not for tourists, then, but for Hawaiians, this symbol would be a precious sign.

Photographs: "Storying the Illustration" and Native Repeopling

Hawaii: Its People, Their Legends features over forty photographic illustrations, several arranged in collage-like fashion—framed in palm, breadfruit, and banana fronds—according to a popular graphic-arts design of the period. The photographer for each picture, with the exception of the frontispiece portrait, is identified at the end of the book—an unusual feature per se. Alonzo Gartley is responsible for fifteen of the images.

How does the visual vocabulary of Emma Nakuina's book reduplicate or contest *legendary Hawai'i*'s reductive tropes, that is, the dominant representation of Hawaiian people as types, and Hawaiian places as tourist sites and dislocated fetishized images? Its strong reliance on halftones and its collage-like displays place *Hawaii: Its People, Their Legends* very much in line with *Paradise of the Pacific* and other early publications of the Hawaii Promotion Committee—the general folder *Hawaii* (1902) and Sereno E. Bishop's *Beauty Spots in Hawaii* (1903) in particular. In the *Hawaii* brochure, however, every picture illustrates such not fully truthful promises as "No Fogs," "No Hurricanes," "No Tidal Waves," "No Sand Storms," "No Frosts," "No Sunstrokes," and "No Malaria." As noted earlier, the organizing principle of illustration in *Beauty Spots* was simply that "the Hawaiian islands are rich in scenery" (3): pictures out of context are essential to the guided fantasy tour that the brochure provides. Photographs in this kind of brochure figured a Hawai'i with only a few Hawaiians, whose lifestyle is discontinuous with the "American Hawaii" of the present.

In Emma Nakuina's book of legends, the photos of people and places advance the project of covertly resisting such pro-annexation promotion of Hawai'i. Though like the volumes discussed in Chapter 3, Emma Nakuina's book does contain at least two images of spear-fishing, *malo*-clothed fishermen (both by Gartley, 29 and 38), the majority of Hawaiians within appear in modern dress and have names. For instance, "Lulia Kalaukoa," the "Hawaiian lei woman," is no dreamy, young girl (10; see Figure 25), and the "Hawaiian Musical Club" (25; Figure 26) is a dapper sextet of well-groomed young men.

Most strikingly, *Hawaii: Its People, Their Legends* features several studio portraits of Hawaiians. At the opening of the book, readers are introduced to "Mrs. Emma Metcalf Nakuina" (frontispiece; Figure 27).[24] The writer's attire is modern, Western, and refined—a visual confirmation of the social status and education that the preface ascribes to her. She is seated in a posture that is appropriate for a lady, but commands attention. From the viewers' perspective, her elegantly upholstered chair faces right; her torso is twisted toward us—arms folded, the right one resting on the arm of the chair—while her head points right, her eyes looking intently toward the facing page where her words begin. Her body language affirms her authority. She wears a double feather lei; such lei are full, and a single color—most probably yellow. These ornaments are symbols of her standing in Hawaiian society. If "feather cloaks, capes, and helmets were sacred insignia of the highest chiefs of Hawai'i," feather lei "were worn by aristocratic women as personal ornaments for the hair or neck" (Roger Rose, *Hawai'i: the Royal Isles* 191). Since featherwork is rarely seen in photos of that time (Davis, personal communication), by wearing this heirloom lei Emma is making a strong statement.[25] There is something reserved about her, in contrast to the open confidence of her high-school days. The rich, dark folds of her sleeves, enlarging her shoulders, suggest the weight of responsibility, and possibly a mysterious sorrow. While reading too much into this image one hundred years later is to be resisted, its deliberateness sug-

Figure 25. Lulia Kalaukoa; Mrs. F. W. Beckely; Kamehameha I; Haka; C. T. Polikapu. By Various Photographers. Designer J. D. Jewett. *Hawaii: Its People, Their Legends.* Courtesy of Bishop Museum.

Figure 26. Hawaiian Musical Club. Unidentified Photographer. *Hawaii: Its People, Their Legends.* Courtesy of Bishop Museum.

gests it deserves more than a glance. Emily Dickinson's "Tell all the Truth but tell it slant" comes to mind when looking at this Mrs. Emma Metcalf Nakuina—perhaps not all the truth, but told definitely on her terms, in the indirect mode, and with multiple layers of *kaona.*

Kamehameha I, Princess Ka'iulani, and other Hawaiian historical figures are also featured, as are photos of two Hawaiian children—Beatrice Taylor and Richard Mossman—and other Hawaiian individuals such as F. W. Beckley and his wife (10, 12; see Figures 25 and 28). These portraits defy the structures of "non-reciprocal order of existence," found in so much colonial photography, and instead visually emphasize Native Hawaiians' "ability to master the codes of social dress and behaviour that characterized civility" (Maxwell 3, 13).[26] *These* Hawaiians do not belong only to the past; they are affected by history and play a part in it as political subjects. Captions identify some as "Hawaiians," and others as "Hawaiian-English" and "Hawaiian-American," a classification that consistently points to their genealogy or ancestry, but also marks— through the "English" and "American" applied, for instance, to Princess Ka'iulani, who died in 1899, and to F. W. Beckley, who was Speaker

Figure 27. Mrs. Emma Metcalf Nakuina. *Hawaii: Its People, Their Legends.* Unidentified Photographer. Courtesy of Bishop Museum.

Figure 28. Beatrice Taylor; Princess Kaiulani; F. W. Beckley; Gov. Boki and Princess Liliha; Richard Mossman. By Various Photographers. Designer J. D. Jewett. *Hawaii: Its People, Their Legends.* Courtesy of Bishop Museum.

of the House in territorial Hawai'i—a break in history and identity that corresponds to the seizing of Hawaiian sovereignty. Finally, these Hawaiians are no strangers to the author. F. W. Beckley is her son Fred, and Mrs. F. W. Beckley therefore her daughter-in-law. These images represent far more than "types." Though the omission of her first husband's name, Beckley, from the writer's name masks the connections, these are Emma's family. This gallery of portraits therefore not only provides a public display of the beauty, diversity, and civility of the Hawaiian people but, for those in the know, a family album as well.

The images of Hawai'i's sites are not as markedly different from the ones found in *Paradise of the Pacific* or other books of translated legends. *The* tourist attractions—the Nu'uanu Pali, Haleakalā and Kīlauea craters, and 'Īao Valley—are featured. But overall, there are fewer coconut trees, more people, and the scenery represented includes Kapi'olani Park, burial caves at Hā'ena, and *heiau* at Kawaihae. More important, no generic Hawaiian cliffs, rivers, waterfalls, or valleys appear. Each place is named in the caption—Nu'alolo cliff, Wailua river, Kaliuwa'a waterfall, Mānoa valley, and more.[27] And rather than further dislocate the images by placing them haphazardly, in *Hawaii: Its People, Their Legends* place and story go hand in hand fairly consistently. A photo of the majestic Nu'uanu Pali dominates the first page of "The Great Battle of Nuuanu"; panoramic vistas of the "Crater of Kilauea" and "Mokua-weoweo's Fires" illustrate the volcano goddess's anger in the section of "Pele and Lohiau" when Pele impatiently waits for her sister to bring her lover back to her; and while reading about the violent death of the high priest and prophet Ka'ōpulupulu in the district of Wai'anae, we can examine a view of its coast.[28]

These images of Hawai'i have a context, their significance emerging "out of place"—as the title of this chapter suggests—and from story. The last paragraph of the introductory chapter, "The Hawaiian People," prepares the way for this linking of storytelling with place:

Every nook, cliff, valley or plain, as well as strip of coast, headland or stretch of water, had its story or legend formerly, and was noted for some heroic deed either performed by a hero or heroine of long ago, or was perhaps the scene of the hapless loves of some unfortunate youth or maiden. Lacking these, they were peopled by strange, supernatural beings, who took on human form at will and exercised great power for weal or woe over the human inhabitants of that locality. (16)

Hawaii: Its People, Their Legends recounts a few of these stories and shows many storied places, nurturing both verbally and visually the Native re-peopling of the land in ways designed to counter its depopulation in much of the pro-annexation literature of the time. For *malihini* (strangers, newcomers), the primary intended audience of the Hawaii Promotion Committee, these photos and stories introduce not simply the beauty of Hawai'i, but a Hawaiian view. The photos help readers place the events of a tale and the actions of Hawaiian gods and heroes—visuals enacting a different epistemology. In short, instead of claiming through visual appropriation, pictures in Nakuina's book perform the work of education. As for those who know the places or the people, these photographs may visually condense the story, reveal a detail not included in the written account, or evoke a memory about the telling of the story in situ. Far from being excluded or ignored, Hawaiians—the people of the land, those in the know—have what Māori Robert Sullivan, when referring to the place of his own people in that larger audience his poetry seeks to address, has called "the best seats in the house."[29]

History and Visual Illustration: The Remainder of Translation

The body of *Hawaii: Its People, Their Legends* contains an introductory chapter, nine stories, and a brief vignette entitled "Kealakakua [*sic*] Bay: Capt. Cook" (63). The stories are well-known *mo'olelo*, many of them as living traditions dear to people in Hawai'i today. Legendary protagonists include Pele, the goddess of the volcano whose fires destroy and give birth to land, her beloved sister Hi'iakaikapoliopele, and their human lover Lohi'au; the beautiful maiden of Mānoa, Kahalaopuna; the mischievous pig-god Kamapua'a; the seer Ka'ōpulupulu; the larger-than-life Kamehameha I, who earned the title of "the Great" for uniting most of the Hawaiian Islands under his rule; and chiefs from different islands who had also battled one another during the eighteenth century. These narratives take readers and prospective tourists to the main Hawaiian islands, so the telling is both a journey in the traditional Hawaiian sense and, like Thrum's or Westervelt's publications, a tourist guide, fulfilling in some way the expectations of the Promotion Committee. But even in the first chapter introducing "The Hawaiian People" (7–16), Nakuina's telling and traveling—her adaptation of "visual illustration"—is already informed by history, and it is not a history that moves toward "sunshine."

In all its numerous editions, another Hawaii Promotion Committee publication, *Hawaii, a Primer*, offered a standard and reassuring description of Emma Nakuina's people: "The Hawaiians are a stalwart, healthy race. They are generous, pleasure-loving, natural musicians and orators, usually well educated. They never were cannibals. They welcomed the earliest visitors gladly, and speedily embraced religion, when brought to them by American missionaries."[30] Fitting this promotional picture (Inserra), Emma Nakuina, in *Hawaii: Its People, Their Legends*, also writes, "The aboriginal Hawaiians were generally a tall, handsome people, of powerful physique; industrious, cheerful, kindly and hospitable to a fault" (9) and "The Hawaiian is hospitable" (14). But hospitality here is attributed to culture rather than to inherent nature or climate—"It is part of his creed, instilled into him for generations" (14). And this hospitality is also presented in sharp contrast to the trials that Hawaiians have suffered historically.

Three examples will suffice. First, with regard to the theories about the origins of the Hawaiian people circulating at the time—Aryans or Lost Tribes of Israel?—"the writer, from knowledge of the customs of her ancestors, is disposed to accept the latter" (7). This theory's actual scientific status is beside the point;[31] what matters for my purposes is that claiming "Hawaiians are descended from one of the lost tribes of Israel" allows for a presentation of her people as "clinging to their beliefs and observances in the face of persecutions" and as "objects of envy" whenever they thrived as a people (7–8). Second, in spite of this history of persecution, Nakuina declares that Hawaiians remained "an industrious people" as "tillers of the soil" and as "skillful and daring fishermen, with a thorough knowledge of the habitat and habits of fishes," and with "stringent laws and regulations for the taking of the fish, looking toward their preservation." These statements are, however, in the past tense, because "Alas! The white man, with his alleged superior knowledge, prevailed on chief and commoner to throw down their wholesome restrictions, as savoring of superstition, with the result that fishes are very scarce in Hawaiian waters, and getting more and more so every year" (11, 13). And third, while "all foreigners" who arrived "in the early and middle part of the last century agree that the Hawaiians were a strong, athletic race," the writer informs us that things are now different, and for the following reasons:

The change of habits and food, the compulsory clothing to come up to the white man's standard of civilization, and not least, the introduction of many new and formerly unknown diseases, with the vices of the white man, the negro, the Chinese and the Japanese, added to his own rather light and natural sins, have played havoc in too many instances with the splendid physique that was the Hawaiian's inheritance. (14)

Today, accounts holding foreign settlement and development responsible for the deterioration of both Hawai'i's natural resources and its Native people abound. But the picture of healthy, beautiful, and knowledgeable Hawaiians becoming few, weak, and poor because of the white man's interventions—yet remaining "hospitable"—was hardly the common fare in literature for early twentieth-century Euro-American tourists.

And yet, Emma Nakuina's text does not present the Hawaiian people as victims. Many of the stories tell of Kamehameha I and other warriors of his time, emphasizing their strength and skills in ways that counter the discourse of feminization pervading publications about the new American "possessions," where women best represented the Native people (Desmond 49-50).[32] And since the volume "is intended only as an appreciation of the people at large" (preface), the writer focuses on storied places—where "every nook, cliff, valley or plain, as well as strip of coast, headland or stretch of water, had its story or legend formerly, and was noted for some heroic deed" (16). Geography, history, biography are all there to be experienced: as Pacific anthropologist and writer Epeli Hauʻofa more recently noted, the land—analogously to books—inscribes oral narratives and history, "provides maps of movements, pauses, more movements" ("Pasts to Remember" 466).

"The Pali of Nuuanu" on Oʻahu is the first volume in this living library. The site of "The Great Battle of Nuuanu" (17), where the warriors of the Oahuan chief Kalanikūpule were "pursued and driven over the precipitous pali, thousands there meeting death" by the army of Kamehameha I in 1795 (20), this place is also first "for scenic beauty and grandeur on the island of Oahu" (17). In ways similar to those in the promotional *Paradise of the Pacific* articles, Emma Nakuina describes the scenic road to the precipice. But she goes on to present the 1795 battle in detail, the Hawaiians appearing not as ghosts still haunting the trails but as heroic warriors whose loss she mourns. The last volume is Kealakekua Bay on the island of Hawaiʻi, where Captain Cook died "at the hands of an outraged people" in 1779. Though the British government "erected a monument to his memory," Emma Nakuina writes that the "Hawaiian people, as a whole, never felt particularly grateful to Captain Cook for discovering them to the European civilized world, nor do they hold his memory in any very great esteem." A more celebrated place lies nearby for she recalls that "the famous Hale-o-Keawe was situated further down the coast" and though destroyed when the "Queen Dowager Kaahumanu" adopted Christianity, it was "the ancient house of the gods" (63). Nuʻuanu Pali and Kealakekua Bay were, indeed, two of the most popular tourist sites. But with Emma Nakuina as interpreter and guide, they re-collect Hawaiian heroism and beliefs—and for tourists, they become disturbingly bloody sites for their way in and out of Hawaiʻi.

In each of the stories, the land as "place" bears testimony to the values and actions of Hawaiians in the face of injustice and violence, displaying and activating the "moral" themes announced in the preface: "sanctity of home, obedience to superiors and full justice are mainsprings of each legend." This is not to say that every story enacts "full justice," or that "obedience to superiors" is an absolute value. Morals are not mechanical, and *kaona* can inflect the telling. But values and their tensions adhere to each storied place.

It is, for instance, to preserve the "sanctity of home" that Pele's parents, we learn from this version, ask her to leave, forcing her to travel from island to island to find a new home for herself and her people. Though Pele's favorite younger sister Hiʻiakaikapoliopele (Hiʻiaka in Pele's bosom or heart) displays steadfast loyalty and obedience as she meets the challenges of returning Pele's lover to her, when Pele violates the sanctity of Hiʻiaka's own home and friendship, Hiʻiaka defies her. In other stories, beautiful and innocent Kahalaopuna obeys her violently jealous husband-to-be, following him away from her home in the valley of Mānoa, where presumably she would have been protected; the trickster Kamapuaʻa protects his family, and especially his grandmother, when struggling against the powerful chief ʻOlopana; the seer Kaʻōpulupulu does his duty even when the chiefs he advises conspire to kill him; and his son, obeying the seer's words, willingly dies; when banished to Lānaʻi, the "wild" Kaululāʻau becomes the protector of fishermen and a "wise and generous ruler" there (58). Warriors from Maui and Hawaiʻi fight each other bravely and to the death for their chiefs in Wailuku, Maui. And an old retainer is willing to sacrifice her life to save a young boy's in a story about an effigy of Kamehameha's "war-god Ku-kaili-moku" (62). The legendary Pele and Kamapuaʻa shape our experience of places in Hawaiʻi, but so do the tears of Kahalaopuna's family, the death at sea of Kaʻōpulupulu's son, the wisdom of Kaululāʻau, the dead bodies damning the waters of ʻIao on Maui, and the battles of Kamehameha.

Unlike Westervelt's paradigmatic translations invoking *legendary Hawaiʻi*, Emma Nakuina's accounts of storied places do not reflect home, heroism, obedience, or justice in the forms and style of the European fairy tale. Whether she represents the land as witness to more ancient events or she recounts battles documented in written history, the frame remains steadfastly historical. This is how the land was formed; this is how it has been scarred and adorned; this is how our warriors of the time of Kamehameha the Great fought to protect their homes or obey their chiefs; this is how Hawaiians have faced challenges and grief. These are no "fairy-stories" nostalgically recalling a simpler "fairy age." Events from the past are made present, as signs requiring interpretation.

Most prominent is Kaʻōpulupulu's message, "I nui ke aho a moe i ke kai, no ke kai ka hoi ua aina," which Emma Nakuina tells us can be "freely translated, 'Be strong and strive to get to the sea, and die in the sea, when the land will then belong to the sea'" (53).[33] I will quote from her commentary at length:

Kaopulupulu's call and advice to his son has been regarded and accepted by all Hawaiians in the nature of a prophecy, presaging the utter extinction of Oahu's autonomy as an independent kingdom. Some believe that the effects of the prophecy will go on forever, and that whoever will exercise sovereignty on Oahu will eventually be superseded by some power from over the seas. So far, from 1783, a hundred and twenty years ago, four changes in government, or rather of the personnel of the governing people, have occurred, and always in the line of advent from over the sea. (53)

Familial struggles among Hawaiians led to the first two changes. Kahekili, king of Maui, took over Oʻahu; then Kamehameha (by some accounts Kahekili's son) from the island of Hawaiʻi defeated Kalanikūpule, Kahekili's son and Oʻahu's chief. A foreign people and country bring about the next two. After "the Kamehameha line became extinct, the white people from over the sea seized the sovereignty and instituted our late Provisional Government and succeeding Republic." And further, "The United States, a power from far beyond the sea, needed Oahu, and she, with the successive powers that had from time to time annexed her to them, was now annexed by one from way, way beyond the sea." These are the facts, but they call for interpretation. "Did a vision of all these happenings flash on the sight of this remarkable old seer [Kaʻōpulupulu] of a hundred years ago? And was this all? Or were there more scenes, as yet unenacted . . . ?" (54). Emma Nakuina mentions how other powers may "cause the United States to give or abandon us"—Japan or Russia, she suspects, though I would add the possibility of Hawaiians from this side of the sea. Whatever the future event may be, this long view makes the American annexation of Hawaiʻi like the other takeovers—transient, or reversible.[34]

Publishing such *moʻolelo* as "legends" in post-annexation Hawaiʻi is a markedly different political gesture from Westervelt's—one that rhetorically resists the projection of a fantasy Hawaiʻi with no Hawaiians. For Emma Nakuina, to appreciate Hawaiian stories is vitally linked to asserting the sovereignty of the Hawaiian people over their knowledge, history, and experience.

At the same time, it is an intimate gesture, a love-filled offering. As the preface to *Hawaii: Its People, Their Legends* declares, "Aloha, the Hawaiian equivalent of affection, love of friends and family, patriotism and devotion, is breathed in every story." This love for family, friends, and nation—and the struggles it demands—is perhaps most strongly dramatized in the ending of "The Great Battle of Nuuanu" story. After the "flower of the Oahu aristocracy" and so many commoners perished, though married to one of Kamehameha's generals, a young chiefess of Oʻahu "called her first-born son Kaheananui [the great heap of the slain], in mournful remembrance of the great heap of the slain Oahuans" (20) and thus "displayed her fidelity to her slaughtered kindred and people" (21). After noting that "It is related that Kamehameha, on hearing of this covert act of feminine defiance, only smiled indulgently

Figure 29. The Pali of Nuuanu. By Alonzo Gartley. *Hawaii: Its People, Their Legends.* Courtesy of Bishop Museum.

and approved of her fidelity to the memories of the dead," Emma Naku-ina ends with a personal observation: "To this act of indulgence I owe much, as the chiefess Kalanikupaulakea was a great grandmother of the writer" (21).

The Nu'uanu Pali now embodies a "legend" or key for reading the *kaona* of Nakuina's succeeding storied places. A memento of Hawaiian history and family history, this story speaks to male *and* female courage in the face of grief, while the teller's personal relation to Nu'uanu as a storied place linked to her very existence adds layers of connotative meanings to the story. Encountering this version of the story can in turn transform our perspective on the Nu'uanu Pali. Because both the writer and the photograph ("The Pali of Nuuanu," Figure 29) invite us to see it not as a precipice, but "a slight cleft or fissure near the top in the face of an almost perpendicular mountain range, forming the *backbone* of the island" (17, my emphasis), Nu'uanu can be revealed as a source of connection and strength, and as a sign of the "covert" and "feminine defiance" that, Nakuina alerts us, runs in her family. No longer exclusively a site of violent death, but also of a family (hi)story in which a more nuanced Kamehameha also grants life, the Nu'uanu Pali now evokes the story of the loyal, defiant chiefess—not entirely unlike her descendant, the writer.

Hawaii: Its People, Their Legends invites us to read Hawaiian places and stories as inextricably related to Hawaiian people through history, blood, and personal experience. Each tale's layered message of *aloha* and justice is as relevant to the home as it is to that larger social world that includes the land and the political sphere.[35] Close to the end of her selected *mo'olelo*, Emma Nakuina reveals again just how personal these (hi)stories are when she notes that the boy who recovered from typhoid fever, possibly thanks to the female retainer's sacrifice, is her son, "the present Speaker of the House of Representatives" (62). Though she does not identify him as the F. W. Beckley whose photograph appears earlier in the book (Figure 28), if we turn back to that page his image now has a history, a story tied to the writer and to "Kamehameha's Last Heiau" (61). If her first acknowledged personal connection to the *mo'olelo* was through her ancestor, the chiefess Kalanikupaulakea, this one is through her son, a political agent in the present, her hope for the future. Kamehameha I and the places marked by his power struggles are part of the *mo'olelo*, literally "a fragment of a story" (Osorio 250), where the words (*'ōlelo*) make up the *mo'o* as "small piece," but also envision the *mo'o* ("lizard" or "dragon") as "succession," as "generational line" and "ridge" (Pukui and Elbert 253).

Though Emma Nakuina offers a range of verbal and visual clues to the epistemological complexities of *mo'olelo*, she does not strive for a "fluent" translation. Protocols of Hawaiian (hi)story inform the telling, calling for reading strategies that acknowledge *kaona* rather than look for shortcuts in the form of comparisons designed to put non-Hawaiian readers at ease. Some Hawaiian words are left unglossed, and Ka'ōpulupulu's prophecy is only "freely translated" into English; while some Hawaiian names are accompanied by their translation, others are not; and a name like Kahalaopuna is never shortened to "Kaha," in the simplifying manner of Westervelt. Finally, although there is personal disclosure, there is no inclination to give away the whole story. Those intended to read a Hawaii Promotion Committee publication, potential tourists expecting a safe and welcoming Hawai'i, were probably left wondering what *aloha*—nowadays employed as *the* slogan or metonymy for island hospitality in the tourist industry—actually meant. Employing the dominant language and engaging with dominant discourses does not mean that Emma Nakuina's translation equates the preservation of Hawaiian traditions with their simplification for the benefit of strangers. Accepting responsibility for Hawai'i, its people, their stories is not at odds with educating the *malihini*, but it cannot be reduced to the Hawaii Promotion Committee's goal of luring and entertaining them.

Those not in the family, already in the story, do not seem to be Emma Nakuina's ideal readers. Even if in English, her writing does not cater to them. But they should be educated—taught about the proud history of her people—instead of being made to feel comfortable with how little they know. Regardless of its institutional provenance, her book provides an opportunity for her to retell in print stories that assert Native agency and "feminine defiance."

Nā Mo'olelo of Resistance

While Thrum's and Westervelt's illustrated translations of legends contributed to the marketing of Hawai'i as a "state of mind" for tourists to acquire—a marketing that continues, in Haunani-Kay Trask's words, to "prostitute Hawaiian culture" today ("Lovely Hula Hands")—the interface of text, image, and *kaona* in Emma Nakuina's volume pictures Hawai'i, its people, and their stories as firmly asserting their resilience and her resistance to such a state. That a Hawaii Promotion Committee publication made such a statement is a testament to Emma Nakuina's knowledge of Hawaiian (hi)stories *and* to her facility with the discursive and visual technologies of her time. That the volume was never reprinted is yet another example of the displacement of a people not only from their land but from their own representation.

Identifying Emma Nakuina as a solitary heroic figure would be only reinforcing a Western model of authorship embodied in Westervelt's pretensions. Just as her "volume is intended only as an appreciation of the people at large," her *mo'olelo* are presented as single instances of the "many versions" available, though the writer promises to recount "the commonly accepted ones" (preface). Unlike Thrum, when she publishes the story of Nanaue for the Hawaiian Historical Society in 1886, she names the individuals who gave it to her—"Kamakau, a woman of Waipio" and D. Napela, who "lived all his lifetime in the vicinity of the scene of the story." Like King Kalākaua, like her contemporaries Moses K. Nakuina and Joseph M. Poepoe, and like Mary Kawena Pukui much later, Emma Kaili Metcalf Beckley Nakuina does not present herself as "author," but as "writer"—a link in the chain of Native Hawaiian tellers who translated *mo'olelo* into print and into English. The work of translation across generations has no straightforward, uniform, or predictable ideological valence. What does link these projects together is the love for Hawai'i, that *aloha* "breathed in every story," and the responsibility to transmit Hawaiian knowledge and history.

Such commitments occasionally make an appearance even in publications like the *Paradise of the Pacific*, where Emma Nakuina and at least two other writers, one of them Hawaiian, published stories that countered the generic fictionalizing of *mo'olelo* that dominated the construction of *legendary Hawai'i*. "The Sacred Pavement of Liloa" (3.11 [1890]: 2) by F. J. Testa and "The Legend of Na-Iwi-O-Pae" written by Emma Kaipu (11.8 [1898]: 117-118) forged strong connections between history, story, and place that did not reduplicate the American "from mist to sunshine" narrative of development.

Quoting from Fornander's *Polynesian Race*, Testa establishes the historical and sacred function of two stone slabs that once constituted the pavement of an important Waipi'o Valley temple and were also associated with the chief Līloa, "sacred in the eyes of his people for his many good qualities." The slabs had been moved to Honolulu, Testa explains, and eventually to "Honuakaha, Her Majesty's premises at the corner of Queen and Punchbowl streets, where they now [1890] lie unnoticed just a few feet away from the 'Transit of Venus.'" Bringing home the political resonance of such neglect, Testa reports: "The expression 'Ka Paepae Kapu a Liloa' as at present used, whether in speaking or writing, refers to the reigning sovereign as to the sacredness of trust imposed upon and reposed in him, and as to the dignity and honour of the position where no intruders are supposed to trespass. It also refers to the pavement and the way that leads up to royalty, and as to the footstool of sovereignty and power" (*ParPac* 3.11 [1890]: 2).[36] Several years later, in 1897, Testa would be one of the co-signers and readers of the "memorial" that articulated the Hawaiian "protest of the annexation aimed at Senator Morgan and his delegates" at a "mass meeting" in October (Silva, *Aloha Betrayed* 151).[37]

Published in August 1898, when the sovereignty of Hawai'i was being ceremonially transferred to the United States, and in the same *Paradise of the Pacific* issue that celebrated the "Americanism of Hawaii" in its lead article, "The Legend of Na-Iwi-O-Pae" was not so politically direct. It did, however, establish a history for the fishhook, fashioned by the chief 'Umi from Pae's bones, and that "is now in the Bishop Museum, where you may see it today." The fishhook is not presented as an object, but as an ethnographic link to such beloved chiefs as 'Umi and his father Līloa, to the Hawaiian practices of fishing and the belief that a hook made of human bone would bring power and plentiful fish to its holder, and to genealogy. "The royal hook," Emma Kaipu writes, "was used by the high chiefs only. This hook was handed down from Umi to all the

Kamehamehas, to Lunalilo, and last to Kalakaua, who gave it into the care of the government curator." The purpose of telling the story and history seems to be to preserve knowledge and *kuleana* ("right, privilege, concern, responsibility, . . . property, . . . jurisdiction," Pukui and Elbert, *Hawaiian Dictionary* 179) in ways that went beyond the hook's physical holding at the Bishop Museum, which had only recently replaced the National Museum. As for the "government curator" of that earlier museum to whom Kalākaua had entrusted the "royal hook," she had to be none other than Emma Kaili Metcalf Beckley Nakuina, who in 1884 had published her own "The Legend of the Fishhook, Called Na-iwi-o-Pae, Now in the Government Museum" (*Annual* 39–40) and had also included a description of the fishhook "made from the thigh bone of a chief called Pae" in her handwritten "Historical Catalogue of the Museum."[38]

F. J. Testa's and Emma Kaipu's *mo'olelo* did not appear in the *Paradise of the Pacific* "Legendary Lore" feature; they really didn't fit. Similarly, later during the territorial days, even if sponsored by the territory's Chamber of Commerce and Merchants' Association, Emma Nakuina's *Hawaii: Its People, Their Legends* contested the marketing of Hawai'i. Her translated legends underscored Hawaiian values, family and patriotic connections, and "feminine defiance." Her *mo'olelo* did not offer a safely primitive Hawai'i for sale, but activated a Hawaiian view of knowledge, (hi)story, and place.

Chapter 5

Stories in Place: Dynamics of Translation and Re-Cognition

Consider that the world is neither flat nor round.
—*Joy Harjo*

Chapter 3 documented the turn-of-the-twentieth-century production of *legendary Hawai'i*, one part of the period's promotional English-language literature about Hawai'i. Violently disrupting Hawaiian traditions of storytelling—*mo'olelo* generally, but *wahi pana* specifically—to benefit non-Hawaiians primarily and to support ideologically the annexation of Hawai'i to the United States of America, Thomas Thrum's and William Westervelt's *legendary Hawai'i* worked to delegitimize Native Hawaiian narratives at the same time that it popularized "legends" as representative of a colonized "Hawaiian culture." Translation—of language, of genre, of epistemology, and of style—enabled this rupture; photography presented the resulting vision of a *legendary Hawai'i* that would appeal to tourists and potential settlers. Chapter 4 documented a complex autoethnographic instance of resistance to this development. Challenging its protocols, Emma Nakuina's English-language collection of *mo'olelo* refused to represent Hawai'i as devoid of its people and their histories. Though not reprinted to this day, with other historical and contemporary Hawaiian counternarratives it invites us to unmake *legendary Hawai'i* by re-visioning and restoring it as an indigenous "storied place."

While the core of this study is a period-specific cultural production, my synchronic approach necessarily raises questions about what preceded the construction of *legendary Hawai'i* and what has become of it today. Had, for example, the tradition of *ha'i mo'olelo* (telling stories, recounting histories) been essentially unchanged by Western contact before then? Since tradition, far from being static or simply conservative, is always a *changing* social and cultural construction, dynamically responding to present need and future responsibilities, the answer to such questions is obviously "no." But what in this case does "no" mean? What do we know about *mo'olelo* traditions at the turn of the twentieth century? And how had they changed during the nineteenth century? As a major force of change in Hawai'i, print almost certainly would have had an effect. And how did the twentieth century—with statehood in 1959, the injection of a rainbow multiculturalism into Hawai'i's "destination image" for tourist consumption, and the emergence of a Native Hawaiian renaissance and sovereignty movement—carry, transform, or challenge these legendary traditions? Though the will to hegemony of *legendary Hawai'i* remains strong in English translation and in the mainstream popular imaginary, Hawaiians have sustained disrupted but not destroyed *mo'olelo* traditions—most visibly through *hula*, the narrative performance of their (hi)stories and poetry. And yet new stories have gripped the popular imagination and even been collected and published as representative of Hawai'i's "supernatural" tradition. How then to evaluate the legacy of *legendary Hawai'i* today?

This final chapter has two main objectives: to limn the difference between the violent disruption that annexation-related politics brought about in Hawaiian narrative traditions, and previous changes inflecting *mo'olelo* in the "contact zone" of the nineteenth century; and to critique current multicultural approaches to "tales of the supernatural" or "contemporary legends" circulating in Hawai'i today, as another unacknowledged, and often unconscious, strategy for perpetuating the effects of that earlier disruption. As I said at the start, this is not a book about Hawaiian *mo'olelo*. Others have the qualifications that I don't possess to conduct in-depth studies of Hawaiian-language narrative traditions. I ground my observations about nineteenth-century *mo'olelo* in what I have learned from their work; my experience with collaborative research and teaching also figures prominently in the following discussion. My overall intention is to insist on a re-cognition of Hawai'i's stories in and of translation that attends to and respects indigenous senses of place, genre, and history.

Both translation studies and indigenous studies have in their own ways moved me to advocate such a "reorientation" (Wood) and re-view. Regardless of whether a specific translated text domesticates, defamiliarizes, or does both, the cultural practice of translation always requires some inscription of naturalized expectations and interests even as it makes its utopian reach toward alterity. In this paradox lies translation's impossibility and its everyday powerful influence. The tensions and challenges are linguistic, epistemological, cultural, ethical, and political, for translating and reading translations both pull what's foreign closer to home *and* broaden one's horizons. Whether that *trans-lation*, that mental move, amounts to crossing or reinforcing boundaries, its valence depends on many specific factors.[1] But the question of *where* "home" is located hierarchically, in the structures of power, is crucial. This question can be posed in several ways. Whose "home" is being translated? Is it the home of the translated, or of the translators, or of the readers, or of all at once? Is the translation for those "at home" or not? How do heterogeneous groups inhabit the place called home? Is "home" an intimate place or a diasporic space? In the larger economy, is home at the center or the periphery? Which symbolic or generic shapes are recognized as best figuring "home," and by whom? What makes the challenges of translation worthwhile is, as Spivak puts it, that "to be human is to be intended toward the other" (*"Planetarity"* in *Death of a Discipline* 72)—but she warns that such a process is never fully realized. Though different readers are at home in different genres, the dynamics of colonialism and cultural imperialism across time have allowed some genres to make their home across the world.

Among those who have found themselves structurally in the position of being "others," Hawaiians and other Native peoples of Oceania have often not embraced the translations and representations purporting to name them and make them intelligible within a dominant framework. In his powerfully visionary and influential 1993 essay "Our Sea of Islands," Epeli Hauʻofa from the University of the South Pacific in Suva, Fiji, confronts the common, "belittling" representation of "Pacific Islands" as "much too small, too poorly endowed with resources, and too isolated from the centers of economic growth" to have sovereignty, independence, or control over themselves. As Hauʻofa tells it, it was when he came to Hawaiʻi and saw how "under the aegis of Pele, . . . the Big Island was growing, rising from the depths of the mighty sea," that he found his way out of the hopeless view he had himself internalized: "The world of Oceania is not small," he recognized, "it is huge and growing bigger every day"; and when he renamed this world to reposition it in the hierarchy, Hauʻofa found that "the myths, legends, oral traditions, and cosmologies of the peoples of Oceania" present a conception of the world that is far from tiny—in fact "boundless" and of epic proportion. "Smallness," Hauʻofa concludes, "is a state of mind," and the people of Oceania need only look to their (hi)stories to overturn confining "hegemonic views" of themselves and their "sea of islands" (28, 30–31, 33, 37).

And as the peoples of Oceania reclaim their own homes, non-Native scholars in a range of disciplines have also taken responsibility for reviewing colonial and other dominant modes of representation—often themselves forms of "smallness" or provincialism—as part of facing the challenge of determining how to think from a different place (*Biography Hawai'i*; Franklin and L. Lyons; Fujikane and Okamura, *Whose Vision?*; Hanlon; Hanlon and White; Jolly; P. Lyons, *American Pacificism*; Maxwell; Minerbi; Schultz; Spahr, *Dole Street* and *2199 Kalia Road*; Stannard, *Honor Killing*; Wilson, *Reimagining the American Pacific*; Wood, *Displacing Natives*). My goal is to practice this kind of *re-cognition*: to consider stories in and of translation in Hawai'i within a framework that does not belittle Native (hi)stories, and considers them "in place," as the title of the chapter suggests.

Translation: Agency in Print

While acknowledging that "in the use of *tradition*" usually "such matters as content and style" are "passed on by the culture, but not invented by the performer,'" when defining "the dynamics of folklore," Barre Toelken argues that "in the processing of these ideas into performance, the artist's own unique talents of inventiveness *within* the tradition are highly valued and are expected to operate strongly" (37). We therefore look to performance for creativity and change, and performances are always inflected not only by individual agency and talent, by audience and contexts, but by their media. What we know of *mo'olelo* today comes partly from the oral tradition and its performance in *hula*, but also from a print tradition dating back well into the nineteenth century, when Hawaiians took up the new technologies of the written and printed word—a print tradition that far exceeds in variety, mass, and detail the non-Hawaiian construction of *legendary Hawai'i*. While *mele*, the songs, have remained fairly unchanged, the prose *mo'olelo* that string them together—and are often not part of *hula* performances—have been subject to more variation. We must ask *what* we know about *mo'olelo* in the nineteenth century, and *how* we know it. On whose practices are we focusing?

Hawaiians of course had been communicating orally for centuries when missionaries arrived in 1820 and sought to establish a written Hawaiian language as a tool for disseminating Christianity among the Natives. In 1834, the first two Hawaiian-language newspapers appeared, both strongly tied to missionary interests.[2] As a number of scholars note, by 1853, "nearly three-fourths of the Native Hawaiian population over the age of sixteen years were literate in their own language," and overall "only Scotland and some of the New England states surpassed the tiny Kingdom" in literacy rates. Hawaiian-language newspapers were in print from 1834 to 1948; over this span of 115 years, approximately 168 different newspapers were published, some running a few months and others for decades. In the early 1860s, newspapers such as *Ka Hoku o ka Pakipika*

(The Star of the Pacific) and *Ka Nupepa Kuokoa* (The Independent) had as many subscribers—approximately 3,000—as the *Pacific Commercial Advertiser*, the most successful English-language newspaper. Hawaiians clearly recognized the power of the printed word. As the "English-mainly" campaign and the annexation debate escalated, the number of Hawaiian-language newspapers multiplied, reaching a high of fourteen concurrent publications in 1896—three years after the overthrow of the Hawaiian monarchy, two years before the official annexation of Hawai'i as a territory of the United States of America, and at the precise moment when English by law became the only official language of instruction in all public and private schools in Hawai'i, thus institutionalizing the suppression of Hawai'i's indigenous language.[3] This had its effects. By 1929—the year of Emma Nakuina's death—only three Hawaiian-language newspapers were circulating. By 1944 there was but one; it closed in 1948.[4]

The extraordinary research by Noenoe Silva and Puakea Nogelmeier has in different ways demonstrated the "live" potential of this archive for a Native-centered exploration of Hawai'i's history and traditions. Scholars in a number of disciplines undeniably face challenges in working with these Hawaiian-language newspapers. Mostly accessible in microfilm, the newspapers lack diacritics, and the nuances of nineteenth-century Hawaiian present problems. But, as of 2005, selected newspapers are available online as both images and, thanks to the efforts of the *Ho'olaupa'i* project of the Bernice Pauahi Bishop Mueseum, as searchable text files, all of which are part of the Ulukau: Hawaiian Electronic Library at http://nupepa.org/.[5]

Work already published makes it clear that in the nineteenth century, when Euro-American settlers were speaking and reading Hawaiian, and when Hawai'i was still a sovereign nation, Hawaiian-language and English-language newspapers together constituted an important site for providing information and for educating and galvanizing the people of Hawai'i. In this hotly contested public sphere, settlers and Hawaiians struggled as they advocated competing systems of governance, land development, language, and culture. According to Hawaiian-language scholar Nogelmeier, any Hawaiian with a strong opinion—whether about politics or a published story—would write to the newspapers, which then published *nā leo* (the voices) of the people, their narratives and counternarratives.[6] In Hawaiian-language newspapers, such narratives might be anecdotes responding to current events, but also *mo'olelo* and *mo'olelo ka'ao*. Grouping story sequences that included legendary or fabulous accounts, these categories did not distinguish between fiction and nonfiction in absolute terms. Among the *mo'olelo*, we find stories about the volcano goddess, Pele; about the pig god, Kamapua'a; and about chiefs and storied places. Furthermore, the term *mo'olelo* was applied to Hawaiian tales that had previously circulated orally *and* to foreign texts in translation.

There were many of these. Well before Hawaiian *mo'olelo* were translated into English-language "legends," Hawaiians were translating outside narratives into Hawaiian and circulating them in print as *mo'olelo* and *ka'ao* often on the front page. Let's take *Ka Nupepa Kuokoa*, "the longest running and most influential of the Hawaiian-language newspapers," which appeared from October 1861 to December 29, 1927 (Forbes, *Hawaiian National Bibliography* 296; Hori). In addition to recording local news and history, and current events from foreign countries ("no [from] Amerika, no Cuba, no Beritania Nui [Great Britain], no Geremananui [Great Germany], no Peresia, no Rusia, no Italia, no Kina [China]," and more), the *Kuokoa* published Hawaiian *mo'olelo* ("a series on the Hawaiian chief 'Umi," for instance, that began in 1862), Hawaiian *mo'olelo ka'ao* from the oral tradition (like Moses Manu's rendition of *Keaomelemele* in 1884–1885), and Hawaiian tales that took on a more literary quality, like *Laieikawai* by S. N. Hale'ole. It also published a large number of translated fictions, including as early as 1861 some European fairy tales: "The Twelve Brothers," "Snow White," "Puss in Boots," and "The Frog Prince" (Schweizer, "Kahaunani"). During the 1870s, the *Kuokoa* offered its readers translations of such German wonder tales as "Ka Wai o ke Ola" (The Water of Life) and "Kanani Hiolanikanahele" (Sleeping Beauty); "na Raianahu ka huhui hoku nani o Pekina," a tale from China, about the beautiful cluster of stars of Peking; "He Iwakalua Tausani Legue malalo o ke kai . . ." (Twenty Thousand Leagues Under the Sea . . .), an adaptation of Jules Verne's popular narrative; and selections from *Arabian Nights*.

This storytelling impetus and range are not peculiar to the *Kuokoa*; together, the Hawaiian-language newspapers are an important site for studying the establishment of a *mo'olelo* print tradition, and for documenting changes in its traditions in the new medium. Though the new technologies of writing and print indisputably lessened the social power of the spoken word, and therefore of history and story as Hawaiians had known them up to 1820, these technologies did not silence Hawaiians.[7] Nor were Hawaiians only the objects of translation. Their own translations of foreign-language narratives into Hawaiian are fruitful sites for exploring the agency of Hawaiian storymakers in print during the second part of the nineteenth century.

Coming to the project with a shared interest in the practice and politics of translation, but with very different relationships to Hawai'i, forms of disciplinary knowledge, and general linguistic competence, Noelani Arista and I recently collaborated in print on reading *He Kaao Arabia*—

Figure 30. September 26, 1874 front page of the *Kuokoa* featuring *He Kaao Arabia*, with a version of the *Arabian Nights* frame story. Courtesy of Bishop Museum.

the translation of a selection of *The Arabian Nights* published in *Ka Nupepa Kuokoa*. The longest section of *He Kaao Arabia* (literally "An Arabian Tale") was published there by S. K. Ulele in ten installments in 1875 as "He Kaao Arabia! No ke Kanaka Lawaia! Ke Kumu o ka Pomaikai," which translates as "An Arabian tale about the Fisherman! The source of Good Fortune" (Figure 30).[8] While not the only translations of *The Arabian Nights* in Hawaiian-language newspapers, these form a cluster that Arista retranslated into English, and that she and I then examined with an eye to their politics of translation. Arista's experience as a translator and her perspective as a Native historian make her nuanced attention to the language of the Hawaiian translators particularly illuminating. While conducting her "exploration of historically-charged negotiations of difference," she "became particularly attentive in [her] own translation to the agency and mediation of the *Kuokoa*

Hawaiian-language translators" (Arista in Bacchilega and Arista 191).[9] For both of us, though in different ways, focusing on this Hawaiian and therefore non-Western translation of one of the most influential texts of Orientalism was an opportunity to "re-locate" the *Arabian Nights* (Marzolph).

Carrying out such a task meant taking into account both the Hawaiians' voluminous production of newspapers and translation in the second half of the nineteenth century and the growing social marginalization of Hawaiian language and culture that was in 1896 institutionalized in the education system. The public sphere of nineteenth-century Hawai'i guided our questions. What were the general *dynamics* of translation at the time? We came to a tentative hypothesis. Depending on whether it was into or from Hawaiian, translation served very different sociopolitical purposes. Taking a cosmopolitan approach to different narrative conventions and cultures—just as their king, Kalākaua, would in the 1880s when he returned from his world tour with novelties such as the telephone, the flush toilet, and electrical lights for his palace— Hawaiians translated a wide variety of texts from English into Hawaiian. Though this open-minded use of translation undoubtedly contributed to the process of acculturating Hawaiians into the settlers' worldview and cultural codes, it was also a sign of pride in Hawaiian language and culture—a "vitality and confidence" that Nogelmeier notices generally in the newspaper writings of the time. Conversely, translation from Hawaiian into English became increasingly symptomatic of a dismissal of Hawaiian language and people as irrelevant to the workings of business and politics in Hawai'i—the move toward an "English-only" policy. This mode of translation speaks to the settlers' felt superiority, and therefore functions as an exclusionary practice, the verbal sign of colonialism being made in the islands.

How did the *Kuokoa* translation of *The Arabian Nights* situate itself within this double project? While, yes, it is acknowledged that these tales were once in Arabic, the Hawaiian translation presents them as stories translated from the English language. The Hawaiian translation is therefore much more focused on relations to the West—Christian morals and politics—than to the fantastic Orient. This translation of *The Arabian Nights* has little to do with the (re)production of Orientalism as sexual and exotic fantasy, and much more to do with the translators' benevolent representation of a foreign imagination, that of "English-language stories," and their Hawaiian transformation of it for specific localized uses. Though it indirectly confirms the reading of *The Arabian Nights* as a Western fantasy of the "Orient," the Orientalism is not the Hawaiian text's motor or appeal.[10]

Is *He Kaao Arabia* an instance of colonial translation in nineteenth-century Hawai'i? At least in the *Kuokoa,* whose declared mission was to "furnish from week to week such reading matter as may tend to develop and enlarge the Hawaiian mind, and enable Hawaiians to think, feel, act and live more like foreigners," Arista notes that translation "was geared to 'teaching' Hawaiians about the superiority of life lived and imported *mai ka 'āina 'ē mai,* 'from foreign lands.'" Thus, "while seemingly attempting to blur the boundaries between Hawaiians and *haole,*" such translation "in fact also solidifies their difference—their separateness and the power relations supporting it" (Arista in Bacchilega and Arista 201).[11] *He Kaao Arabia* does further the project of acculturating Hawaiian readership to the ways of Euro-American settlers, but it does more than that. The selection of stories, I believe, is a way for Hawaiian translators to exercise their agency by using the tales as statements on the present political dramas. Arista foregrounds the translators' indigenous agency within the larger politics of translation of the time, showing how some of the word choices that allude to the Hawaiian past and its idioms are acts of "cultural re-membering" (Stillman, "Re-Membering the History" 2001). At least some Hawaiian readers would welcome such assertions of the relevance "of Hawaiian ways of knowing" into their present. It is our understanding, then, that for Hawaiian translators and readers, *He Kaao Arabia* was a form of acculturation *and* creative resistance.

Translation: Genre in Place

Hawaiians in the second half of the nineteenth century exercised at least some agency in their translating and distributing of a wide range of foreign stories. Reading those stories certainly had an impact on Hawaiians' imagination and storymaking. The process of writing and printing also transformed the experience and rituals of storytelling; the constraints of serialized publication, for example, influenced the rhythms of story production and reception. And yet, while change was inevitable, it did not result in a sudden erasure of Hawaiian narrative traditions; in fact, according to Nogelmeier, "The writings submitted to the 1860s newspapers show a new and extended mixture of traditional oratory and modern Western written forms rather than a replacement of the older traditional forms by newer styles of presentation" (137).[12] The presence in Hawaiian-language newspapers of poetic address and of words that relied on complex cultural knowledge; the extensive public dialogue resulting from readers commenting on published stories by writing letters to the newspapers; and the many intertextual references "connecting multiple newspapers to a single discussion"—all these strategies preserved Native storytelling and knowledge in Hawaiian-language writing (Nogelmeier 137, 152–53).

In the introduction to her 1996 English-language translation of the anonymous "He Moʻolelo Kaʻao o Kamapuaʻa" (A Legendary Tradition of Kamapuaʻa) published in 1891 by *Ka Leo o ka Lahui* (The Voice of the Nation), Lilikalā Kameʻeleihiwa explains that "Because it is not a simple recounting of a memorized story, as would have been told orally, but rather a reworked version meant to be eloquent and moving when read, we know that the art of Hawaiian storytelling was alive, changing, and adapting itself to written form in 1891" (xvi). Kameʻeleihiwa's edition aims to combine a literal (that is, not fluent) translation with annotations on the cultural, sexual, and poetic complexities of the text's metaphors, and its relevance to the political struggles of the time. In my undergraduate Oral Narratives and graduate Folklore and Literature courses, students have uniformly found her translation much more interesting and lively than the shorter, simpler Kamapuaʻa translations by Thrum and Westervelt. The *kaona* of place names is evident because several storied places—Kaliuwaʻa foremost but not alone—are a focus of narration that the translation does not gloss over. But we also talk in class about the conventions of serialized writing that are present. The writer refers to himself as such (Kameʻeleihiwa, *A Legendary Tradition of Kamapuaʻa* 2, 58), and often addresses his "reader" in formal ways: "You perhaps should know, O friendly readers of this story . . ." (7); or "at this point, if it pleases the readers, there is a short clarification below" (41). "Aole i pau," translated as "It is not finished" (17), is a formula for telling Hawaiian readers that the tale was "to be continued." Students' observations confirmed Kameʻeleihiwa's assertions about the vitality of Hawaiian storytelling. The power of the spoken word survives in the published name chants, Tina Bushnell recognized, because in this Kamapuaʻa written narrative a spoken name has a force and effect of its own: depending on whether his protective grandmother or his antagonistic cousin Pele performs his name chant, it empowers or disempowers the pig god. And while the narrative displays some *ʻōlelo noʻeau* (Hawaiian proverbs and poetical sayings, in Pukui's translation; see Kameʻeleihiwa, *A Legendary Tradition of Kamapuaʻa* 23, 24, 27, 99), Maile Gresham noted that to read "The time it took for Kamapuaʻa to return was faster than a steamship travels" is to encounter modernity.

To explore these changes and issues of genre in class, I focus on *Laieikawai* (*Lāʻieikawai* in current orthography), whose publication marked a particularly significant "first" in Hawaiian storytelling and literature because, having appeared in 1862 in the *Hoku o ka Pakipika* (only a few installments) and the *Kuokoa* in serialized form as *Ka Moolelo o Laieikawai*, it was then published as a book entitled *Ke Kaao o Laieikawai* in 1863. In the words of its publisher, Henry Whitney, *Laieikawai* was "the first Hawaiian story book ever printed, relating to their ancient traditions,

customs, sayings and doings."[13] "Kakauia mailoko mai o na Moolelo
Kahiko o Hawaii Nei"—"Set down from the ancient history of Hawai'i"
(Forbes's translation, 3:348) or "Composed from the old stories of
Hawaii" (Hale'ole/Beckwith translation 341)—this text was written by
S. N. Hale'ole (Haleole in nineteenth-century orthography), a historian,
teacher, and *Ka Hoku o ka Pakipika* newspaper editor who had been edu-
cated at the Lahainaluna Seminary with Malo and Kamakau. It was first
translated into English by Martha Warren Beckwith for the Bureau of
American Ethnology of the Smithsonian in 1919, with the translation
facing the Hawaiian text.[14]

As "probably the first literary effort by a native Hawaiian, which has
received compensation, the manuscript having been purchased from
the author," *Kuokoa* publisher Whitney writes, "It will, we hope, form
the pioneer of more valuable works." And yet, while the publication of
a book by a Hawaiian in Hawaiian that was a *mo'olelo ka'ao*, and not a
compendium of information or a translation, was recognized as a
momentous event, descriptions of *Laieikawai* reveal different agendas.
The book is in Hawaiian language; and yet, by focusing on its "authenticity" and the past in his 1862 English-language announcements, the
publisher anticipates the rhetoric of Thrum and Westervelt: "This volume narrates one of the ancient legends written in the most polished
and pure style of the language. Being the first book of the kind ever
published in the vernacular, and also one of the most popular of the
legends of this people, it will be valued by foreigners and natives, that
desire to see its records preserved in this form" (as quoted in Forbes 3:
348). In contrast, Hale'ole's "Foreword" reads: "Ua hoopuka ka mea
nana i pai keia buke me ka olioli nui, ka makamua o ka hoao ana e hoo-
lako i buke hoonanea na na kanaka Hawaii." (343 "Olelo Hoakaka" in
Hale'ole/Beckwith; "The editor of this book rejoices to print the first
fruits of his efforts to enrich the Hawaiian people with a story book";
"Foreword" in Laura Green's translation as acknowledged in Beckwith's
edition, 342).[15] Hale'ole's stated purpose is to give "i ka lahui Hawaii,
ka buke e pili ana i ka hoonanea'ku i ka noho ana, e like ma ka na haole,
he mea ia nana e hanai mai i ko kakou mau manao i ka ike a me ka
naauao" (343; "the people of Hawaii a book of entertainment for leisure moments like those of the foreigners, a book to feed our minds
with wisdom and insight" 342); to foster "ke aloha o na poe o Hawaii
nei, no ko lakou mau kupuna a me ko lakou aina" (343; "in the Hawaiian people the love of their ancestors and their country" 342); and to
secure "i mau buke hou na keia lahui, ma kana olelo iho—ka olelo
Hawaii"(343; "to the people more books of this same nature written in
. . . the Hawaiian tongue" 342). The Hawaiian people are the beneficiaries of his "story book"; and Hale'ole's explicit intention is to inaugu-

rate a Hawaiian national literature, suggesting that while he did not receive the recognition that the Brothers Grimm have, his project was similar.

Laieikawai features the homonymous heroine, "ka Hiwahiwa o Paliuli, Kawahineokaliula," the "Beauty of Paliuli, the Woman of the Twilight." Symbolic thunder and a rainbow over the island of Oʻahu announce the birth of the high-ranking and beautiful Lāʻieikawai and Lāʻielohelohe, but the twin sisters must be separated and hidden because their lives are at risk. Their powerful grandmother takes Lāʻieikawai to the island of Hawaiʻi, where she leads a secluded and protected life in the forest of Paliuli, with multicolored birds as her attendants. Suitors woo her unsuccessfully for she is befriended by the sweet-scented Maile sisters who— led by the youngest, Kahalaomāpuana—protect Lāʻieikawai's virginity. When however Lāʻieikawai is abducted by a surfer, a "wily rascal of Puna," her grandmother and the high chief to whom she had been promised abandon her; and when her surfer lover sees her twin sister's beauty, he leaves Lāʻieikawai too. But the five Maile sisters and her *moʻo* uncle stand by her. The brave Kahalaomāpuana goes on a challenging quest for a husband who deserves Lāʻieikawai, returning with her own divine brother, Kaʻōnohiokalā, "The Eyeball of the Sun," who marries the beautiful chiefess, takes her to the heavens, and punishes her enemies. But Lāʻieikawai's tribulations are not over for her husband, also smitten with her sister's looks, pursues Lāʻielohelohe. Ultimately his parents punish the unfaithful Kaʻōnohiokalā, transforming him into the first *lapu*, or ghost, condemned to roam in darkness forever. The twin sisters are reconciled; Kahalaomāpuana's wisdom is recognized; and Lāʻieikawai is worshipped as the "Woman of the Twilight" until her death.

Laieikawai may have been what Whitney called "one of the most popular of the native traditions," but to think of it simply as a transcription of an oral narrative is to deny Haleʻole any agency or artistry.[16] He called the publication a difficult undertaking, requiring support and perseverance to overcome "na pilikia" (troubles). Martha Beckwith called his book the "composition of a Polynesian mind working on the material of an old legend and eager to create a genuine national literature" ("Introduction" 294). As an authored narrative anchored in *moʻolelo* as traditional story, *Laieikawai* explicitly presents itself as literature in print.

As with other writers of *moʻolelo* and *kaʻao*—and for that matter his contemporaries like Charles Dickens in England—Haleʻole's need to adapt to the constraints of serialization affected the book's form as well. A tale that supposedly could be told in six hours (Beckwith, "Introduction" 293; Forbes 3: 348), is distributed over thirty-four chapters, often bridged by transitions like this:

(Ma ka Mokuna V o keia Kaao, ua ike kakou ua hiki aku a [sic] Aiwohikupua ma Laupahoehoe; maanei e kamailio iki kakou no Hulumaniani ka Makaula nana i ukali mai o Laieikawai, mai Kauai mai, ka mea i olelomuaia ma ka helu mua o keia Kaao.) (395; parentheses in original)

In Chapter V of this story we have seen how Aiwohikupua got to Laupahoehoe. Here we shall say a word about Hulumaniani, the seer, who followed Laieikawai hither from Kauai, as described in the first chapter of this story. (394)

The retention of this metacommentary not only shows how Hale'ole negotiated the demands of *Laieikawai*'s first publication in weekly install-ments; it also self-reflectively calls attention to the challenges print posed for the pioneering writer and readers. Just as Samuel Kamakau "saw himself as a *kākau mo'olelo*, a writer of *mo'olelo*, a formal, self-proclaimed title that he used often" (Nogelmeier 195), Hale'ole is con-scious of his role as editor, shaper, and writer—and of his responsibility to offer "punihei" (fascinating) insights to his Hawaiian readers in this new medium.

For students, it is obvious that the Hawaiian writer is *adapting to* print, and they also quickly notice that some of *Laieikawai*'s stylistic and sym-bolic elements parallel those of the European tale of magic, a genre that had already found its way into the Hawaiian-language newspapers of the time and that had great contemporary currency as foundational to "national" literatures. In class, however, we resist the easy conclusion that Hale'ole is adopting this genre's protocols to write a locally set "Cinderella-like" story that anticipates Westervelt-like readings of Hawaiian stories as "fairy tales." Instead, we re-cognize Hawaiian agency by approaching *Laieikawai* as the product of a more engaged intertextu-ality; in other words, we look at how Hale'ole may be *adapting* the fairy tale by setting it within a framework of Hawaiian logic and epistemology as well.

The parallels are indisputable. *Laieikawai* thrives on externalization, symbolism, and wonder—the characterizing features of the European tale of magic (Lüthi). The heroine's beauty, and her closeness with nature (the rainbow, birds, and fragrant plants) confirm her special status in ways that parallel Snow White's naturalized beauty ("a child as white as snow, as red as blood, and as black as the wood of the window frame," *The Annotated Brothers Grimm* 243; Tatar's translation). Especially in contrast to her sister's obedience, Lā'ieikawai's disobedience also marks her as an "unlikely" heroine—again fully within the tale-of-magic tradition. In both *Laieikawai* and the tale of magic, the natural world, from the sun to the forest, is alive in "wondrous" ways fully accepted or naturalized within the narrative world. Like the tale of wonder, the narrative focuses on a beautiful girl's initiation that in its challenges and accomplishments crystallizes significant social values for both genders. And, like the classic tale of magic, the prose is relatively terse, so as to maximize the power of symbol and metaphor.[17]

Hale'ole may have acculturated these fairy-tale elements from the existing translations of fairy tales from the European and the *Arabian Nights* traditions into the Hawaiian language. But, if we focus on his goals, agency, and milieu as the primary ground for interpretation, these fairy-tale elements in *Laieikawai* can also be seen as working *for* Hawaiian social values and epistemology. Let's take sexual symbolism as an example. The value of virginity is foundational to many European tales of magic with female protagonists ("Snow White," "Rapunzel," and "Cinderella"); in fact, it defines innocence and womanhood. In *Laieikawai*, while the heroine's sexual purity certainly matters, she must be guarded primarily *because*, a woman of high rank, her marriage and progeny will have political and spiritual value.[18] Hawaiian sexual restrictions and mores had primarily to do with rank, family influence, and political alliances. Preserving the *ali'i* (chiefs) and their *mana* (spiritual power) was their goal; not directing the lifestyles of all women. Purity was a political force. In the mid-nineteenth century, then, when missionaries were actively seeking to redefine marriage in Hawai'i in terms of Christian morality, and to put what they saw as deviant sexual behaviors on trial (Merry), *Laieikawai* appears as a beautiful fiction that symbolically asserts the Hawaiian sacred linking of sexuality not to moral virtue, but to rank and power.

Another example. Just as *'āina* and "land" are not semantically or symbolically equivalent (see Chapter 2), neither are *nahele* and "forest." Lā'ieikawai's seclusion in Paliuli may seem like Snow White's stay with the dwarves in the forest of the Brothers Grimm tale, or the protected slumber that the thick and thorny forest offers Sleeping Beauty/Briar Rose during her long wait for the prince. But Snow White cooks and cleans for the dwarves, domesticating the surrounding wilderness, male desire, and herself. And while the dwarves do guard and worship her beauty after she has tasted the poisoned apple, she lies in a crystal coffin—a framed *objet d'art* quite other from the surrounding natural world. Snow White is attractive because she does not belong in the forest or in the dirt of a grave. She is unnatural, and so is Sleeping Beauty. In a similarly aestheticizing scene, vines protect Briar Rose from unwanted suitors while she is asleep, but the thorny forest actually surrounds a *castle* that insulates her from the outside natural world. She lies in a comfortable bed, perfectly coifed.

Lā'ieikawai's stay in Paliuli is described quite differently. As we have come to expect in Hawaiian culture, her relationship to nature is *familial.* Lā'ieikawai's forest hut is "ua uhiia me na hulu melemele o ka Oo"

(Hale'ole/Beckwith 401; "covered with the yellow feathers of the *oo* bird" 400), and she herself is found "e kau mai ana iluna o ka eheu o na manu e like me kona ano mau, elua hoi mau manu Iiwipolena e kau ana ma na poohiwi o ke Alii, e lu ana i na wai ala lehua ma ke poo o ke Alii" (435; "resting on the wings of birds as was her custom; two scarlet *iiwi* birds were perched on the shoulders of the princess and shook the dew from red *lehua* blossoms upon her head" 434). The image of the young woman lying on bird feathers is not only beautiful, but a sign of her high standing in the social and natural world. No barrier lies between her and the birds or the flowers; she is with them, honored by them, part of their world. Lā'ieikawai's name also links royalty and nature within her, since the *'ie'ie* vine is a "red-spiked climbing pandanus" that was symbolic of royalty and sacred.[19] To the rescue of the *'ie* leaf (lau + 'ie = lā'ie) come her five sisters—four types of *maile* (the fragrant myrtle vine), and the strong but "sweet-scented hala" (pandanus tree; Figure 31), Kahalaomāpuana. The text therefore offers a multi-sensory experience of Paliuli, though many of us in the classroom today have to re-view the story's cast through visuals to access the multiple meanings of the Hawaiian names that identify characters as flora or fauna *and* high-ranking humans. The Paliuli forest provides more than shelter to Lā'ieikawai: she is supported by its intertwining of the social and natural world. Only by recognizing these culture-specific connections can we come to agree with Dennis Kawaharada's suggestions that "this is not the dark dangerous forest of European folktales, but a sacred place, secluded but life-giving," and that stories such as *Laieikawai* "depict the forest as a place where human beings belong" ("Alive in Story" 53 and 66).[20]

This belonging comes to life in the narrative because of the forest's and its inhabitants' specificity. Located on the island of Hawai'i in the district of Puna, Lā'ieikawai's refuge is not "a" forest—as in any forest we can freely imagine. We learn about its geography and vegetation, the journeys one must take to get there, and the birds that fill it with song and color, as we read about the heroine's romances. "Place" is thus narrated so that experience-based knowledge about it is transmitted, and this is true of the story's other places, and of the journeys that characters take from island to island. Telling stories *in* place, the text of *Laieikawai* begins in Lā'ie, on the windward side of O'ahu, the heroine's and her twin sister's birthplace, and the place name continues to preserve their memory. Chapter 1 begins: "I ke kamailio ana i keia kaao ua oleloia ma Laie, Koolau" (Hale'ole/Beckwith 345) or "This tale was told at Laie, Koolau," (344) where as the tale goes the twins were born. A place close by retains the twins' mother's name, Mālaekahana; and Lā'ieikawai's

Figure 31. *Hala* plant. Courtesy of Lynn A. Davis.

name associates her with water (*ka wai*) because she is initially hidden in the nearby "water hole of Waiapuka" (348), where rainbows would gather in her presence. As heroine and vine, Lāʻieikawai is rooted in a specific place (Lāʻie), then nurtured in another (Puna).[21] Appropriately, Hawaiian studies and Hawaiian language classes often include field trips to "storied places." Haleʻole's imaginative book therefore is not a "fairy tale" (though that may be a most readily available framework for contemporary Western readers to make sense of it), but a Hawaiian narrative that firmly maintains its ground in a Hawaiian sense of place, while possibly, and, if so, actively, adapting fairy-tale elements to its own protocols.

Overall, my observations about print, agency, and genre in nineteenth-century literary translations into Hawaiian, nineteenth-century *moʻolelo* in print, and selected twentieth-century translations of them into English aim to reinforce three related points. First, Native Hawaiian culture was not caught in some ahistorical "ethnographic present" when Thrum, Westervelt, and others rewrote it for Euro-American popular consumption; for their own ends, Hawaiians had been actively adapting new media and forms brought by settlers.[22] Second, Emma Nakuina's intervention in the production of *legendary Hawaiʻi* at the turn of the twentieth century was itself part of this larger Hawaiian narrative tradition of agency in print. And third, modern editions of nineteenth-century *moʻolelo* and *moʻolelo kaʻao*—and especially when they are bilingual, like Haleʻole's *Laieikawai* or Moses Manu's *Keaomelemele* (translated by Mary Kawena Pukui and edited by Puakea Nogelmeier) and Hoʻoulumāhiehie's *Hiiakaikapoliopele* (edited and translated by Nogelmeier)— offer excellent pedagogical opportunities in a folklore and literature class for exploring dynamics of change, genre, place, and translation. These texts, the Kamapuaʻa and the Pele and Hiʻiaka stories, and many nineteenth-century Hawaiian narratives were adapted to print, while still strongly relying on and preserving knowledge of *wahi pana*.

Whether one knows Hawaiian language or not, reading these texts offers an opportunity to appreciate how Hawaiians did bring their views of place into the medium of print and, more generally, to re-view stories in place—to see not only where they were told and where their events occurred, but also from where the impulse to publish emerged, and what kinds of sensory and "legendary" experiences of a Hawaiian place these stories evoked. For most of us, this will require venturing away from the touristic image that confines Hawaiians to premodern simplicity and becoming familiar with a much-needed counternarrative to the domesticating logic of *legendary Hawaiʻi*, which inflects readings of Hawaiʻi's popular culture to this day.

Re-Cognition of Storied Places Today

"No place I have ever lived is so haunted by spirits, real or imagined, and in such a diverse array," Rick Carroll proclaims at the beginning of *Chicken Skin: True Spooky Stories of Hawai'i* (1996): "There are as many different ghosts here as there are ethnic groups. . . . Hawai'i's ghosts are very cosmopolitan" (xvi). Also in 1996, Glen Grant—who collected and published ghost stories in Hawai'i for some twenty years—wrote that "As the Native Hawaiian beliefs interfaced with the immigrants' beliefs in the supernatural, a new form of 'ghost story' was born in Hawai'i which intricately blended the different cultures' common beliefs in spirit return. . . . Everyone [in Hawai'i] seem[s] to have a ghost story either personal or within their family . . ." (*Obake Files* xiv, xvi).[23]

Over the years, *Honolulu* magazine, the successor of *Paradise of the Pacific*, has from time to time featured the phenomenon of ghost stories in Hawai'i—often enough with Glen Grant as authoritative guide. "The Ghosts of Honolulu" (1990) is an account of—and advertisement for— what was then Grant's walking tour (Wittig-Harby); "Haunted Hawai'i" (1991) by Tomi K. Knaefler summarizes many of Grant's "spooky stories" along with stories collected from noted individuals, including Hawaiian novelist John Dominis Holt. There are more. "Ghost Stories" (2004) by short-story writer Cedric Yamanaka stands out, because it offers an unusually varied array of stories about "playful" ghosts told by your "everyday folks." As you might predict, all of these articles appeared in the October issues of this glossy monthly—a tribute to the Halloween mood.

"We Hawai'i residents love our ghost stories" (Yamanaka 31). Sure. Teaching at the University of Hawai'i at Mānoa over the last twenty years in Honolulu certainly acquainted me with the abundance of ghost stories in contemporary Hawai'i, and more specifically, of contemporary supernatural legends that take on distinctly "localized" and/or ethnically marked forms. These stories straddle "the boundary between the rational and the supernatural, varying in focus from teller to teller" and raise questions about what purports to be our rational and science-based contemporary world (Lindahl in Bennett and Smith xiii).[24] In a well-known 1972 essay, folklorist Katharine Luomala pointed out versions of the popular "Vanishing Hitchhiker" contemporary legend in Hawai'i, where the goddess Pele appears as the savvy hitchhiker testing the driver's generosity and respect.[25] Students eagerly discuss other stories: the silent female Japanese "Faceless Ghost," sighted in the bathroom of the Waialae Drive-In theater, and more recently in the bathrooms in the nearby Kahala shopping center and in the Kailua McDonald's; "The Needle in the Movie Theater" AIDS-related rumor that in Hawai'i for some reason applied only to Signature Theatres, first-time competitors in the 1990s to the Consolidated Theatres' monopoly; the numerous hauntings in the university dormitories.

But other classroom experiences have made me wary of the multicultural narrative that often seems to frame these stories. According to Glen Grant—whose audio tapes, radio storytelling programs, commercial tours, and videos flooded the market in the 1990s to the point that some students would cite his versions and views as the "true" ones— "Ethnic boundaries have been transcended by Japanese ghosts, which have become Island phantoms" ("Japanese Obake in Hawaii"), and "The fact that the word *obake*, supernatural creature, is so well known among all races in Hawai'i as a term for 'ghost' reveals the influence the Japanese community had in keeping the underground faith alive" (*Obake Files* xv). I suspect, though, that this "transcend[ing]" of boundaries, and this use of the *obake* terminology, did not come to haunt Hawai'i in straightforward or innocuous ways. In my 1998 Oral Narratives undergraduate class, for instance, a "local" Japanese-American student began her presentation on stories about the Old Pali Road in Nu'uanu on the island of O'ahu (Figure 32) by stating confidently, "Everyone has a really spooky feeling about it." A usually soft-spoken female Hawaiian student interrupted her: "What? I love it. I go there to meditate because it is so beautiful. How can you say that?" Neither a matter of personal taste or experience, nor concerned with the "truth" of a particular story, this disagreement was about a sense of place. Saying that the place may have a different "feel" at night than in the daylight did not make much of a difference; other students intervened, and we avoided polarization—barely—but I think of that exchange often, for it has crystallized for me the conflicted, politically charged dynamics of the historical process that Grant describes as harmonious. In this "multicultural" process haven't Hawaiian beliefs and people been taken over and displaced, their language silenced, their culture reinterpreted and colonized? Though the answer may not be a blanket "yes," I believe this question must be asked in a settler society, whose pervasive cultural values have become not only more recognizably Euro-American, but also Japanese-American (Trask, *From a Native Daughter* and "Settlers of Color"; Fujikane and Okamura, *Whose Vision?*; Morales).

Tales of Supernatural Hawai'i and Multiculturalism

In a 1983 article for the *Hawaii Herald*, a newspaper that self-identifies Hawai'i's Japanese Americans as its readers, Glen Grant first began to shape his readers' understanding of "localized" ghost stories within a multicultural framework:

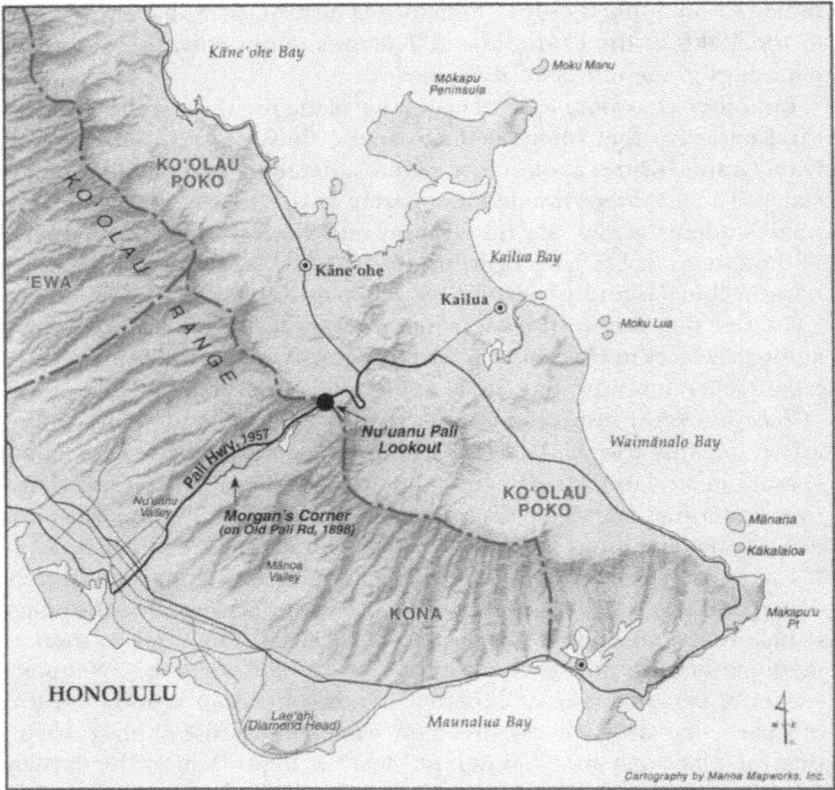

Figure 32. Old Pali Road, Pali Highway, and Pali Lookout. Courtesy of Jane
Eckelman, Manoa Mapworks.

The great majority of urban and rural ghosts found in contemporary Hawaii are
Hawaiian in origin. After a thousand years inhabiting the land, it is only natural
that the legends, myths and supernatural perceptions of the Native Hawaiian
should form the spiritual bedrock of modern occult occurrences. But Hawaiian
spirits are tolerant and there is also room in the Islands for the supernatural
traditions of later immigrants. ("Japanese Obake in Hawaii")

This tolerance, Grant writes, transforms "Japanese ghosts" into "Island
phantoms." As Grant's publications and ghost-story enterprises multiplied, a new version of *legendary Hawai'i* emerged, offering a *multicultural*
tradition of the supernatural as an important part of his narrative of
popular culture in Hawai'i. Here is how it goes. Hawaiian "supernaturalism was later infused with the rural folk religions of the immigrants from
China, Portugal, Japan, Korea, Okinawa, Puerto Rico and the Philip-

pines who came to work in a sugar plantation industry. As the Native Hawaiian beliefs interfaced with the immigrants' beliefs in the supernatural, a new form of 'ghost story' was born in Hawaii which intricately blended the different cultures' common beliefs in spirit return" (*Obake Files* xiv). A bit later, in *Glen Grant's Chicken Skin Tales* (chicken skin = goose bumps), he writes that: "Hawaii's 'Chicken Skin' stories persist as a living spiritual tradition of open-hearted and free-minded Islanders who know intuitively that the spirits of the ancient people have not wholly left the *aina*, the land, which they once in life loved so dearly. In addition, the family spirits of the many immigrant cultures of Asia, the Pacific, Europe and the Americas which came to Hawaii added to this supernatural mixed place" (vi).

Dressed up in multiculturalism, this *supernatural Hawai'i* replicates *legendary Hawai'i* in three ways. First, though Hawaiian traditions and beliefs are "the spiritual bedrock" of "modern occultism," the implication is that, while they should be treated with respect, their significance rests primarily in a *long-gone* past. Second, Hawaiian beliefs are *dislocated* or assimilated into an umbrella supernaturalism, where the relationship to land as *'āina*, for instance, has no particular currency. What allows for Grant's successful blend of traditions is therefore his operating assumption that within Hawai'i there is now a common approach to spirituality and place, especially among nonwhites. And third, Hawaiians are *hospitable*. Having accommodated several waves of immigration, Hawaiians are no longer major players in "cosmopolitan" contemporary Hawai'i. Within this narrative, where strife and violence are definitely out of focus so as not to disturb newcomers and visitors, Hawaiians may be "honorary icons," but the heroes come from abroad. Folklorists call this the *localization* of Japanese or American tales of the supernatural in Hawai'i; "immigrant" stories are now the force, having taken on new life in a "mixed plate" representation of culture.[26]

Like the earlier re-framing of *mo'olelo* into legends and fairy tales, the marketing of today's "stories of the supernatural" as *Obake* on the one hand, and *Chicken Skin* stories on the other is also telling. *Obake*—Japanese "weird things" (Grant, *Japanese Obake*) or "ghosts" (Carroll, *Chicken Skin*)—are the protagonists of several Grant collections published in the 1990s, but he insists that these stories rest upon and "incorporate" Hawaiian beliefs and tales. Thus, we find very different Hawaiian beings under the *obake* umbrella: the *lapu*—ghost, apparition, phantom—and *'uhane*—soul or spirit of the deceased,[27] but also the *'aumakua* (family or personal god, deified ancestor, who might assume nonhuman shapes), and the *kupua* (demigod or cultural hero, especially a supernatural being possessing several forms).[28] In Westervelt's early twentieth-century packaging, Hawaiian traditions were incorporated into the universally appealing genre of the fairy tale. Now in the name of a local "multiculturalism," they are subsumed under the ethnically marked Japanese denomination of *obake*.[29] Grant's other commodified generic label—he copyrighted "Chicken Skin"—groups contemporary supernatural tales of Hawai'i, giving a "local" spin to the generic "goose bumps," but still effectively avoiding having to distinguish between traditions or specific genres of belief narratives in Hawai'i. "'Chicken Skin' is the sensation that sweeps over your body whenever you come close to the borderland between reality and mystery. 'Chicken Skin' reminds us that we still do live in a world where occasionally, the shadows do indeed talk back" (*Glen Grant's Chicken Skin Tales* v).[30]

What attitude toward this "talking back" of the supernatural does such a narrative of multiculturalism promote? Grant wisely acknowledged that "personal-experience" narratives—what folklorists call "memorates"—"demanded a different attitude and more respect than the 'friend of a friend' tales concerning Morgan's Corner" (Grant, *Obake Files* xi). But "Fun, sometimes silly, often spooky," contemporary legends function primarily as entertainment.[31] Writing about the setting of a tale on which I intend to focus, Grant says that: "Morgan's Corner remains for me nothing more than a place for urban legends. This location is nothing more than a dark parking lot for the imagination to get carried away in and for tales to be exaggerated and embellished through the enthusiasm of each storyteller. . . . Oh, this hairpin turn of nightmares is one more thing to me. It is a place I would never go alone at night" (*Glen Grant's Chicken Skin Tales* 174). In Grant's usually sensational retelling of these tales, the exciting experience of a "frisson" is *the* primary goal. The successful reception of the story, then, rests almost exclusively on the individual teller's tone and style, rather than on the social dynamics played out in the articulation of place, stories, and personal beliefs. As with *legendary Hawai'i*, the author exercises his creative license to entertain readers who enjoy eerie tales and visitors who want to experience a particular kind of excitement while touring Hawai'i.[32]

But I would argue that, whether told as memorates or "friend of a friend" tales, these "localized" ghost tales or tales of the supernatural do not innocuously conflate different Euro-American, Asian, and Native Hawaiian belief traditions. Histories of colonization, settlement, and Native resistance bring competing experiences, goals, and commitments to the telling and valorizing of contemporary supernatural legends in present-day Hawai'i—regardless of whether they are told informally, scripted in newspapers, performed during commercial tours, recorded on audiotapes, or published in collections. We are not therefore looking so much at a process of "localization" of Euro-American or Asian legends taking on local color, but at narrative performances of epistemological and social struggles. Or as Bill Ellis puts it, "Legend telling embodies a complex event, in which the performer not only narrates a story but also gains (or fails to gain) social control over a social situation. The best tellers—and the most popular legends—have the potential to transform social structures. Hence legend telling is often a fundamentally *political* act" (xiv). Similarly, scholarly or popular representations of such narratives are also political acts that can obfuscate or foreground this struggle for social control. And, as I see it, applying a script of multiculturalism to Hawai'i's contemporary supernatural legends actively ignores these political and narrative dynamics, thus continuing to relegate Hawaiian culture to the past.

"My intentions have always been simple," wrote Glen Grant, "I record, preserve and tell the supernatural lore of the islands because I love ghost stories" (*Glen Grant's Chicken Skin Tales* viii). But given his great investment in publishing and promoting "Chicken Skin," this statement is at a minimum disingenuous. As a nonlocal, non-Native scholar like Grant, I seek, contra his framework, an alternative approach to *supernatural Hawai'i* and its narrative of multiculturalism. In doing so, I must acknowledge (once again) that I cannot speak for any of these groups—and some Hawai'i-born and raised students love *obake*—but I also acknowledge the responsibility for responding to published accounts that unwittingly contribute once again to the dispossession of a Native group by "celebrating" only its past. I now turn to re-viewing today's *supernatural Hawai'i* in light of what I have come to understand as a Native Hawaiian view that is both place-centered and historicizing. From this perspective, the telling of old and contemporary "legends" appears as a potentially transformative act—an argument for repopulating present-day Hawai'i with a Native spiritual and material presence, for refusing to forget that Hawai'i is an indigenous place.

"Morgan's Corner" as Storied Place

As reported by a student in 1998, the story of "Morgan's Corner" begins, "A young couple were making out at Morgan's Corner. It became late and time for the girl to go home. When the young boy tried to start the car it would only make a clicking noise." A 1987 version only says "a girl and her boyfriend were driving one night when their car stalled." But no matter how much sexual transgression is a coded trigger for the following ghastly events—the social warning most interpretations see at work in this story—in Hawai'i, the couple is always at Morgan's Corner. "Everyone by now has heard about a place called Morgan's Corner on the Nu'uanu Pali Road," Burl Burlingame writes, "There are a hundred variations of the story, but most involve a dark Pali [cliff] road"

Figure 33. Old Pali Road, 1925. Courtesy of Bishop Museum Archives.

(reprinted in Carroll, *True Spooky Stories* 89). A well-known "spooky" spot on the island of Oʻahu, Morgan's Corner is significantly in the vicinity of a hairpin turn where trees arch over the road, adding shade during the day and mystery at night to the spot (Figure 33). Though the road is not highly frequented now—drivers take the highway—the turn itself, near a house that Dr. James Morgan built in the 1920s, was known as a place where drivers should slow down. Most versions of the story I have heard or read place Morgan's Corner on the Honolulu side of the island near Dr. Morgan's house. But some take place at another "Morgan's Corner" on the Kailua side.[33] "Morgan's Corner is probably the spookiest place on Oahu, even though few agree on exactly where it is. It's likely more a state of mind." That's how Honolulu journalist Burl Burlingame, who has researched "Morgan's Corner" for several articles over the years, opens his most recent piece, "Morgan's Corner Has a Deadly Reputation," as part of his series "X Marks the Spot," "a weekly feature documenting historic monuments and sites around Oahu" (*Honolulu Star-Bulletin*, Travel Section, May 1, 2005).

Even those unfamiliar with the Hawaiʻi location will recognize the story. In a lonely and dark place, a couple are parked. When they decide to leave and the car does not start, the young man goes looking for help, while his girlfriend remains in the car. She becomes scared by a persistent dripping, or in some versions scratching, on the roof of the car. Eventually she falls asleep. The policeman who wakes her in the morning tells her to get out of the car and not look back. She does look, of course—and "there is her boyfriend's lifeless body hanging upside down from a tree branch, over the car, his fingernails scratching on the roof and his blood running down the windshield" (Brunvand 45). This account, from the *Encyclopedia of Urban Legends*, summarizes a well-documented contemporary legend in the United States, in which an isolated place for "parking" is part of the formula for building an eerie feeling. Identified as a version of "The Boyfriend's Death," this tale closely resembles most of the versions of "Morgan's Corner" I have encountered.

If, however, we consider "Morgan's Corner" from within a Hawaiian narrative economy, an exotic locale for a Euro-American legend becomes visible as a Hawaiian "storied place" on the Nuʻuanu Pali Road. In this sense, then, "localization," while an important methodological concept in folklore studies, when it identifies a "localized" version of an international contemporary legend in a place with Hawaiʻi's history, runs the risk of ignoring or even dismissing the Native epistemological framework that is already in place. If this assumption is true, then presumably approaching place as the backbone of Hawaiian narratives (Malo; Pukui, Elbert, and Mookini; Luomala, "Creative Processes") may actually lend historical and semantic depth to the analysis of contemporary narratives in Hawaiʻi—including vaguely genre-centered "chicken skin" or "spooky" tales.

Let's for example see what happens when "Morgan's Corner" is viewed as one of the stories told about the Nuʻuanu Valley and Pali, an area of many cherished places, and one of the richest in lore on the island of Oʻahu (Handy, Handy and Pukui 233). Though celebrated for its "scenic beauty and grandeur," the Nuʻuanu Pali was and is more than photogenic material. To reach urban Honolulu from the wet, well-cultivated area of Koʻolau Poko (the windward, south-eastern district), and vice versa, the Koʻolau range of mountains (see Figures 1 and 32) must be crossed. Until quite recently, this crossing over was a challenge. Before 1830, Hawaiians bringing produce to town had to "climb up the walls of the escarpment to reach a pass leading to Nuʻuanu Valley's gentle slopes falling to Honolulu" (Dorrance 49). During the nineteenth century, "a succession of efforts converted the hazardous 800-foot climb to a six-foot wide path carved into the side of the pali" (Dorrance 49), until what is now called the Old Pali Road—a two-lane road—opened in

1898 to horses and buggies and automobiles. Finally, since 1957, the Pali Highway and its tunnels have made commuting easier, and tourists crowd the windy terrace overlooking the old path and the astoundingly beautiful windward coast every day. Yet for many residents, a sense of challenge still persists; going over the Pali was and is a journey.

As a real and metaphoric borderland, the Nu'uanu Pali has always been a place where one could meet death, and certainly should expect danger. Several sources indicate that Hawaiians wanting a safe journey left offerings to the two stone *akua*, or powerful beings, who guarded the cliff (these *akua* have since been removed; see Sterling and Summers). The indelible memory of the 1795 battle between the chief of O'ahu, Kalanikūpule, and the rising power, Kamehameha, who would unify the islands in large part thanks to this victory, also points to the abyss that lies before you when you make the big decision to cross a certain line. At the moment of their defeat at the hands of Kamehameha's warriors, Kalanikūpule's forces were either driven over the precipice or chose to dive from it. According to the *mo'olelo* of the place, the gigantic dog Kaupe was said "to stop carriage and horseback riders." An omen of death, the dog thus guarded the passageway, and "If a man met Kaupe first, he never made the descent of the steep mountain trail to the other side, but turned around" (Armitage and Judd 69). Another widely circulating contemporary belief is "Do not take pork over the Pali at night." Your car might stall. This speaks to the consequences of angering a god: the most common explanation is that Kamapua'a, the pig god of the wetlands, does not belong in the drier area of Kona where the fiery Pele dominates. Or, to put it differently, don't pollute.

When re-viewing these narratives and beliefs associated with the Pali, the point is not to ask oneself whether they are "true." The continuing appearance of such stories does suggest that the Nu'uanu Pali remains a windy place of passage where a sudden move—of one's foot on the steep climb, of one's political leader in the struggle, or a thing transported in a car on impulse—can have awful consequences. This perception has had material results. In the 1950s and 1960s, the Pali was the scene of "suicide leaps" off the windy lookout before safety measures were increased, and today young people still challenge each other to go there on special nights, hoping and fearing they will see the Nightmarchers, the warriors of the night, who in this case could be the dead warriors of Kalanikūpule. These different forms of ostension confirm and reproduce performatively the intensely liminal dimension of this storied place. When viewed within this historical pattern context, then, the generic warning to teenagers against transgressing sexually in a tale like "Morgan's Corner" is not simply localized but *transformed* by Hawaiian cultural markers.

Figure 34. Lanihuli. Swirling Heavens. By Anne Kapulani Landgraf. Courtesy of artist and University of Hawai'i Press.

But I would further argue that "repeopling" Hawai'i as an indigenous place in this instance also requires us to consider the other very different stories still told or not told about the larger valley of Nu'uanu. Many speak of beauty and record a reciprocally nurturing relationship between Hawaiians, all living beings, and the land. Moses Manu's *Keao-melemele* offers a numinous view of Nu'uanu, where for instance the peak Lanihuli is a guardian of the golden-cloud heroine (Figure 34). In short, the presence of the supernatural cannot always be reduced, or trans-lated, into a "spooky" feeling. To cite only a few examples, in Pū'iwa near the Nu'uanu stream a loving father tells his daughters where to bury him after his death. Once there, he turns into a new significant resource, the *wauke* (paper mulberry) bush used to make the *kapa* cloth for which Hawaiians had and have multiple uses. The *menehune*, small industrious beings who may have been a people conquered and enslaved by the Hawaiians, fought a giant in Nu'uanu, and apparently people paid homage to the stone that was hurled to kill him (Sterling and Summers 303; other stories resonate with "sword in the rock" and recognition motifs). Attractive but tricky *mo'o* women (reptilian or mer-maidlike beings) guard some of the Nu'uanu pools. The playful

Pūehuehu spring is the water gift of Papa, the female earth power, to a compassionate and generous farmer (Sterling and Summers 295–296). In fact, larger Nuʻuanu is filled with *heiau*, guardian stones, waterfalls, and places of "rest" where the unexpected can be encountered.

These storied places are not only haunted by fearful ghosts, but peopled by guardians or helpers—for Hawaiians, by family. Unhappy ghosts in Hawaiian stories are actually in the minority, and their presence or violence is a symptom that some balance has been upset, a transgression has occurred, or a power struggle is at hand. In the *Honolulu* article about "spooky stories," John Dominis Holt was quick to assert that "most Hawaiian spirits are friendly and caring" (Knaefler 48). As I read it, then, the Hawaiian student's protest in my class was a reclaiming of the Nuʻuanu Pali away from dominant cultural representations informed by capitalistic or dollar-mediated approaches to Hawaiʻi's land. Though she undoubtedly had some personal associations with the place, they operated within familial closeness to storied places and *ʻāina* that—as illustrated in Hawaiian *mele*, *oli*, and *moʻolelo*—differs radically from the nineteenth-century exploitative approach that Europeans and Americans brought to the islands, and that also necessarily shaped the Asian immigrant experience of Hawaiʻi as plantation, and themselves as imported labor.

Let's also consider the Hawaiian insistence on the metaphorical and historical significance of place names. Nuʻuanu is "cool terrace" or "cool height" (Sterling and Summers; Pukui, Elbert, and Mookini), referring to the cold wind that sweeps the top of the Pali—haunting, if you will, the passageway. Furthermore, one of the older Hawaiian names of the *pali*'s terrace, *Kanuku o Nuuanu* (Sterling and Summers 223), as "tip, end; . . . gap" (Pukui and Elbert 272) can be read as pointing to Kalanikūpule's "great decision" evoking a significant rite of passage in Hawaiʻi's history (Landgraf, "Ka Nuku," "The Mountain Pass," in *Nā Wahi Pana O Koʻolau Poko* 98).

What then happens if we apply this principle to a non-Hawaiian denomination, and ask, "Why Morgan's Corner?" Familiar with names like "Freddy" that invoke a kind of horror in popular American film, one student guessed that the place and the story's title indicate that Morgan must have been the boyfriend's name. But Burl Burlingame has connected "Morgan's Corner" with a 1948 crime. Two young Hawaiian men broke into the house of a wealthy and older white woman, Mrs. Therese Wilder, who lived across the street from Dr. Morgan. They assaulted her, then gagged and tied her up, and left. When found days after the attack, she was dead.

The reputation of "Morgan's Corner" had preceded Mrs. Wilder's death. Indeed, the map of the crime accompanying a 1948 newspaper report specifically identifies "Dr. Morgan Home" as the main point of reference in that area for Oʻahu residents at the time ("Police Seek," *Honolulu Star-Bulletin*). Even if young tellers today do not know about the Palakiko-Majors assassination, "Morgan's Corner" still carries in its title and location traces of this violent historical event. "So listen carefully if you happen to stop at Morgan's Corner one dark night," Burlingame concludes in a "chicken skin" mood: "Is that the muffled mutter of the wind or the lonely screams of Therese Wilder" ("Morgan's Corner" G3). And in 2004 another student drew a different connection during class discussion (English 380) between the "Mrs. Wilder" story and the "Morgan's Corner" contemporary legend when she associated "the image of hanging people at 'Morgan's Corner'" with "a case in the 1940s about two Hawaiian thieves who were to be hung." The student suggested that given the proximity of the crime scene to Morgan's Corner, "it is believed to be a historic incident that led to the hanging legends of 'Morgan's Corner' at Nuʻuanu." Though this student did not know the details, when referring to the "image of hanging people" she was clearly reaching for a felt cultural memory of another trauma tied to the Wilder case—one that made legal and social history in Hawaiʻi.

James Majors and John Palakiko, the two Hawaiian youths accused of murdering Mrs. Wilder, were sentenced to hang. This sentence fomented a heated public debate over racial discrimination in Hawaiʻi's court system, a debate reminiscent of the very different and extremely controversial circumstances of the 1932 Massie/Kahahawai rape and murder trials—to which the Wilder case was contrasted right away (Okamura; Stannard, "The Massie Case" and *Honor Killing*). After several appeals, in 1954 their sentences were commuted to a prison term not because the facts were successfully disputed, but because of evidence of police brutality, faulty procedures, and language translation issues—and the pressure of 16,000 signatures on a petition requesting clemency. On the heels of this case, the death penalty was abolished in Hawaiʻi (Arinaga; Matsuda; *Biography Hawaiʻi*). Perhaps then the hanging boyfriend in the contemporary "Morgan's Corner" has some metonymic contiguity with what would have been—had it occurred—a rather haunting hanging that took on "legendary" proportions in Hawaiʻi's prestatehood strained racial dynamics. The name "Morgan's Corner," most commonly associated today with a generic contemporary legend, can therefore serve for some also as a reminder of violence and racial conflict, a reminder speaking to the institutionalized suppression of Hawaiians not only in so-called "antiquity," but in relatively recent history.

Storied places and their "supernatural" beings cannot be confined to the past as residual and scattered beliefs. Hawaiian familial and intimate relations to land can function as forms of resistance and the assertion of

Native claims. If in her 1904 account of the Nuʻuanu Pali battle Emma Nakuina exercised "feminine defiance," in the present, Haunani-Kay Trask's poetry invokes Pele to come from Halemaʻumaʻu, for "Night is a sharkskin drum / sounding our bodies black / and gold" (*Night Is a Sharkskin Drum* 5). And also in the present, my students' various comments on Nuʻuanu and its stories point to competing "senses of place."

In the 1990s, another student in an uncommon version of "Morgan's Corner" claimed that the boyfriend's attacker is "half-human, half-beast"—an intimation, perhaps, of the reappearance of a powerful Hawaiian shape-shifter, like the dog Kaupe, who guards the Nuʻuanu Pali, and whose apparition is an omen of death. I am not suggesting that today's Hawaiians all believe these other "supernatural" stories to be true—as in other systems of belief, some do, some don't, others are skeptical, others don't know them. But I have begun to see how, among the multivalent associations clustered around the telling and the reception of "Morgan's Corner," this possible allusion to Kaupe could be a covert political claim, could test listeners' knowledge and attitudes without seeming to, or could even offer a way to find family and allies in unexpected places.

While undeveloped at this point, this hypothesis points to alliances outside of Hawaiʻi. Scholars have made parallel observations about Native American versions of "The Boyfriend's Death": one in New Hampshire, in the place "where the last white man of the region was killed by Indians"; another, a Navajo version, where "the murderous entity at the haunted site" is "'the hairy one,' or skinwalker, a character from Native traditions of legends" (Brunvand 283). I therefore join other folklorists working to unsettle the dichotomy of "local versus global" perspectives on the contemporary legend (Goldstein; Langlois) and suggest that an intertextual analysis of Hawaiian and Native American stories would, in an alternative *international* arena, bring into focus epistemological dynamics as well as political claims at work in places where different peoples live with the legacy of American settlement.[34]

That Hawaiʻi is a "legendary place" means different things depending on one's relationship to the islands, one's understanding of legend as an emergent or residual genre, and one's culturally grounded epistemology and belief system. Seeking to contribute to the larger project of "repeopling" Hawaiʻi as an indigenous place in the present, I have focused in this chapter on a supernatural contemporary legend, suggesting that we consider it within a Native Hawaiian place-centered narrative economy and a historicizing politics of place. Since places and place names record cultural change and struggles, and since reclaiming land is crucial to Hawaiians' struggle for sovereignty today, I have also argued that indigenous and settler narratives of place in Hawai'i often articulate competing relationships to nature, expose different layers of located history, and make implicit claims to replace one another. These narratives, including "localized" contemporary legends, play a crucial role in the everyday articulation of epistemology and cultural values. For folk narrative scholars focusing on Hawai'i, then, turning from "localization" to "storied place" as an analytical framework allows us to mark the dynamic persistence or insistent re-emergence of a Native Hawaiian epistemology and worldview *into the present.* Doing so also offers us the opportunity to register the social struggles and tensions that these everyday narratives—and their histories—silence and/or voice. The telling of these stories is not simply an instance of localization. It can be a sign of, and in some cases an argument for, the articulation of an indigenous epistemology and relationship to the land. As the struggle for Hawaiian sovereignty intensifies, and our process of reeducation develops, I hope that these storied places will seem to be populated by "specters"—I am of course thinking of Marx's famous opening here—only from an exclusionary settlers' perspective that will itself become progressively obsolete.

Notes

Chapter 1. Introduction

1. Though increasingly residual in folklore studies, well-established views of tradition present it as the passing down or transmission of a time-honored cultural practice, or as a cultural element "rooted in the past but persisting in the present in the manner of a natural object." Whether they foreground process or product, in these views tradition is bound to the past, and tracing the trajectory of its social force would seem to point one way only to an older time when that tale had a reason for being, a reason we conjure when honoring it in the present. The above definition in quotation marks is included by Richard Bauman in his article "Folklore," but it hardly reflects Bauman's position (31).

In contrast, my work is informed by an approach that Henry Glassie's article in the 1995 special issue of "Key Concepts" of the *Journal of American Folklore* crystallizes.

2. For the scholarly definition of this concept, which I will not be using in my work, see Eric Hobsbawn and Terence Ranger, *The Invention of Tradition*: " 'Invented tradition' is taken to mean a set of practices, . . . which seek to inculcate certain values and norms of behaviour by repetition, which automatically implies continuity with the past. In fact, where possible, they normally attempt to establish continuity with a suitable historic past" (1). In "Elision or Decision: Lived History and the Contextual Grounding of the Constructed Past," Laurence Marshall Carucci also makes a distinction akin to the one I am emphasizing on the grounds that "historical recollections are inherently embedded in the present" (82). Laiana Wong writes: "It would be a mistake to assume that the inability to authenticate tradition on an absolute level eliminates its role in shaping the attitudes of a community" (103). See note 16 for how the label "invented traditions" has been discussed in Hawai'i.

Richard Bauman offers a concise articulation of the role that "traditionality" has played in folklore: "The term tradition is conventionally used in a dual sense, to name both the process of transmission of an isolable cultural element through time and also the elements themselves that are transmitted in this process. To view an item of folklore as traditional is to see it as having temporal continuity. . . . There is, however, an emergent reorientation taking place among students of tradition, away from this naturalistic view of tradition as a cultural inheritance rooted in the past and toward an understanding of tradition as symbolically constituted in the present" ("Folklore" 31). See *In Search of Authenticity: The Formation of Folklore Studies* by Regina Bendix, especially 211–18, for an exemplary reflection on "tradition" within the history of the discipline of folkloristics. To mark the shift away from a naturalizing time-oriented definition, she cites Dell Hymes who had urged in 1975, "let us root the notion [of tradition] not in time, but in social life. Let us postulate that the traditional is a functional prereq-uisite of social life. . . . It seems in fact that every person and group makes some effort to 'traditionalize' aspects of its experience" (211–12).

3. As Richard Bauman and Charles Briggs have theorized, contemporary folkloristics seeks to consider how the contextualized interplay of tradition and performance "bears upon the political economy of texts" ("Poetics and Per-formance as Critical Perspectives on Language and Social Life" 76).

4. I acknowledge that "colonialism" may not tell the whole story and may at times—especially when Hawai'i was a sovereign nation—obscure the role of Hawaiian agency and the difference between different types of domination; the rights of Hawaiians were eroded while Hawai'i was a sovereign nation. Some may argue that we need a new term rather than "colonialism" to describe the Hawai'i situation, but the continued dynamics of domination point to "colonial-ism" at this point. See Spivak, *Critique of Postcolonial Reason* for an effort to dis-criminate among types of colonialism (especially 172–73).

5. In Western folkloristics, a textbook definition of this genre is that "legends are stories people tell about events that purportedly really happened. However, one of the identifying marks of a legend is that, in the telling people bring up the issue of whether or not the story is true" (Adams, "Folk Narrative" 25). In contrast to tales of magic or folktales whose fictionality demands suspension of disbelief, legends are *belief narratives*, but they can be told or transmitted by non-believers; they raise the question of belief (some believe, others don't, and oth-ers are skeptics), and they have local, historical, religious, or personal "truth elements" and significance. The genre as studied by folklorists includes a wide range of belief narratives: supernatural legends, place-centered ones, and the now ubiquitous "contemporary" legends. In that they may feature supernatural beings, legends can hold religious and cultural value that is similar to that of myths, but myths—within Western classification—narrate a much more distant past and are often part of a ritual or ceremony. See Linda Dégh's *Legend and Belief* (2001) for an extended discussion of and perspective on how folklorists have defined the legend.

6. Noenoe Silva's "Kanaka Maoli Resistance to Annexation," published in the first issue of *'Ōiwi: A Native Hawaiian Journal* (1998), was the product of groundbreaking research that documents Hawaiian resistance to the overthrow, the republic, the imprisonment of Queen Lili'uokalani, and annexation. Partic-ularly meaningful is her recovery of two of the three groups' anti-annexation petitions that collectively show 38,000 signatures; the Native Hawaiian popula-tion at the time was approximately 40,000. See also Tom Coffman's *Nation Within: The Story of America's Annexation of the Nation of Hawai'i* (1998), an award-winning book that is written in a refreshingly journalistic style and acknowledges its reliance on Silva's original research for documentation of resistance. More recently, Silva has published the book, *Aloha Betrayed: Native Hawaiian Resistance to American Colonialism* (2004), that further documents Hawaiian struggles well before and after the monarchy's overthrow.

7. As Osorio shows in *Dismembering Lāhui,* the erosion of the political rights and participation in government of Hawaiians began long before annexation. By 1887 with the Bayonet Constitution, the electorate was limited on the grounds of race (Hawaiians, Americans, and Europeans only, while Asians were implicitly excluded) and property both (Osorio 240–49), a combination that qualified only a small number of Hawaiians. The electorate was of course only male.

European and American settlers throughout the nineteenth century were certainly not all of a kind or all of one mind about Hawai'i. Osorio discusses the strife between "Hawaiianized" pro-annexation settlers and, e.g., Walter Murray Gibson, who, having arrived in Hawai'i in 1861, became King Kalākaua's closest counselor and nevertheless viewed the Hawaiian as "an interesting yet feeble younger brother, a subject of an oceanic empire" (quoted in Osorio 199 from Gibson's diary). See also Niklaus R. Schweizer's *Hawai'i and the German Speaking Peoples*.

8. Trask, *From a Native Daughter: Colonialism and Sovereignty in Hawai'i* 16. The first edition of this powerful book was published in 1993 (Monroe, Me.: Common Courage Press). I quote throughout from the 1999 revised text.

9. It is important to acknowledge that "rural Hawaiian communities where Hawaiians have maintained a close relationship to the land through their subsistence livelihoods have played a crucial role in the survival of Hawaiian culture" (McGregor 195). In "Waipi'o Valley, a Cultural *Kīpuka* in Early 20th Century Hawai'i," McGregor makes a strong case for cultural *kīpuka*—isolated rural Hawaiian communities that were relatively untouched by development—like Waipi'o Valley as "traditional centres of spiritual power . . . from which native Hawaiian culture can be regenerated and revitalised in the contemporary setting" (196).

10. See the first chapter of Nogelmeier's 2003 Ph.D. dissertation "Mai Pa'a i ka Leo: Historical Voice in Hawaiian Primary Materials, Looking Forward and Listening Back." Nogelmeier defines this *discourse of sufficiency* as "the long-standing recognition and acceptance of a small core of Hawaiian writings from the 19th century as being sufficient to embody nearly a hundred years of extensive Hawaiian auto-representation" (2). The canonized and translated sources Nogelmeier refers to are the selected works of Malo, Kepelino, Kamakau, and 'Ī'ī; but "these works make up only a fraction of one percent of the available primary materials" (3). Native ethnomusicologist Amy Ku'uleialoha Stillman's research on Hawaiian-language songs has also spoken to the importance of expanding the pool of textual documentation for Hawaiian history and of recognizing "cultural resilience and resistance to assimilation" in Hawaiian-language sources ("Of the People Who Loved the Land" 85).

11. One of the meanings for *moo* is "A history. See mooolelo. A connected story"; and *moo-o-lelo* is defined as "*Moo* and *olelo*, discourse. A continuous or connected narrative of events; a history. *Luk.* 1:1. A tradition. *Mat.* 15:2. In modern times, the minutes of a deliberative body; a taxation list" (Lorrin Andrews 399).

Hawaiian classification recognizes that the *mo'olelo* as (hi)story is different from the *ka'ao* that is nowadays commonly accepted as fiction, but *mo'olelo ka'ao* blurs the distinction. These storytelling modes take the form of prose but also of *mele* (song) or *oli* (chant), with much more variation in prose than in the poetic verses of *mele* and *oli*.

12. While I was not familiar with the work of cultural geographers when I started this project in the 1990s, both humanist and critical cultural constructs of "place" have played a role in the development of my perspective.

13. Osorio writes about the effects of colonialism in Hawai'i: "The mutilations were not physical only, but also psychological and spiritual. Death came not only through infection and disease, but through racial and legal discourse that crippled the will, confidence, and trust of the Kānaka Maoli [Native Hawaiian] as surely as leprosy and smallpox claimed their limbs and lives" (3). *Dismem-*

bering Lāhui takes on the project of comprehending the story of the Bayonet Constitution—which the Hawaiian League, a group of Euro-American business-men and missionary offsprings, forced King Kalākaua to sign in 1887—within the context of nineteenth-century changes in Hawaiian society *and* of fore-grounding Native resistance to colonialism. His last chapter, "Ho'oulu Lāhui," reproposes King Kalākaua's motto, "increase the nation," with a strong empha-sis on the Hawaiian people's pride and identity today and, as I read it, is sus-tained by a sense of tradition, in Glassie's words, as "the creation of the future out of the past."

14. Ku'ualoha Ho'omanawanui's manuscript "'This Land Is Your Land, This Land Was My Land': Kanaka Maoli Versus Settler Representations of 'Āina in Contemporary Literature of Hawai'i" is forthcoming in *Asian Settler Colonialism in Hawai'i*, ed. Candace Fujikane and Jonathan Okamura. See especially pp. 4–5 of manuscript. Commenting on the more collective, rather than individual-centered, approach to authorship in Hawaiian culture, both past and present, Ho'omanawanui writes: "there has been a presumption on the part of colonial academic authorities that mo'olelo belong to an unowned oral tradition. Dr. Noenoe Silva says [in a personal communication to the author] that haole schol-ars 'don't notice or credit the vast majority of mo'olelo and mele published from 1834–1948 which are SIGNED with author and composer names. It serves the colonial project to pretend there are no authors. It facilitates both colonial theft of *kūpuna* knowledge, and it aids in perpetuating the myth of backwardness and savagery'" (5). This is not to say that the practice of not naming or acknowledg-ing individual storytellers and poets was a *haole* exclusive; examples can be found in some Hawaiian-language newspaper *mo'olelo* that are assumed to be tran-scribed or authored by Native writers, who were—whatever their politics—influenced by and "educated" in the Western ways.

15. Neither is my main point to classify certain narratives as "folklore," but to see what results asking questions that methodologically come from folkloris-tics can yield. In fact, I am arguing to adopt the Hawaiian concept of *wahi pana* as a way to contest the imposition of Western genres on Hawaiian orature or narrative traditions.

16. Regina Bendix's *In Search of Authenticity* "deconstructs authenticity as a discursive formation" that has historically marginalized folklore in the social world and folklore studies in the academy. But Bendix also states that such deconstruction "cannot simply invalidate the search for authenticity. This search arises out of a profound human longing, . . . and declaring the object of such longing nonexistent may violate the very core around which people build meaningful lives" (17). The question becomes "not 'what is authenticity?' but 'who needs authenticity and why?' and 'how has authenticity been used?'" (21). Thus the project of "questioning 'tradition'" becomes "an examination of the 'tradition' of the discipline itself" (213).

Interestingly enough, Bendix cites the anthropologist Jocelyn Linnekin's 1983 statement "in her study of Hawaiian identity . . . that 'the selection of what constitutes tradition is always made up in the present'" to exemplify "a chal-lenge of both the notion and the scholarly practice of separating the genuine from the fake" (212). However, in 1990 and 1991 Linnekin was taken to task by Haunani-Kay Trask, who pointed out, within a critique of anthropology, how Linnekin's comments on "the invention of tradition" in the case of the sacred-ness of Kaho'olawe—a small Hawaiian island whose use as a site for bombing practice on the part of the United States military troops Hawaiians and other concerned citizens were protesting at the time—was used by the U.S. Navy to "argue that the Hawaiian assertion of love and sacredness regarding Kahoʻolawe was 'fakery'" ("Politics in the Pacific Islands: Imperialism and Native Self-Determination"). In situ, then, Linnekin's scholarship was used to reinstitute the power of the authentic versus the fake, rather than challenging its authority. In spring 1991 *The Contemporary Pacific* published a dead-end "dialogue" featuring Trask, Roger M. Keesing, and Linnekin. Jeffrey Tobin commented on and contextualized this exchange in his 1994 essay "Cultural Construction and Native Nationalism: Report from the Hawaiian Front."

While Linnekin protested that she was not responsible for the navy's misuse of her work, I find this case instructive in a number of ways and bring it up to emphasize how the politics of location necessarily test disciplinary projects and ethics not so much on the basis of their statements—well-intentioned as they may be—but on their uses and effects. As scholars we cannot control these uses in absolute terms, just as storytellers cannot control their listeners turned tellers; however, we can make our best effort to ask "who needs authenticity and why?" and "how has authenticity been used?" in the framework not only of our scholarly disciplines but of the *localized*, historical and present, asymmetry of power relations outside academia. See Charles L. Briggs, "The Politics of Discursive Authority in Research on the 'Invention of Tradition.'"

17. The discussion of normativity and consensus in folklore and literature dynamics has a long history. My point is not to recast folklore into an exclusively conservative mode, but to note how the storyteller's "authority" is not located in "authorship."

18. For "emergent" in relation to "pre-emergent," "dominant," and "residual" as I also use them in this book, see Raymond Williams, *Marxism and Literature.*

19. The range of folklore & literature approaches in recent American folkloristics is wide; it includes work by Daniel R. Barnes, Mary Ellen Brown, Trudier Harris, Bonnie Irwin, Cathy Lynn Preston, Danielle Roemer, Bruce Rosenberg, Susan Stewart, Mark Workman. Frank de Caro and Rosan A. Jordan's introduction in the recent *Re-Situating Folklore* provides a useful overview (1–22), though folklore *in* literature is their main focus.

20. The spirited Belgian scholar André Lefevere introduced the term and outlined the new tasks of "translation studies" as a discipline that deals with "the problems raised by the production and description of translations" (quoted in Susan Bassnett-McGuire's *Translation Studies* 1).

21. Tejaswini Niranjana's work focuses on the colonial work of translation in India (see *Siting Translation*, 1992), Kwame Anthony Appiah in Ghana ("Thick Translation," 1993, reprinted in Venuti's 2000 *Translation Studies Reader*). The work of Noelani Arista, Puakea Nogelmeier, and Noenoe Silva also focuses on translation as colonial tool in Hawaiʻi. In addition to Spivak and Venuti's interventions, see Susan Bassnett and Harish Trivedi, eds., *Post-Colonial Translation: Theory and Practice* (1999) and Eric Cheyfitz, *The Poetics of Imperialism: Translation and Colonization from* The Tempest *to* Tarzan (1997).

22. In "Prefaced Space: Tales of the Colonial British Collectors of Indian Folklore," Sadhana Naithani outlines how the prefaces of these late nineteenth-century and early twentieth-century collections narratively construct an Orientalized India, a heroic British collector, and a precious but valueless tradition of "Indian" tales.

23. See Niranjana's *Siting Translation* (3, 47–86) for ample discussion of ethnographic translations as applied to colonial India.

24. Spivak, *Critique of Postcolonial Reason* 161, n. 71.

25. Eric Cheyfitz states that English colonizers could recognize cultural differences, "even as they translated these differences into their terms" and that "unless we are attentive to the repressed problem of translation," we will continue "to forget the other side of the story" (*The Poetics of Imperialism* 8–9).

26. I realize that Venuti and Spivak are writing from different traditions, the former adapting Lecercle and Deleuze and Guattari, the latter rewriting Marx, Lacan, Derrida, Klein, and feminist thought. However, the projects of these two intellectuals seem to me to resonate together, especially in their advocacy of a politically activist and ethical task for translators and their demystifying concern for the often unrecognized role that translation plays in the "globalization" of comparative literature. Spivak's numerous reflections on translation include the introduction to *Imaginary Maps: Three Stories by Mahasweta Devi* and specific pieces such as "The Politics of Translation" (1993); "Translation as Culture" (1999); "Questioned on Translation: Adrift" (2001); and "Translating into English" (2005), which I first read in typescript. Translation is also very much at stake in *A Critique of Postcolonial Reason* (1999). *Death of a Discipline* is an exceptionally brilliant reflection on comparative literature in global and planetary terms, working against a globalizing economy of translation. For Venuti, see "Translation, Community, Utopia" in *The Translation Studies Reader;* and *The Scandals of Translation: Towards an Ethics of Difference* (1998).

27. See Jane C. Desmond's *Staging Tourism: Bodies on Display from Waikiki to Sea World*, especially xvii–xxi, for a synthesis of tourist research from the 1970s through the 1990s.

28. In *Staging Tourism* (15), Desmond quotes MacCannell to define "reconstructed ethnicity" as "the maintenance and preservation of ethnic forms for the persuasion or entertainment not of specific others . . . but of a 'generalized other' within a white cultural frame" (*Empty Meeting Grounds* 168). Kirshenblatt-Gimblett writes: "Tourism is an export industry" that functions by "import[ing] visitors to consume goods and services locally" (*Destination Culture* 153).

29. Cited in Desmond (5) from Kye-Sung Chon's "The Role of Destination Image in Tourism: A Review and Discussion," *Tourist Review* 2 (1990): 2–9.

30. This essay first appeared in *Border/Lines* 23 (1991/1992): 22–34 and is republished in Trask's *From a Native Daughter: Colonialism and Sovereignty in Hawai'i.* I cite from the 1999 revised text.

31. The last words of this essay are: "If you are thinking of visiting my homeland, please do not. We do not want or need any more tourists, and we certainly do not like them. If you want to help our cause, pass this message on to your friends" (146). As Trask explains earlier in the essay, her "use of the word *tourism* in the Hawai'i context refers to a mass-based, corporately controlled industry that is both vertically and horizontally integrated such that one multinational corporation owns an airline and the tour buses that transport tourists to the corporation-owned hotel where they eat in a corporation-owned restaurant, play golf, and 'experience' Hawai'i on corporation-owned recreation areas and eventually consider buying a second home built on corporation land. Profits, in this case, are mostly repatriated back to the home country," which can be "Japan, Taiwan, Hong Kong, Canada, Australia, and the United States" (139). Recognizing that, as Desmond puts it, "tourist experiences are actively constructed by the industries themselves" (*Staging Tourism* xviii) is an "off-putting," bubble-bursting but necessary step in making choices about why and how we want to seek "the other." For Natives, as Trask states, to become aware that they are partici-

pating in the commodification of culture for exportation is a step toward "decolonization" (145). In its refusal to perform the "soft" and willingly "for sale" image of Hawai'i, Trask's essay is appropriately "hard" in its rhetoric.

32. Momiala Kamahele's essay, "'Ilio'ulaokalani: Defending Native Hawaiian Culture," documents the political action of a coalition of *hula hālau* in the late 1990s to "defend Native Hawaiian traditional and customary rights to gather resources that ensure the practice of hula and sustain our culture" (41). Trask also mentions organizations such as the Ecumenical Coalition on Third World Tourism (Bangkok), the Center for Responsible Tourism (California), and the Third World European Network as "band[ing] together to help give voice to Native peoples in daily resistance against corporate tourism" ("'Lovely Hula Hands'" in *From a Native Daughter* 138). And mostly referring to European tourist destinations, Regina Bendix provides documentation of "critical narrations of life with the tourists" ("Capitalizing on Memories" 478).

Furthermore, I would not want to equate cultural commerce in general with commodification, as if all cultural displays that participate in an economic exchange—and that could include museums in general as well as Native festivals, art exhibitions, concerts, or culture-related businesses—were *automatically* objectified and expropriated from their tradition bearers. See Barbara Kirshenblatt-Gimblett's "Mistaken Dichotomies" (1988) as a warning to folklorists against the purism that sustained an unhealthy separation between folkloristics in the academy and folklore in the applied sector. In "Tourism and Cultural Displays: Inventing Traditions for Whom?" (1989), Bendix questions the "direct, economically motivated connection between tourism and displays" (132) by examining the "affirmation of local and national cultural identity in the face of seasonal mass foreign invasion" in Interlaken, Switzerland. Bendix argues that "cultural displays require staging and thus negotiation of some sort" (143) and that European examples of cultural tourism can provide useful insights along those lines. This is a corrective to a totalizing model that leaves "local" cultures with no agency in the face of tourism, and I think it is an important point. But we must also recognize that the ways in which corporate tourism in Hawai'i contributes to the colonization of Hawaiians do not apply to Switzerland.

33. In the "marketing of heritage" that pertains to commercial hula, "the complexities of who and what are Hawaiian are lost. Hula as an enactment of attachment to the islands, or as an act of resistance to assimilation and decimation, is invisible" (Desmond, *Staging Tourism* 28). However, this invisibility may depend more on the tourist's gaze than on the agency of the performers. For instance, Maiki Aiu, the much honored and loved "mother" of the Hawaiian hula renaissance, danced in commercial shows while at the same time teaching in the first modern *hālau*. Even in Waikīkī today, some Hawaiian *kumu hula*, or teachers of hula—and I am in particular thinking of Coline Aiu, Maiki's daughter, whose *hālau* I've been fortunate to attend—provide in their introductions to specific dances information that *could* prompt viewers to find out more about the history of Hawai'i and the views of those who are fighting for Hawaiian sovereignty. Resistance may be more or less adamant, but it does not automatically disappear even in a commercial or tourist-oriented context.

34. See Andria Imada's 2004 essay "Hawaiians on Tour" for a study of hula as entertainment during territorial times.

35. Regina Bendix astutely explores the complex "interrelationship of narration with the endeavor of tourism" and the "aura of the tourist experience" in her 2002 essay, "Capitalizing on Memories" (471).

36. See also Anne McClintock's *Imperial Leather*, ed. Elizabeth Edwards, esp. 64–65; *Anthropology and Photography, 1860–1920*, Lynn Davis's *Nā Pa'i Ki'i: Photographers in the Hawaiian Islands, 1845–1900*; and Scott McQuire's *Visions of Modernity: Representation, Memory, Time and Space in the Age of the Camera* for analytical and bibliographic information on photography and colonialism.

37. Using Bernard Smith's phrase in *European Vision and the South Pacific* (New Haven, Conn.: Yale University Press, 1985), Jane Desmond writes that the Hawaiian "native" is an example of "soft primitivism" in that it presents the tourist with "a non-threatening, alluring encounter with paradisical exoticism" (4).

38. As Maxwell explains truth is based in the case of photography on empiricism and positivism (11–13).

39. Sanford Dole, the first governor of the Territory as of 1900, had also headed the "provisional government" that deposed Lili'uokalani in 1893 and presided over the running of the "republic" until 1900. While the American resolution to annex Hawai'i took place in 1898, President William McKinley signed the Organic Act to set up a territorial government in Hawai'i in April of 1900.

40. I believe that Davis does not mention Kalākaua's *The Legends and Myths of Hawaii: The Fables and Folk-Lore of a Strange People* because it contains only two photographic illustrations and not because R. M. Daggett was involved in its editing and production.

41. By the 1890s, the invention of the "Instamatic" camera makes it possible to have one's pictures printed without personally having darkroom equipment; women and working-class people in the West are also beginning to practice photography.

42. Lawrence Venuti eloquently discusses the "ethics of location" in his work on translation.

43. Countering these views of myth, from her early study of the Virgin Mary to her work on gender and fairy tales, and the recent *Fantastic Metamorphoses, Other Worlds*, Marina Warner's interdisciplinary and historicizing approach to myth and stories—their verbal and visual transformations, "congeners," transmigration, and pleasures—has been inspirational in many ways.

44. During the Q&A period of "Conversations on Indigenous Issues and Settler Viewpoints" (Center for Hawaiian Studies, April 15, 2003), Candace Fujikane perceptively asked Gayatri Chakravorty Spivak: "Earlier you asked the question, 'Where is there a place where people are not settlers?' What are the implications of this question for the distinction between Native and settler?" According to my notes, Spivak replied, "In this time and place, yes, I agree completely with the importance of that distinction between Native and settler," and eloquently added that, because we are "not only settlers," "we owe our children not to teach them what will burden them if we succeed."

45. As Hawaiian scholars and activists have repeatedly stated, this transformation involves Native Hawaiians and non-Natives in different ways. Ku'ualoha Ho'omanawanui strongly critiques Glen Grant's 1998 introduction to Thomas G. Thrum's *Hawaiian Folk Tales* where "sitting quietly in the vicinity of a beach" and experiencing "the transforming power of the sacred narratives which for centuries have excited the souls of Polynesians" are presented as a lasting conversion that provides an immediate connection with the land ("'This Land'"). My goals in rereading Hawaiian legendary traditions are much more limited and, I trust, quite different from Grant's.

Chapter 2. Hawai'i's Storied Places

1. According to nineteenth-century Hawaiian historian Davida Malo (1795–1853), each *moku*, or island, was divided into *kalana*, or districts, and Ko'olau Poko was one of the six districts on O'ahu. Each district in turn includes many *ahupua'a*, that is, as Kame'eleihiwa explains, "usually wedge-shaped sections of land that followed natural geographic boundaries, such as ridge lines and rivers, and ran from mountains to sea. . . . Ideally, an *ahupua'a* would include within its borders all the materials required for sustenance—timber, thatching, and rope from the mountains, various crops from the uplands, *kalo* from the lowlands, and fish from the sea" (*Native Land and Foreign Desires* 27).

2. Marketed as an ideal gift for the holiday season, Landgraf's book was praised as "peel[ing] back layers of romanticized, urbanized Hawai'i to reveal its essence" (Jan Rose) and "giv[ing] voice to the silent places of windward Oahu" (Tenbruggencate). Having received positive reviews in Hawai'i newspapers and magazines, the book quickly became a 1995 local best seller and was awarded the 1995 Ka Palapala Po'okela Award for Excellence in Illustrative Books, administered by the Hawaii Book Publishers Association. Exploring the dynamics between the book's success and its politics would be productive in itself, especially if other Hawaiian artists' work were also to be considered, but that is not my project here. See Ty-Tomkins, Burlingame ("From a Hawaiian Point of View"), and Fulland-Leo in addition to Rose and Tennbruggencate for published reviews. Burlingame's article also reports from an interview with Landgraf. An early version of this chapter is in Davis's *Photography in Hawen'i* (2001).

Landgraf has also published "Ē Luku Wale Ē . . . Devastation upon Devastation," poetry in Hawaiian and English accompanying black-and-white photographs of O'ahu places as affected by pollution, building, and redistribution of water. These images were part of her 1998 exhibit with Mark Hamasaki of photographs documenting the building of the controversial H-3 freeway and constitute a powerful statement on the devastation of Hawaiian culture and land. Landgraf's work is also exhibited at the Center for Hawaiian Studies at the University of Hawai'i at Mānoa.

See also Cashman et al., *ReViewing Paradise*, an introduction to and discussion of the collective exhibit of photographers Kimo Cashman, Gaye Chan, Mark Hamasaki, Renee Iijima, Karen Kosasa, Stan Tomita, Ann Kalupani Landgraf, John Morita, and Kainalani Young that was held at the Honolulu Advertiser Gallery in Honolulu (April 27, 1995–June 28, 1995) [Honolulu: s.n., 1995]. The booklet includes statements by the artists (Landgraf's on 9–10) as well as the reprint of Dennis Kawaharada's essay "Toward an Authentic Local Literature of Hawai'i" (13–17), which had been presented and distributed at the 1994 conference on Hawai'i's literatures held at Kapi'olani Community College in Honolulu.

Landgraf's more recent mixed-media work, *ku'u ewe, ku'u iwi, ku'u koko/my umbilical cord, my bones, my blood*, was on view in the John Dominis and Patches Damon Holt Gallery of the Honolulu Academy of Arts from May 14 to September 21, 2003—while I was revising this chapter. Her book *Nā Wahi Kapu o Maui* also came out in 2003 with 'Ai Pōhaku Press and is beautifully introduced by Kihei de Silva.

3. As discussed in Chapter 1, a number of factors have contributed to the colonization of Hawai'i: Hawaiian depopulation brought on by Western diseases, the missionary squelching of Hawaiian religion and overall culture, the

privatization of land, the American-based interest in a capitalist economy of sugar plantations, the overthrow of the Hawaiian monarchy (1893), the banning of Hawaiian language from public and private schools, and the political annexation of Hawai'i by the United States (1898) against the will of the majority of Hawaiians as indicated by their petitions.

The U.S. Justice Department has recognized that the United States has a "trust obligation to indigenous Hawaiians because it bears responsibility for the destruction of their government and unconsented and uncompensated taking of their lands." This responsibility is stated in various acts (the Hawaiian Homes Commission Act of 1921, the Admissions Act of 1959); it is also the reason for the establishment of the Office of Hawaiian Affairs (OHA) in 1978 and for the 1993 bill signed by President Clinton apologizing for the 1893 overthrow. In reaction to this acknowledgment of political injustice as well as to increasing support for some form of Hawaiian sovereignty, Hawaiian-only OHA elections and Hawaiian-only admissions to Kamehameha Schools (built and funded through Bernice Pauahi Bishop's trust for the education and benefit of Hawaiians) have recently been under legal attack on the grounds that they are discriminatory and thus unconstitutional (*Rice v. Cayetano* and *Earl Arakaki et al. v. the State of Hawai'i*).

Land issues have been central to the process of colonization and are central today to obtaining sovereignty and justice for the Hawaiian people (see Kame'eleihiwa, *Native Land and Foreign Desires*, and Trask, *From a Native Daughter*). "Over a million acres of so-called 'trust' lands [were] set aside by Congress for Native beneficiaries but leased by their alleged 'trustee,' the state of Hawai'i, to non-Natives" (Trask, *From a Native Daughter* 16).

4. In dealing with apparently stable material objects such as photos, it is important to keep in mind that "context is creative, suggestive and provocative" (Edwards "Visuality and History" 49).

5. My focus here is not on landscape painting, an immense subject in itself, but I do want to note that photography extends the work of paintings here. At a time when sketches, engravings, paintings, lithographs, and photographs were all being reproduced to illustrate the printed word, recognizing this continuity is significant. See David W. Forbes's *Encounters with Paradise* for an excellent commentary on the first exhibit of visual representations of Hawai'i and a catalog of the exhibit. Particularly relevant to my point would be *Kilauea by Day* and *Kilauea by Night* (1842 oil canvases by Titian Ramsay Peale); the 1865 majestic *Manoa Valley from Waikiki* by Enoch Wood Perry Jr.; Edward Bailey's 1870 oil *Iao Valley*; the 1869 watercolor *The Pali* by Nicholas Chevalier and *View of the Pali* painted around 1886 by Jules Tavernier. For a study of landscape within the European tradition, see Ann Bermingham's *Landscape and Ideology: The English Rustic Tradition, 1740–1860*.

6. In *The Lure of the Local: Senses of Place in a Multicentered Society* (1997), Lucy Lippard notes that landscape, commonly used to refer to "place" but also "nature, view, scenery," has come to include "everything you see when you go outdoors—if you are looking" and "can only be seen from the outside, as a backdrop for the experience of viewing" (8). Mary Louise Pratt makes an equivalent point about "panoramic views" or "sweeping prospects" in the literature of exploration: "This discursive configuration, which centers landscape, separates people from place, and effaces the speaking self, is characteristic of a great deal of travel writing in the last century" ("Scratches on the Face of the Country; or, What Mr. Barrow Saw in the Land of the Bushmen" 143).

This understanding of landscape is not held by all. In her 1965 article "Creative Processes in Hawaiian Use of Place Names in Chants," Katharine Luomala quoted from Geoffrey Grigson's *Places of the Mind* (London, 1949) to the effect that "the 'beauty' of a landscape comes from ourselves, how much in one way or another we project ourselves into a landscape, which then reflects our own being back to our eyes. . . . [Landscape] is a very personal affair, [it] is you and me" (241). This approach to landscape seems akin to the "affective fallacy" and entails *projection* of the individual's feelings on to the representation of nature rather than, as in the Hawaiian view, a *relation* that—as will become clear in the ensuing discussion—is both familial and historical. A much stronger and complex reading of landscape in Romantic "local poems" is available in the classic essay by M. H. Abrams, "Structure and Style in the Greater Romantic Lyric," where the sublime human-nature encounter is not a simple projection, but structured by a mnemonic relation that is not the same as the Hawaiian one I have been describing.

7. See Lew Andrews, " 'Fine Island Views.' "

8. See Lynn Ann Davis's *Nā Pa'i Ki'i: The Photographers in the Hawaiian Islands, 1845–1900* for a detailed study of photography in Hawai'i as well as the more recent *Photography in Hawai'i*, which provides an extensive bibliography as well as case studies on early and contemporary photographers in Hawai'i.

In my sketch of "landscape" photography in Hawai'i, I consciously run the risk of generalizing in order to point out Landgraf's critical turn away from the "landscape" perspective even as she engages in some of its defining practices—large-format camera and often expansive take. Obviously, not every landscape photographer or photograph, especially as we move to recent times, will fit the bill. Others, most notably Wayne Levin, Mark Hamasaki, Kimo Cashman, and April Drexel have also in recent times critically revisited the Hawai'i "landscape" tradition, but Landgraf's photography distinguishes itself because of her explicit and sustained dialogue with traditional narratives.

I also do not, with the generalizations about *external* landscapes in Western nineteenth-century photography of Hawai'i and about the concurrent naturalization of Native culture, mean to suggest that Hawaiians have only been objectified in photographic images: obviously, this is less true of those who could afford and valued having their portrait taken. And there are also specific landscape instances in which passersby disrupt the one-way view of the photographer by either searching for the same view as the camera's from within the frame (e.g., Weed's "Aldrich House" in Davis, *Nā Pa'i Ki'i* 30) or pausing out of curiosity to look at back at the photographer, at "the antics of the *haole pa'i ki'i* on the rooftop nearby" (Hugo Stangerwald's "Honolulu" in Davis *Nā Pa'i Ki'i* 27). Nevertheless, Leslie Marmon Silko's assertion that "the Indian with a camera is an omen of . . . the time when the indigenous people of the Americas will retake their land" (178) echoes strongly in Landgraf's photographic practice.

9. "The linkage of performance, photography, tourism, and the production of the iconic image occurred even more explicitly in the Kodak Hula Show, which began in 1937" (Desmond 105). Desmond refers to it as the "longest-running Hawaiian cultural show on the islands." In an August 9, 2003, lecture at the Honolulu Art Academy, DeSoto Brown from the Bishop Museum Archives showed some clips of early Kodak Hula Shows. They were held near the Waikiki Natatorium and then moved into Kapi'olani Park in the late 1960s by ordinance of Mayor Frank Fasi. There was a necessary, war-related break from 1941 to 1949.

10. I am not referring to the experience of the dancers here, which could be

much more varied and self-motivated, but to the staging and choreographing of the event.

11. I found Lippard's contrast between "landscape" and "place" in her examination of contemporary visual arts in the United States very helpful. Then, from my position in Hawai'i, I had to work out how to read her assertion that place also "bear[s] the record of hybrid culture" (Lippard 8). While I agree that narratives of place expose different layers of located history, I am not using the term "hybrid" in my analysis of Hawai'i as it could lead either to a quiescently "multicultural" understanding of the present cultural dynamics or to the endorsement of a competition between indigenous and settler narratives of place.

12. As Steven Feld and Keith H. Basso note in their introduction to *Senses of Place* (1996), discussions of philosophies of place in relation to power and authority dynamics have recently abounded in cultural geography and other disciplines, particularly ethnography. I use "sense of place" in the experiential, sensory, and culturally bound meaning that Feld and Basso ascribe to it. Tim Cresswell's *Place: A Short Introduction* offers a critically shrewd synthesis of changing approaches to "place" in the disciplinary history of human geography. "*Sense of place*, really, is a collection of feelings about locality, about how we as individuals and as members of a community relate to that locality which ties in with our senses of *identity*" write de Caro and Jordan in their chapter, "Finding a Sense of Place: Folk Ideas and the Lore of Place in Written and Visual Arts Texts" (*Re-Situating Folklore* 234), where they recognize the long-term interest that folklorists have had in the concept. Katharine Luomala's approach to place names in Hawaiian chants was already in the 1960s ("Dynamic" and "Creative Processes") attuned to the "emotional" dimension of "place."

Given the polymorphous appeal of "sense of place," it is not surprising that the term has also been used and abused within the tourist industry. A letter to the *Honolulu Advertiser* recently noted: "An assistant manager of a major hotel chain makes inquiries about receiving a liquor license for a topless entertainment show. And then he assures us that the show will have a Hawaiian sense of place. Too often political and business leaders are using that phrase to cover up their own personal agendas" (July 6, 1999, A7).

13. Kawaharada's book makes use of Landgraf's photographs as illustrations of his discussion of specific "storied landscapes," for instance, the powerful Kualoa and the sands of Māhinahina (*Storied Landscapes* 42–43). Kawaharada's reference to "storied landscapes" is equivalent to my use of "storied places." I have chosen the latter not only because it stands in explicit contrast to "landscapes," but because it is, together with "celebrated" or "legendary places," the common translation of *nā wahi pana* (Pukui and Elbert, *Hawaiian Dictionary*). Kawaharada's terminology does not contrast landscape and place, but it has the advantage of foregrounding *land* as an issue.

Kawaharada's perspective is nevertheless quite different from Ku'ualoha Ho'omanawanui's ("This Land"). The point she makes that " '*āina* does not translate to 'landscape' because landscape implies a pristine panoramic view of land (or 'nature') devoid of human beings" while *kanaka maoli* "are descended from the land and are *related to* and not *separate from* elements of 'nature'" eloquently articulates a distinction that my work seeks to support. As I point out in various sections of this volume, I have learned much from Ho'omanawanui with whom I have exchanged drafts and published work over the years. For yet a different approach see Wilson, "Shark God on Trial."

14. See Burlingame's review of Landgraf's book, "From a Hawaiian Point of View."

15. Given her reliance on Grigson's understanding of "personal" (see note 6 above), Luomala's wording would seem to point in the direction of primarily individual emotional experience. Nevertheless, "personal" evokes the animated and kin qualities of "nature" and can—though Luomala's wording does not explicitly—extend to nature as familial.

16. This strong attention to place and localization is not exclusive to Hawaiian narrative traditions and has been noted in the Pacific more generally as well as among Native Americans. See Feld and Basso's work, but also *Emplaced Myth: Space, Narrative, and Knowledge in Aboriginal Australia and Papua New Guinea*, ed. Alan Rumsey and James F. Weiner. For a theoretical discussion: Steven Edmund Winduo's "Unwriting Oceania: The Repositioning of the Pacific Writer Scholars Within a Folk Narrative Space" and David Welchman Gegeo's "Cultural Rupture and Indigeneity: The Challenge of (Re)visioning 'Place' in the Pacific." The important relationship between place and story in constituting local history has been noted in other cultures as well that are beyond the scope of my analysis.

17. While Kawaharada does not read Landgraf's photograph explicitly in this way, his discussion of her photos is part of the third essay in *Storied Landscapes*, entitled "Voyaging Chiefs in Kāneʻohe Bay" (33–49) and ends with a discussion of "The Modern Revival of Voyaging." It is significant that Kawaharada was an actual participant in that revival. Citing Ben Finney's well-known publications on the Hōkuleʻa, Kawaharada writes, "Those who thought that the oral traditions recounting such voyages [from Hawaiʻi to Tahiti] were fictions and who doubted that traditional navigational techniques could be used to guide sailing canoes across 2,400 miles of open ocean were proven wrong" (48). See also Kawaharada's chapter "Crossing Seas" on the present-day value of voyaging traditions in *Local Geographies* (2004).

18. Samuel Mānaiakalani Kamakau's writings in the nineteenth century feature prominently within this tradition just as Mary Kawena Pukui's do in the twentieth.

It is important to note, as Richard Hamasaki does, that studies and translations of Hawaiian literature in the 1980s and 1990s continued to "build on extensive research of the ancient genres of Hawaiian and Polynesian traditions, studies initiated by Professor Rubellite Kawena Johnson . . . and others before her such as Samuel Mānaiakalani Kamakau, Martha Beckwith, Abraham Fornander, Mary Kawena Pukui, and Samuel H. Elbert" ("Mountains in the Sea" 192). Increasingly, the recent work with Hawaiian-language newspapers and documents conducted by a new generation of Hawaiian scholars, such as Noelani Arista, Kuʻualoha Hoʻomanawanui, and Noenoe Silva, as well as by Hawaiian-language scholars like Puakea Nogelmeier has also profoundly affected the discussion of politics and culture in pre- and post-annexation Hawaiʻi.

19. Luomala identifies "at least five uses of localization" in Beckwith's discussion ("Dynamic" 141). In addition to their "allusive interest," they are: "to display the narrator's knowledge and name-creating ability"; "to [connect] with the actual physical description of a locality"; "to identify the route of travel for the characters"; and "to help establish the reliability of the narrative" (142).

20. Part of the Appendix was reprinted as "Connotative Values of Place Names" in *Directions in Pacific Traditional Literature*. The passage I quoted appears on page 124 of this edition.

21. Thomas G. Thrum's "Hawaiian Place Names" offers literal translations

and basic information about location, but nothing else. It is this flatness consti-
tutive of what Johannes Fabian has called the "ethnographic present" that
Pukui, Elbert, and Mookini had to work at undoing in their *Place Names of
Hawaii*.

22. See Stillman's essay "Re-Membering the History of the Hawaiian Hula."

23. In his discussion of other genres and cultural contexts, folklorist and lin-
guist W. H. F. Nicolaisen makes significant observations about the condensation
of experience "through toponymic encapsulation" and the persuasive power of
"designated locatability" in the construction of the past "through story both as
time and space" ("The Past as Place" 9 and 13). See also Nicolaisen, "Maps of
Space—Maps of Time."

24. As a way to overcome these problems, Luomala proposes that a "search
for the expression of universal emotions can be a key to let one into a world of
unfamiliar art" ("Creative Processes" 235); thus her essay focuses on expressions of sorrow as related to place names in chants. While the emotional relation
to place is an important aspect to consider, I would argue that key to understanding unfamiliar art is the acknowledgment of difference—as culturally constitutive of expression.

25. This kind of dialogue is still very much part of *oli* and hula performances,
though it may not be recognized by wider audiences.

26. As author Maxine Hong Kingston wrote in a short 1978 piece about this
"pointed island offshore": "Mokoli'i Island, but nobody calls it that. . . . 'Chinaman's Hat,' people say to visitors, 'because it looks just like a Chinaman's hat.
See?'" (*Hawai'i One Summer* 29–30). Kingston's reaction to and reappropriation
of the nickname is telling of today's power dynamics in Hawai'i and remains for
me quite problematic: having grown up in California, at first Kingston clearly
finds "Chinaman's hat" to be a derogatory term; then, like Landgraf, she gets
close in order to know the island—its waters, beach, blowhole, fishermen,
sharks; finally, she tells of hearing a "howling like wolves, like ghosts, ... It was,
I know, the island, . . . the voice of our island singing" (33). But her getting
close is not actually like Landgraf's: Kingston's piece strongly asserts the need
to recognize islands as "living, sacred earth" (33), but hers seems to be primarily
a poetic move as her somewhat disconcerting reference to Odysseus's sirens
indicates, and the "we" her "our" evokes is at best only implicitly inclusive of
Hawaiians. In the 1998 volume where this piece is reprinted, the accompanying
black-and-white photo by Franco Salmoiraghi, "Chinaman's Hat, O'ahu," seems
to romanticize the tiny island as a world of its own.

27. As Kawaharada remarks, fish-attracting stones "have become the source
of modern legends" involving the misfortune of those who did not recognize
the power of these beings (*Storied Landscapes* 10; see also Sterling and Summers
258–59). Landgraf's focus does not include multiethnic legends of Hawai'i's
recent past which also inform these places in the present.

28. Edith Kanaka'ole's video recorded interview by Homer Hayes, in Hilo,
Hawai'i (1978). She went on to tell the story of how Kahuku on the island of
Hawai'i was a "flatland" in the old days and hills were formed from Kamapua'a's
rooting as he tried to hide from Pele who was following him. This story included
information about where Pele's territory ended—at Wailuku River—and the pig
god's began. Pele was chasing after Kamapua'a outside her territory and, after
her foot accidentally touched the water of a stream, she returned to her domain.
As a young child, Edith Kanaka'ole was told this story by her mother; as an adult
she composed a *mele* from it and presented it at a workshop to exemplify how
stories and literature are the foundation of *mele*.

29. *Holo Mai Pele* was performed on at least three islands in 1995 and 1996: Hawai'i, O'ahu, and Maui. The Blaisdell Theater was packed for the performance in Honolulu. For the first time in recent history, the *mo'olelo* of Pele and Hi'iaka was performed as an extended narrative and theatrical representation—rather than as separate *mele* or *oli*. The three-hour epic performance worked on a number of levels: dance, song, chant, theatrical performance, summarized narration in English, costumes, reconstructed staging of social practices (games and competitions for instance), and special lighting effects from Western theater. The video introduces the performance and then synthesizes it into a one-hour production. The book is framed by Pualani Kanaka'ole Kanahele's introduction to the tradition of hula, Hālau o Kekuhi, and Pele. It is significant that a Hawaiian writer with strong editing credentials, Mahealani Dudoit, was called by the *kumu* to edit the English-language text. Together the book and the video make for excellent classroom use, especially when juxtaposed with Nathaniel B. Emerson's 1915 English-language book *Pele and Hi'iaka*. See also Pualani Kanaka'ole Kanahele and Duke Kalani Wise's *Ka Honua Ola: The Living Earth* (1992) for an earlier poetic and analytical study of Pele by this *kumu hula* and a bibliography of stories associated with Pele.

30. I am quoting from James F. Weiner's "Afterword" to the already mentioned volume *Emplaced Myth* (Rumsey and Weiner 235). He distinguishes in discussing Papua New Guinea between those who can learn about storied places "only through the verbal accounts that people bring back for revelation in the public space" and those who "have the immediate intimacy of ritual-productive-manipulative engagement" (235). The context for his statement applies foremost to secret knowledge and places that are restricted in Papua New Guinea, while I have been referring more generally to "storied places," the sacredness and history of which are not uniformly secret, and clearly Landgraf by employing a camera and print sources is not engaging in an experience of "immediate intimacy," but one heavily mediated by colonial history. Nevertheless, as I see it, the distinction between levels of relation to a place and differences among claims on which such a relation can be established applies to both contexts.

31. See M. K. Palikoolauloa's letter listing the various storied places of Kaliuwa'a as it is reproduced in Hawaiian and English in Rubellite Kinney Johnson's *Kūkini 'Aha'ilono* (180–83).

32. Some of Kamakau's articles in the Hawaiian-language newspapers *Ka Nupepa Kuokoa* and *Ke Au Okoa* were translated by Mary Kawena Pukui for *Tales and Traditions of the People of Old* and edited by Dorothy B. Barrère. The phrase in quotation marks is from Barrère's "Preface."

33. For a thorough investigation of Kamapua'a stories as connected with Kaliuwa'a see John Charlot's *The Kamapua'a Literature*, especially 47–60. Charlot also comments on the telling of the stories in location (33 and 47) and refers to Westervelt (*Hawaiian Legends of Old Honolulu* 248) and Luomala ("Dynamic" 152). Also extremely useful is Melia Lane's "Cross-Reference of Descriptions of Kaliuwa'a" (1979). There are several English-language translations of Kamapua'a literature. Kame'eleihiwa's 1996 text is particularly successful because of its annotations in relating the importance of place names and *wahi pana*.

34. Bishop Museum Archives, Hawaiian Ethnographic Notes (HEN) collection, I: 2197.

35. Siikala, "Oral History and Landscape: Narratives in the Southern Cook Islands." Anna-Leena Siikala and Jukka Siikala's book *Return to Culture* was published too late for me to integrate their perspective into this study, but it

includes within its "Strategies for Reproduction" section a chapter on "spatial memory and narration" (112–31), which ends: "In giving meaning to tangible objects and locations, in transforming them into indexical signs of crucial actions in the past, narratives create a landscape in which time and space melt together into mental maps of the universe and the social world. At the same time, the indexicality and its tendency to restrict circulation of the narratives creates the basis of contestation. The right location becomes as important as the events themselves" (131).

36. I am grateful to preservationist and artist Lynn Davis for sharing her insight that in Landgraf's book "text and image respond to each other at a poetic edge" (July 8, 1998 conversation).

37. Silko's work on Pueblo echoes here again. She writes: "in the case of many of the Pueblo narratives, it is impossible to determine which came first, the incident or the geographical feature that begs to be brought alive in a story that features some unusual aspect of this location" (33). She also states that her project in "An essay on Rocks" is "coaxing the photographs and the narratives to work as one" (24).

38. See Larry Kimura's "Native Hawaiian Culture."

39. *Ka Leo Hawai'i* was originally broadcast by Larry Kimura, at present Professor of Hawaiian Language at the University of Hawai'i at Hilo, in 1971 on KCCN AM 1420. There was a hiatus in the late 1980s when he moved to Hilo; then Puakea Nogelmeier, Tuti Kanahele, and Hau'oli Akaka revived it, with the same title, on KINE FM 105.1. Currently not on the air, the program featured Hawaiian elders telling their experiences in Hawaiian and other Hawaiian-language dialogues.

40. "Hidden meaning, as in Hawaiian poetry; concealed reference, as to a person, thing, or place; words with double meanings that might bring good or bad fortune" (Pukui and Elbert, *Hawaiian Dictionary* 130).

41. On these struggles and their cultural history, see videos such as *Kaho'olawe Aloha 'Āina* (1992), *Mākua Valley: Yesterday and Today, What About Tomorrow?* (1996), and *Mele Aloha: 'Āina Songs and Hula of Hawaiian Resistance* (2002); the 1984 book edited by Rodney Morales *Ho'iho'i Hou: A Tribute to George Helm & Kimo Mitchell*; and Marion Kelly and Nancy Aleck's *Mākua Means Parents: A Brief Cultural History of Mākua Valley* (1997).

Chapter 3. Production of Legendary Hawai'i

1. *The Kahala Hilton Video Tour* (VHS video recording; Honolulu: Kahala Hilton Corporation, [1989?]) is in the Wong Audiovisual Center at the University of Hawai'i-Mānoa. I came across it while conducting a broad search on "legends" and "places" in Hawai'i.

2. As is the case with the name Punchbowl replacing Pūowaina in another part of the Kona district, where the city of Honolulu is, the subdivision of Kāhala also superimposes itself on the *ahupua'a*, an often self-sustaining, wedge-shaped land section that extended from the uplands to the ocean, and in the process erases it. From what I can tell, the hotel is at one far end of the Wai'alae Iki *ahupua'a*, possibly crossing over to Wailupe. In the case of Kāhala, the *ahupua'a* is replaced with the mapping of an area that extends itself along the coast and is defined by the desirability of oceanfront and ocean-view real estate. Kāhala is the name of a fish, the amberjack. In the case of Punchbowl, the National Cemetery of the Pacific within the crater becomes the redefining monumental land-

mark to the exclusion of the *makai* (in the direction of the sea) areas of Pūowaina.

3. Texts I will be discussing more fully in Chapter 5, such as Hale'ole's *Laiei-kawai* and the *mo'olelo* of Kamapua'a, are among the nineteenth-century Hawaiian-language publications that strongly relied on knowledge of *wahi pana*. For Kamapua'a, we have at least three Hawaiian-language versions: Fornander's, G. W. Kahiolo's 1861 story in *Ka Hae Hawaii*, and the anonymous one in *Ka Leo o ka Lāhui* in 1891.

A number of texts recounting Pele traditions also found their way into print during that time, and we have already gotten from Landgraf's work a glimpse of how important place is in the context of Pele's and Hi'iaka's epic travels. Ku'u-aloha Ho'omanawanui is researching these different texts, starting with Kapihe-nui's 1861–1862 text published in *Ka Hoku o Ka Pakipika*, and comparing the Hawaiian form of these *mo'olelo* with the shape that English-language translations have taken, starting as early as 1883 in the *Pacific Commercial Advertiser*, of which Walter Murray Gibson was in charge at the time (Bishop Museum talk with Noenoe Silva in April 2003 and dissertation in progress). Puakea Nogelmeier's bilingual edition of the text as published in *Ka Na'i Aupuni* is forthcoming.

4. Fornander is a most significant and interesting figure for the preservation of *mo'olelo* and Hawaiian knowledge. However, I am not focusing on his work here because it is primarily outside of the time frame that is most relevant to my study and because—like Nathaniel B. Emerson, the translator of Malo's *Moolelo Hawaii* as *Hawaiian Antiquities* (originally published in 1903) and redactor of the very influential *Pele and Hiiaka: A Myth from Hawaii* (Honolulu, 1915)—Fornander was primarily a scholar and did not participate in the popularizing and commercializing of *mo'olelo* that Thomas G. Thrum and William W. Wester-velt best represent. See Helen Chapin's discussion of Fornander (48–52) as the editor of several publications, including the *Weekly Argus* (January 1851–September 1853) where he "castigated . . . the Protestant missionaries for preaching that national calamities were a 'divine judgment' on Hawaiians" (51). Chapin draws on Eleanor Davis's *Abraham Fornander: A Biography* (Honolulu: University of Hawai'i Press, 1979). I will note only in passing some of the ways in which Fornander's ethics and rhetoric differed from that of later collectors and translators.

5. A good two-thirds of the stories in the 1888 Kalākaua volume are part of Skinner's compilation. Many of the tales are drastically shortened and their order of presentation is different, which speaks to a number of issues: the editing for content and the dismissal of style and form that would also characterize many future renditions of Hawaiian *mo'olelo* in English; the ease with which cultural appropriation could take place as long as it was not plagiarism explicitly as defined by copyright law; and the lack of interest that Skinner's volume shows in the historical dimension of Kalākaua's project.

6. Amos P. Leib noted, on the one hand, that "Fornander speaks of Kalā-kaua's 'extensive erudition in Hawaiian antiquities' (*Polynesian Race* I:xi)" and, on the other hand, that "Daggett was probably the writer of the two. Besides 'editing' this book, Daggett wrote poetry," and William Ellis should have been credited for the story of Pele and Kahawali ("Hawaiian Mythology in English Translation" M.A. thesis, June 1947, 31–32). In his 1949 book *Hawaiian Legends in English*, which is currently available in the expanded 1979 edition (Leib and Day), Leib omits Fornander's comment on Kalākaua's knowledge. See note 26.

7. In the chapter "The Merry Monarch: Genealogy, Cosmology, Mele, and

Performance Art as Resistance" (*Aloha Betrayed* 87–122), Silva details how "Kalā-kaua vehemently insists through these activities that the Kanaka Maoli are proud of their past (which is not forgotten) and so already consider themselves the equals of the Europeans and Euro-Americans" (116).

8. Jonathan Osorio has persuasively suggested that post-contact Hawaiian history enacted a struggle over the meaning and the very existence of *lāhui*—nation, but also "'gathering,' 'people,' 'tribe,' and even 'species'" (253–54)—and that, during Kalākaua's reign the infamous Bayonet Constitution of 1887, by which political power was placed in the hands of a group of Euro-American businessmen, marked the "dismemberment" of the *lāhui* and the violent translation of it into a modern and foreign nation.

9. "Annexation of Hawaii to the United States" (*Annual* [1899]:72–79) closes with the following statement about the ball with which the day ended: "This state function was very generally attended by all classes and nationalities of the community, and consequently was quite democratic, though throughout the day's exercises the Hawaiians were, comparatively, sparsely represented, except as silent and distant observers—and who could blame them?" (79).

10. "A file of this *Annual* is an indispensable part of every library of Hawaiiana. A few years ago the League of Nations secretariat sent for a complete file to add to the library of that organization at Geneva" (Kuykendall, "Thomas George Thrum" 46).

11. *Annual* (1884):49; (1894):142; (1899):72; and (1907):106.

12. *Annual* (1879):59; (1881):59; (1880):61. See "Reference List of Principal Articles that have appeared in prior Hawaiian Annuals, 1875–1923, classified under their respective subjects" in the 1924 *Annual* 175.

13. One *moʻolelo* included in the "Historical" articles section was the "History of Umi" translated by Professor Alexander in the *Annual* (1888):78 ("List of Principal Articles," 1924 *Annual* 177).

14. *Paradise of the Pacific* 2.5[1889]:4 and 1.1[1888]:3. Paul Lyons notes that in much writing of the time about Oceania, including Mark Twain's lecture, "the turn toward colonial humor in discussing the 'recently ended' cannibalism . . . rechannels the fear-driven semiotics into literary tourism, with its search for authentic remnants of primitivity" (*American Pacificism* 20). The book presents a wide-ranging and persuasive critique of what Lyons calls "histourism" in order to make visible both masculinist and nationalistic dimensions of U.S. travel literature in its history of Oceania.

15. *Paradise of the Pacific* 6.5 [1893]:8; 10.11[1897]:164.

16. This information is provided in the 1900 December issue (13.12:8). Providing general data about editorial changes and their connections with politics and support from the legislature is beyond the scope of my comments on *Paradise of the Pacific*, but it would further bolster an understanding of the important role this magazine played in public discourse.

17. "Happy Hawaii" and "What the Hawaiian Islands Offer to American Capitalists," *Paradise of the Pacific* 2.9[1889]:1 and 3.1[1890]:1.

18. *Paradise of the Pacific* 1.12 [1888]:1; 9.8 [1896]:113; 9.9 [1896]:132; 9.9 [1897]:130.

19. *Paradise of the Pacific* 11.8 [1898]:113; 8.3 [1895]:35. The February 1896 issue of the magazine references the following mention in the British publication *Folklore*, "Only a few days ago came The Paradise of the Pacific, a monthly, Frank L. Hoogs, published at Honolulu. It is printed upon a fine quality of paper and is first-class in all respects. We heartily welcome the publication, coming to

us as a representative from our neighbor republic out in the midst of the Pacific" (*Paradise of the Pacific* 9.2 [1896]:20).

20. *Paradise of the Pacific* 10.7 [1897]:100; 11.6 [1898]:83.

21. The anecdote ends with what is supposed to be its lesson, "Thou shalt not prevaricate. Thou shalt not lie." But the division of the printed words suggests a joke: "Tho usha lt no tprevari ca te. Tho usha lt no tl ie."

22. This Euro-American frame ("in the olden times") and vocabulary ("fairies") characterizes many other authored texts for children that can be found in the twentieth century retelling or even inventing of "Hawaiian traditions." *Old Time Hawaiians* by Mary S. Lawrence (Boston and New York: Ginn and Co., 1912) is an interesting example of retellings for children because it was produced specifically "to supply the children of Hawaii with a history of their own race" and was used at Kamehameha School for Girls. Several photos of Hawaiian boys are captioned "Menehunes."

23. *Paradise of the Pacific* 3.2 [1890]:6–7; 3.11 [1890]:1; 4.3 [1891]:1; 5.3 [1892]:1; 3.3 [1890]:2.

24. See "The Legend Trees of Hawaii" (*Paradise of the Pacific* 18.4:11 and 11.8:16) in 1905.

25. Others like William B. Sabin (see "Beneath the Banyan: Stories of Hawaii Founded on Her Ancient Legends" 14.7 [1901]:18–21) and Emma L. Dillingham ("The Hidden Spring" 15.12 [1902]:45–47) also published "legends" in *Paradise of the Pacific* during those twenty years, but Westervelt's contributions dominate the period. Over and above the sixty seven pieces I mentioned, he published at least fifteen more articles with a historical or more broadly Polynesian focus and at least two pieces that are labeled as "fiction" ("Old Man of the Mountain" 14.10 [1901]:11–13) and "historical fiction" ("The Sons of Kii" 14.5 [1901]:11–16) in the Leib and Day bibliography (113 and 114).

26. Leib's book, originally his 1947 Master's thesis at the University of Hawai'i, was published by the University of Hawai'i Press in 1949; its second edition includes a substantial supplement to the first bibliography and an introduction by A. Grove Day who was invited to complete the work after Leib's death in 1977. Both were professors of English at the University of Hawai'i.

27. Thrum's edition was based on work done by W. D. Alexander, John Wise, and Martha W. Beckwith on Fornander's manuscripts. I am not including an analysis on Fornander's work because he died in 1887, prior to the time frame on which I am focusing. Needless to say, the publication of Fornander's *Hawaiian Antiquities and Folk-lore* as translated and annotated by Thomas G. Thrum in 1916–1920 for the Bishop Museum did make an important contribution to the developing interest in Hawaiian folklore, but mostly in a more strictly scholarly context. See the *Fornander Collection of Hawaiian Antiquities and Folk-Lore* as recently reissued with Hawaiian and English text (1999).

28. Robert J. Morris persuasively points to Thrum's mistranslation of same-sex pronouns and relations in Hawaiian stories. Morris also shows how this misgendering that embodies the norms of Christianization and heterosexuality was and is widespread in English-language translations from Hawaiian. See Hall and Kauanui, Lyons (*American Pacificism*), and Silva ("Pele, Hi'iaka, and Haumea") for further discussion of same-sex sex relations in texts from Oceania and in Western representations of the Pacific or Oceania.

29. His translations of Henry Drummond's "Greatest Things of the World" and "Teachings of the Apostles" (*Men in Hawaii* 3:859) are available at the UHM Hamilton Library.

30. My references will be to the 1916 edition because it contains a greater number of photographic illustrations. The only other difference is that the second chapter in the 1915 edition, "Wakea the Polynesian," is retitled "The Migration of the Hawaiians" and positioned first in 1916.

31. William John Thoms' letter to the *Athenaeum* (August 22, 1846) seeks to replace the Latinate "Antiquities" and "Popular Literature" with a "good Saxon compound" that would identify the customs and beliefs of the people including but not privileging their literature. Thoms wrote to the readers of the *Athenaeum*: "I am not without hopes of enlisting your aid in garnering the few ears which are remaining, scattered over that field from which our forefathers might have gathered a goodly crop."

32. "As 'good' natives, Hawaiians were positioned as alluring soft primitives, the perfect hosts for elite tourists' escape from modernity's workaday ennui" (Desmond 97). Jane C. Desmond sees the tourist image of the Hawaiian "native" as an example of what in *European Vision and the South Pacific* Bernard Smith called "soft primitivism": "a non-threatening, alluring encounter with paradisical exoticism" that is female or feminized and brown, rather than black (Desmond 4). See also Rona Tamiko Halualani's discussion in *In the Name of Hawaiians* of nativism and the *aloha* spirit as constitutive of the dominant discourse of the tourist industry in Hawai'i today.

33. The contrast between the paratextual apparatus of Westervelt's volume and Abraham Fornander's preface to his *Account of the Polynesian Race* is quite striking. Fornander begins: "When a gentleman, whose genius and talents have secured for himself one of the curule chairs in the republic of letters, introduces a blushing aspirant, his name becomes a voucher for the respectability of the latter, ... But we are not all born with a silver spoon, and many an author, like myself, has had to bear the double burden of introducing himself as well as his subject." Fornander goes on to assert, "I should state my right to present [myths and legends of Polynesia], how I came about them, and also the lights that guided me and the aids that assisted me on the journey" (iii).

34. Or as another reviewer put it, "In popularizing these materials, he has won for himself a position of pre-eminence in Polynesia" (H. D. Skinner 141). Thrum's 1923 second *Folk Tales* book—along with Padraic Colum's *At the Gateways of the Day: Tales and Legends from Hawaii* (1924) and William Hyde Rice's *Hawaiian Legends* (1923)—was also reviewed in the 1925 *Journal of American Folklore* by Beckwith. She called him "an able transmitter of things Hawaiian, through life-long acquaintance with the language and life of the people" and stated that "much of the material is of fresh interest" partly because it made available texts "after the old tradition" of Kamakau and Fornander (326). Thrum's first book was reviewed positively in the *Journal of the Polynesian Society* (16 [1907]:105), but was otherwise noted only in *Dial, Book Review Digest*, and the *Independent* in New York.

Since they have been referenced, I want to clarify that Colum and Rice started publishing legends in the 1920s when Thrum's and Westervelt's careers were coming to an end; the circumstances of their production of translated legends were different, and examining them thus falls within the purview of another project.

35. Numerous other strategies that Thrum and Westervelt employ in their translations could be analyzed to show how Hawaiian narrative and rhetorical strategies are violated: abbreviation of names and episodes, elimination of repetition, biblical or mythological comparison, generalizing descriptions, and

more. I will refer in passing to some of these in Chapters 4 and 5 as contrasts to Nakuina and others, but because of my focus on place, I am most interested in "visual illustration."

36. "The people went up by the way of 'the big canoe of Kaliuwaa.' The face of the pig was turned upwards, and the people climbed up on the nipples of the pig, lest they be captured by the king" (Kame'eleihiwa, *He Mo'olelo Ka'ao o Kamapua'a* 35). Kame'eleihiwa glosses: "ka wa'a nui o Kaliuwa'a" as referring "to an upright section of the cliff, just to the left of the falls, which looks like a canoe hull."

37. The "early writer" presents only one version of the Kamapua'a and Pele encounter (a peaceful marriage) and ignores the many in which the struggle between the two is ongoing or their lives continue in separate domains.

38. Access to Kaliuwa'a Valley, now known mostly as Sacred Falls, has been closed down due to a deadly rockslide in the 1990s. Silva reports an 1861 disdainful comment by John Emerson on the offerings at Kaliuwa'a as an example of Hawaiian "uncivilized" behavior (*Aloha Betrayed* 58–59).

39. See Wright for *Legends of Ma-ui*; the anonymous review of *Hawaiian Legends of Volcanoes* in *Folklore* 28 (1917): 111–112; of *Hawaiian Folk Tales* in *Dial* (1907):1035.

40. Caspar Whitney devoted a chapter of *Hawaiian America* to "The Passing Hawaiian," explaining that Hawaiians had "excellent qualities" (67), but their "improvidence and indolence are by no means traits of modern development" (68) and would soon account for their disappearance.

41. The 1897 *Paradise of the Pacific* article "Trip Around Oahu" by Walter H. Baugh, illustrated by a Williams photo of "Kapena Falls," presents several paragraphs about the Pali:

We are off for a four days' drive from Honolulu in an easy phaeton, drawn by two high-headed steeds, and in two hours are standing speechless upon the precipice of the Pali. . . . The Pali, that ancient lofty peak, upon whose volcanic crags is written the story of the bloodiest conflict that crimsons the pages of Hawaiian history. . . . For the moment one stands where the greatest Hawaiian chieftain [Kamehameha I] stood in victorious defiant attitude, but one views with sealed lips other scenes than he in his insatiate blood carnage.

First the eye catches toward the orient the vast Pacific lying in peaceful composure a sea of inimitable beauty; just a little way out lies an island, a small earth and stone protrusion upon whose sloping side stand a few graceful but, [sic] lonely cocoanut [sic] trees; . . . . From the summit of the Pali one also looks down upon sweet homes nestled in bowers of palms and flowers, cocoanut [sic] groves and golden yellow fruits; the city of Honolulu with her harbor . . . , a spectacle to arouse and inspire the dullest brain. Just to the other side lies another picturesque panorama, little verdant valleys stretched down from mountain side in graceful undulations to dip their green swards in the foaming surf. (10.5:69)

42. "The Nuuanu Pali" by Chas. Warren Stoddard (with accompanying image "Nuuanu Pali," Photo Eng Co., NY; *Paradise of the Pacific* 1.8 [1888]:4) from which I just quoted continues:

Some of us went on wheels and some on saddles. Corkscrews and sandwiches were not forgotten; nor field-glasses, the most indispensable of all. . . .

Under the shadow of a great rock we camp, and then climb the little rise to the brow of the precipice, and look over into the other world. For a long time we are silent. . . . Microscopic pilgrims toil up the long stairway—fugitives from the mysterious land yonder; we are almost surprised to find that they are human, like ourselves. While some come back to us from the tour of this newly discovered country, others are going thither—passing down into the silence and the serenity of the enchanting distance, and becoming as ghosts in dream-land. The havenward [*sic*] vista is glorious. The harbor as seen from the Pali reminds one of the Vesuvian bay, and the golden-crested combers play like sheet lightning upon the surf.

What a pilgrimage it is, and who that has made it will ever forget it?

Chapter 4. Emma Nakuina's Hawai'i

1. See Niklaus R. Schweizer's *Turning Tide*, especially 301–9.

2. Thurston showed a cyclorama of the Kilauea volcano, where the Volcano House is located, as part of his promotion of the islands at three fairs and always with dancers (Davis, personal communication). Hawai'i had been promoted through photographic displays at other exhibitions, "including Vienna (1873), Philadelphia (1876), and Paris (1889)" (Davis, "Illustrated Books" 289). These exhibits along with King Kalākaua's 1874 trip to the United States were part of the Hawaiian king's own promotion of Hawai'i. Right at the time of annexation, Hawai'i was also represented at the 1898 Trans-Mississippi Exhibition in Omaha, Nebraska; Crampon reports that "more than 900,000 persons visited the Hawaii exhibit" (222).

3. Twain was in Hawai'i in 1866, lectured extensively about his experience afterwards, and wrote the "No alien land in all the world has any deep, strong charm for me but that one" as part of a speech made in New York (Hodge and Ferris 62).

I find it interesting that at least one of these early Hawaii Promotion Committee publications presented personal narratives in the form of letters to relatives and friends who could not join the fortunate tourist in her journey. Perhaps following in the steps of Isabella Bird's popular *Six Months in the Sandwich Islands*, the fictitious visitor and letter-writer is a female; eventually the journey takes a romantic turn as Miss Carson announces her engagement to a young East Coast visitor she has met in Hawai'i (*Letters from Hawaii*, 1905).

Among its activities, the Promotion Committee was also buying and distributing copies of *Paradise of the Pacific* to libraries and clubs in the United States. The Hawaii Promotion Committee changed its name to the Hawaii Tourist Bureau in 1919, the Hawaii Visitors Bureau in 1945, and the Hawaii Tourism Authority as attached to the Department of Business, Economic Development, and Tourism (DBEDT) in 1998. Numbers of visitors per year went from approximately 2,000 in 1892 to 5,000 in 1902; 6,200 in 1912; some 50,000 in 1952; some 500,000 in 1965; some 4,000,000 in the 1990s; and some 6,000,000 in 2003 (Crampon; Desmond; Hawaii Visitor Research Report for 2003 by DBEDT).

4. Armitage went on to publish with Henry Judd, *Ghost Dog and Other Hawaiian Legends* in 1944.

5. Shaffer argues that "tourism—both the production of the tourist landscape and the consumption of the tourist experience—was central to the development of a nascent national culture in the United States. Tourism not only reshaped and redefined the built and natural environment of the United States, transforming the symbolic value of American landscape, but also influenced the way people defined and identified themselves as Americans" (6).

6. In another publication of the Promotion Committee: "The rugged mountains, broken on their slopes by great gulches, picturesque by reason of the foliage, and the fantastic shapes of cliffs and ravines, offer many attractions to the pedestrian. For more reasons than one Hawaii is destined to become an American mountain climbers' paradise" (*Hawaii* 4).

7. "Intertwined with this celebration of nature were ideals of the primitive as represented by Native Americans and the ruins of Native American cultures" (Shaffer 189).

8. Shaffer suggests that in the United States "[F]olklore and folk customs were of particular interest because they revealed the diverse traditions that underlay regional and local cultures. . . . Folk material included local legends, tall tales, ghost stories, jokes, and animal tales. Indian legends and 'Negro lore' were of particular interest, and supplementary manuals instructed field workers on the fine points of interviewing former slaves and documenting landmarks associated with Indian lore" (215).

9. In 1887, *He Buke No Ke Ola Kino No Kamalii* was published, a translation of Dr. William DeWitt's work on children's health by Emma M. Beckley and Harriet Green under the superintendence of W. D. Alexander.

10. Emma attended Punahou at an early age (1852–1854) and then for high school (1861–1865). Maile Gresham ascertained dates in the *Catalogue of the Teachers and Pupils of Punahou School and Oahu College* (Honolulu, 1866) for Emma's attendance; and in the "Instructors and Staff from 1841" (Punahou Archives 7), a typed list compiled by Punahou staff from various sources (copied by Gresham in November 2004) for W. T. Brigham's teaching record.

Though taken in 1865, Charles Weed's photo (Figure 22) is labeled "Mrs. Emma Metcalf Beckley (Nakuina)," but she was married to her first husband (Beckley) in 1867, and to her second (Nakuina) in 1887.

11. Metcalf's obituary describes him as a man of "conspicuous" abilities who came to Hawai'i in 1842 as a civil engineer and was also superintendent of public works and marshall of the islands for a few years. "About the year 1855 he commenced the Kaupakuea Plantation on Hawaii, which he continued to carry on till his death. Few men have done more to develop the resources of this group than he, and few have more thoroughly studied its wants and necessities. He possessed a vigorous and powerful pen, and contributed some interesting articles on our agriculture and resources" (*Pacific Commercial Advertiser* [*PCA*], September 1, 1866, 3). He died in Oakland, California, and Emma was there with him.

12. George Beckley became commander of the first fort in Honolulu in 1816 and "introduced a Western uniform" to the Hawaiian soldiers, thus earning himself the name of *Humehume* (cover up); he also probably designed the first Hawaiian flag. His wife was the chiefess Ahia, whose family was close to Kamehameha and who accompanied him often on trips to China, South America, and Mexico, and dressed both in "Spanish" and Hawaiian style. About George and Frederick William Beckley, see *PCA*, September 11, 1875; *Friend*, February 1, 1881; *PCA*, January 8, 1881; *Hawaiian Gazette*, January 12, 1881, p. 3, col.1; and Lam's "Six Generations of Race Mixture in Hawaii."

13. "Honor Memory of M. K. Nakuina," *PCA*, August 7, 1911, 1, 4. For information about Moses K. Nakuina, see also *PCA*, August 4, 1911, 10; *Friend*, August 1906,12; "About Moses Kuaea Nakuina" in Mookini and Nākoa 141–42; Wood's "Hawaiian Texts in an American Context"; and *Moses Kuaea Nākuina: Hawaiian Novelist* by John Charlot (2005).

The first 1902 *mo'olelo* by Moses K. Nakuina was translated into English as *The Wind Gourd of La'amaomao* in 1990 by Esther T. Mookini and Sarah Nākoa thanks to the publishing efforts of Dennis Kawaharada of the Kalamakū Press and the support of John Charlot. In her introduction, Mookini explains: "Set on Hawai'i, Kaua'i, and Moloka'i, the story concerns the close relationship between the *aliʻi* [chief] and his *kahu iwikuamoʻo*, or personal attendant, and their responsibilities to each other and the people they ruled. . . . The story also illustrates the importance of ancestry in Hawaiian society in establishing status and access to privileges and power" (vii). The story contains wind chants that "attest to the intimate knowledge the Hawaiians had of their natural environment and to their belief in the power of words to control its elements" (ix). Mookini also reports that a gourd called "the wind gourd of Laʻamaomao" was given to King Kalākaua in 1883 and donated by Princess Kalanianaʻole to the Bishop Museum in 1923.

"Stories of the Menehunes: Hawaii the Original Home of the Brownies" was published by Thomas Thrum and Moses Nakuina both in the *Annual* ([1895]:112–17) and the *Paradise of the Pacific* (8.2 [1895]:17–18, 25). Several translations by Moses Nakuina also appear in the 1907 *Hawaiian Folk Tales*.

Moses Nakuina sued Thomas G. Thrum in November 1901 for "wickedly and maliciously intending to defame and injure him" when Thrum discharged him from the position of deputy registrar of conveyances. Nakuina detailed Thrum's allegations of how Nakuina had conspired against him, incited the other Native Hawaiian employees to disobey Thrum, and asserted that "race prejudice must be at the bottom of the business" of Nakuina's "conspiracy" and "deep hatred" for him. In 1903, the Circuit Court found for the plaintiff Nakuina in his case for slander, but he was awarded "damages in the sum of ten dollars" rather than the ten thousand he had requested (*Thrum, T. G., ad Nakuina* Case no. 5027). It is difficult to understand what this all means, but we must take into account that Hawaiians had to take an oath of loyalty to the territorial government and those who did not were fired. Moses Nakuina was dismissed in 1901 by Thrum, and his alleged accusations of Nakuina's disloyalty, disobedience, and racial prejudice suggest a larger political dimension when read in this context. Moses Nakuina—who would go on to become a member of the House and with Prince Jonah Kalanianaʻole Kūhiō of the Republican Party a fervid supporter of prohibition—defended himself, and successfully.

Some would say he was not one to rock the boat; but those were difficult and complicated times, and he did take great pride in his Hawaiian culture and knowledge. John Charlot's study of him as a Hawaiian novelist emphasizes Moses Nakuina's purpose "to correct the negative stereotypes of Hawaiians and their culture, a stereotype that would intensify through much of the twentieth century" (34)—and that would be a purpose I think Moses and Emma would have shared.

14. About Fred W. Beckley, see *Men of Hawaii* 3: 261, 263; *Honolulu Star-Bulletin*, December 21, 1943, 6; *Paradise of the Pacific* 35.2 (1922):3–14; 45.12 (1932):25–28; *PCA*, Dec. 22, 1943, 5, 13; April 12, 1925, 3; April 16, 1925, 3; and April 17, 1925, 5; and *Journal of Hawaiian and Pacific Folklore & Folklife Studies* 2, pt 2 (1991), sec. A. There is much more research to be done about Fred Beckley.

15. From 1870 to 1907, the position of commissioner of private ways and water rights in Hawaiʻi was considered a judicial one since it involved hearings and determinations. See "The Courts of Hawaii" by Jno. T. Morgan and W. F. Frear (*Paradise of the Pacific* 12.5 [1899]:69–70) and Wells A. Hutchins's *The Hawaiian System of Water Rights* report (Honolulu, 1946). In the 1907 *Picturesque Hawaii*, we read "Mrs. Nakuina holds a unique position in the Territorial government. She is a water commissioner and sits as a judge to decide cases where the rights are in litigation, and is considered an able and most just official, her decisions seldom, if ever, being set aside." ("Native Chiefs of Honolulu" 3).

16. "Brigham Bellows" and an editorial strongly criticizing Brigham's statements appeared in F. J. Testa's *Independent* on April 13, 1897. For letters by W. T. Brigham and various Bishop Museum trustees, including Charles Reed Bishop, I am relying on letters in the Institutional Records and the Brigham papers at the Bishop Museum Archives, specifically: BPBM Letters in BK I, 1894–1897, 204, 223; BPBM Letters in BK II, 1897–1898, 10; MS SC Brigham, box 3.7 and 3.24.

17. *PCA,* June 8, 1907, 4.

18. See Emma Nakuina's profile in Peterson's *Notable Women of Hawaii.* Other relevant information is to be found in "Native Chiefs of Honolulu" (*Picturesque Honolulu,* 1907); "Emma Metcalf Nakuina" in *Women of Hawaii* (1938); Clarice B. Taylor, "Caretaker Emma Metcalf Nakuina" in the series "Tales About Hawaii," *Honolulu Star-Bulletin,* May 17, 1961; Roger G. Rose, *Symbols of Sovereignty. Feather Girdles of Tahiti and Hawaii,* especially 34–37, and 40–42; and *A Museum to Instruct and Delight,* 4–5, 66–67; Donald D. Johnson, "Notes on the History of the Hawaiian Historical Society," *Hawaiian Journal of History* 16 (1982); Janice Otaguro, "Unsung Heroines: Five Hawaiian Women Who Made History, But Not Necessarily the History Books," *Honolulu* (March 1990), especially 51; Victoria Nālani Kneubuhl, "Emma Metcalf Beckley Nakuina Hawai'i's First Woman Judge"; and Bacchilega, "Emma Nakuina: A Remarkable Woman of Hawai'i." Charlot mentions Moses marrying "his second cousin, the prominent and redoubtable Emma Metcalf Beckley" and notices among her accomplishments that "she was an important writer on Hawaiian history and traditions–which she advocated teaching in the schools" (*Nākuina* 4, 38–39, n. 13)

I also consulted obituaries in *Ke Alakai o Hawaii* ("Hala ia kamaaina kahiko o Honolulu nei," May 2, 1929); *Ka Hoku o Hawaii* ("Ua Make Mrs. E. B. Nakuina," April 30, 1929); *Honolulu Advertiser* ("Death Takes First Hawaii Woman Judge," April 28, 1929); and *Honolulu Star-Bulletin* ("End Comes to Mrs. Nakuina," April 27, 1929). The sentences I quote were translated by Noelani Arista and Sahoa Fukushima.

19. She co-translated a medical book into Hawaiian, and yet I have not found any article or *mo'olelo* attributed to her in the Hawaiian language. This could be because most contributors to the Hawaiian-language newspapers were men, or because women contributors did not sign as such; but perhaps she did not publish in the Hawaiian language, and if so why not? I cannot say, except that her father was a strong influence on her, she did have to use English in her legal profession, had the English-language skills to write effectively, and was proud of her ability to do so.

In the final stage of this book's production, Noenoe Silva's research on Hawaiian-language newspapers confirmed what we had suspected: Emma Nakuina published one piece using her Hawaiian name Kaili, "Hiiaka: A Hawaiian Legend by a Hawaiian Native" (*PCA,* 1883), an unusually long version in English of the Pele, Hi'iaka, and Lohi'au story that is quite different from the one included in her 1904 book.

20. In a progressive move to make Hawaiian *mo'olelo* more accessible to English-language readers in the 1990s, Dennis Kawaharada edited *Nanaue the Shark Man and Other Hawaiian Shark Stories [by] Emma M. Nakuina and Others,* but no further information about her was offered, and her name remained folded into an unindividuated tradition.

21. Copies of the book in Hamilton Library have no front cover. The gold embossing probably enhanced the value of the cover as souvenir as of itself.

22. "The Royal Arms of Hawaii, to be Presented in Features of Program for Kauikeaouli Centenary," by Mrs. Emma Nakuina, *PCA*, March 15, 1914, 1. This piece was reprinted verbatim and with no acknowledgment in "Hawaii's Royal Coat-of-Arms by Albert Pierce Taylor, Librarian, Archives of Hawaii" in Thrum's *Annual* (1927):68–73. Earlier descriptions had appeared in the *Annual*, and both Nakuina and Taylor quote an 1845 letter. Taylor states: "Upon the dethronement of Queen Liliuokalani in 1893, the royal coat-of-arms with all things royal, was no longer used" (73).

23. When King Kalākaua requested some changes in the royal standard, "the writer, with the king's chamberlain, the late Col. Charles Judd, were commissioned to take one of the new standards to Kona to be unfurled on Kaiulani's twelfth birthday, which was celebrated at Kaawaloa, in Kona, with great pomp and a revival of old ceremonies. By an oversight, the standard of the mother was taken, instead of that of the princess, and unfurled" *PCA*, April 15, 1914.

24. This portrait may echo that of King David Kalākaua in the 1888 *Legends and Myths of Hawaii*, a display that in the context of his Hawai'i for Hawaiians campaign "testified to the 'civility' of his people" and was "politically expedient" (Maxwell 196 and 197). Of course, featuring the author's picture was and is a widespread design and marketing strategy.

25. Princess Ruth Ke'elikōlani and Queen Lili'uokalani had posed with featherwork—capes and *kāhili*—as symbols of their royal status.
    Clasping Emma Nakuina's neck and half hidden by the lei, there may also be a *niho palaoa*, a carved whale tooth worn by high chiefs, but it is hard to be sure.

26. According to Anne Maxwell in her excellent study *Colonial Photography & Exhibitions*, studio portraits as a genre were preferred by colonized peoples who had an interest in being photographed around 1900. Studio portraits were seen as a "mechanism by which to recover pride and dignity"; by choosing clothing, colonized subjects exercise some "semblance of control." King Kalākaua and his family made a strategic use of such portraits, even in the 1888 *Legends* book.

27. The four river scenes grouped in a collage accompanying the "Legend of Kaliuwaa" are the exception (49); there is no caption, and in the list of illustrations they are identified as "Amateur Shots" of "Scenes in Hawaii."

28. *Hawaii: Its People, Their Legends* 17; 32–33, C. H. Merriam and A. Gartley; 53, "The Coast of Waianae," Honolulu Photo Supply Co. This matching is not always at work: the Kauai "Canyon of the Makaweli" accompanies the Mānoa-based "Valley of the Rainbows" story (43), but so do several images of this O'ahu valley.

29. Reading at the Korean Studies Center, University of Hawai'i at Mānoa, January 30, 2003. This kind of reorientation and rhetoric will be discussed further in Chapter 5.

30. This passage is from the third edition of the *Hawaii, a Primer*, but the paragraph was widely duplicated with only minor variation in other editions and promotional brochures.

31. She explicitly positions herself against Fornander's theory here. See K. R. Howe's *The Quest for Origins: Who First Discovered and Settled New Zealand and the Pacific Islands?* (Honolulu: University of Hawai'i Press, 2003) for a readable overview of old and new theories.

32. See Desmond 49–50 for a discussion of this "educational" mode, for instance in *Pictorial History of America's New Possessions*, edited by Murat Halstead in 1899: "Publications like *Our Islands and Their People* helped situate Hawai'i as a subjected colony in public discourse and focused attention on Hawaiian

women as beautiful, desirable natives, precisely the soft primitivism that would come to dominate later tourist advertisements" (50). I am indebted to Nadia Inserra for pointing out in class the discontinuity between Nakuina's portrayal of strong Hawaiians and the *legendary Hawai'i* trope of soft primitivism.

By foregrounding Nakuina's focus on Hawaiian warriors, I do not mean to suggest that Emma Nakuina favored violence. She is reported in *Paradise of the Pacific*, just before annexation took place, as addressing the congregation at Kaumakapili Church with a list of "blessings of the past year": no epidemics, no "horrors of starvation," no floods, and no "deadly conflict." "Peace has smiled upon us while we have the knowledge that in Cuba, that land now torn by internal dissension in the attempts of the people to free themselves from the oppressive yoke of a cruel mother country, families have been rent asunder and relative has pitted himself against relative, neighbor against neighbor and friend against friend" (11.2[1898]:20).

33. See Samuel M. Kamakau's *Ruling Chiefs*, especially 133–34, 136–40. The English-language translation of the prophecy there is: "Take a deep breath and give your body to the sea; the land is the sea's" and Kamakau's commentary (again in translation) reads: "The words . . . contain an inner meaning which relates not alone to the conquests of Ka-hekili and Kamehameha as the chiefs who came by the way of the sea and took the island of Oahu, but also to the events of these days [1867] in which we are now living" (140). In Mary Kawena Pukui's *'Ōlelo No'eau* a slightly different version "E nui ke aho, e ku'u keiki, a moe i ke kai, no ke kai la ho'i ka 'āina" (no. 363) is translated as "Take a deep breath, my son, and lay yourself in the sea, for then the land shall belong to the sea" (44).

34. In *Storied Landscapes*, Dennis Kawaharada reads three of Emma Nakuina's tales—"Ka'ōpulupulu," "Punahou," and Kahalaopuna"—as expressions of "grim fatalism" (29). In particular, about "the fatalistic ending" of her versions of "Kahalaopuna," he writes that it "suggests a parallel to the loss of Hawaiian traditions and the overthrow of Hawaiian sovereignty by American colonizers at the end of the 19th century" (28). While I find the chapter "'Aumākua of Kona, O'ahu," in which this interpretation is embedded, most insightful in drawing connections among places, beliefs, and stories, I am not sure that her looking to future changes that would destabilize the United States' power in Hawai'i can be read only as "grim fatalism." I agree that political commentary is integral to Emma Nakuina's writing and that she protests the American annexation, but I do not see clear evidence of her expressing no hope.

35. There is another instance in which Emma Nakuina presents personal experience, the only one where she uses the first person. Having praised Hawaiians as builders of canoes and voyagers, she writes: "I remember a pair of double canoes on my father's plantation that were over eighty feet in length. One had been broken in a storm through the unskillful handling of a foreigner. The unbroken mate was used singly, as a lighter to carry sugar from the plantation to schooners or steamers" (13). Her Harvard-educated father owned a sugar plantation, and that too is part of her story. But her memory of the canoes points to how Hawaiian knowledge inflected that experience.

36. The Līloa stones were later taken to the Bishop Museum where they resided into the 1990s. Four British expeditions were organized for the 1874 "Transit of Venus," and one of the stations was in Honolulu, near princess Ruth's residence. For information about the "Transit of Venus," see Chauvin's article in the *Hawaiian Journal of History* (1993).

37. F. J. Testa was the editor of *Ka Makaainana*, an anti-annexation Hawaiian-language newspaper, and of *Buke Mele Lahui* (1895), which gathered nationalist and *aloha 'āina* songs in support of the queen (Silva, *Aloha Betrayed*).

38. The handwritten annotated and itemized list of artifacts and geological specimens at the Hawaiian National Museum of which Emma Nakuina was curator from 1882 to 1887 is available at the Bishop Museum Archives (MS. HI.H.112).

Chapter 5. Stories in Place

1. "Because translation traffics in the foreign, in the introduction of linguistic and cultural differences, it is equally capable of crossing or reinforcing the boundaries between domestic audiences and the hierarchies within which they are positioned" (Venuti, "Translation, Community, Utopia" 477). Venuti is referring here to sociocultural hierarchies that make any domestic readership a heterogeneous community. My reference to "crossing or reinforcing" boundaries is not specific to any one heterogeneous community, but I find Venuti's language suggestive.

2. Sections of this chapter are drawn from "*The Arabian Nights* in a Nineteenth-Century Hawaiian Newspaper: Reflections on the Politics of Translation," an essay Noelani Arista and I co-authored (*Fabula* 2004); and from my "Gli spettri e la politica dei luoghi alle Hawai'i" ("Specters and the Politics of Place in Hawai'i") that appeared in the Italian international journal of North American Studies, *ÁCOMA*. In late 2005, Arista, Sahoa Fukushima, and I collaborated on a revised version of the *Fabula* essay for a collection edited by Ulrich Marzolph that is forthcoming with Wayne State University Press.

3. During that same time, fostered by Hawai'i's immigration and sugar plantation economy, "Pidgin" or Hawai'i Creole English became the more common alternative to the English language, allowing Hawaiians, Japanese, Chinese, Portuguese, and Filipinos to communicate in noninstitutional settings. As Ku'ualoha Ho'omanawanui remarks: "Most Hawaiians in the first half of the twentieth century turned away from their language and social customs to blend into the 'melting pot' propaganda" of the time ("Ka Ola Hoa" 165). It is only after statehood that Hawaiian cultural and political activism resurfaced and has brought about, especially since the 1970s, a revival of the Hawaiian language, hula, music, navigation, education (Hawaiian immersion and charter schools), religion, and a sovereignty movement.

4. See Esther K. Mookini's pioneering *The Hawaiian Newspapers* (1974), Rubellite Kawena Johnson's *Kūkini 'Aha'ilono* (1976), Helen Chapin's *Shaping History: The Role of Newspapers in Hawai'i* (1996), M. Puakea Nogelmeier's dissertation "Mai Pa'a i ka Leo: Historical Voice in Hawaiian Primary Materials" (2003), and Noenoe Silva's *Aloha Betrayed* (2004). Other scholars such as Arista, Ho'omanawanui, and Kame'eleihiwa have been making extensive use of the Hawaiian-language newspapers.

The first Hawaiian-language newspapers were *Ka Lama Hawaii* (founded by Lorrin Andrews for the Lahainaluna Seminary) and *Ke Kumu Hawaii* (Mookini iv–v, 22, 24–25). From 1834 to 1861, newspapers were issued by Protestant or Catholic institutions or by the Hawaiian government. The year 1861 marked the advent in the public sphere of two "new" kinds of newspapers. One, *Ka Hoku o ka Pakipika* (The Star of the Pacific), was the first newspaper to be published by a Native Hawaiian (Mookini vi–vii; Silva, *Aloha Betrayed* for further discussion).

The other, *Ka Nupepa Kuokoa* (The Independent), was issued by the printer, Henry Martyn Whitney; the son of a missionary, he started the English-language newspaper that under various titles has been running in Honolulu since 1856 and explicitly wanted to establish a "free press" in Hawai'i. (He also published the first tourist guide to the islands in 1875.) See also Maenette K. P. Benham and Ronald H. Heck's *Culture and Educational Policy in Hawai'i: The Silencing of Native Voices* (1998) for a "critical account of two centuries of education in Hawai'i" (P. Lyons, " 'They Will Eat Us Up': Remembering Hawai'i").

Quoted and summarized information in text comes from: Lucas 2; Benham and Heck 72; Nogelmeier 119–20; Lucas 2–8 for the "English-only" campaign; Mookini ix, x.

5. In 1997 the University of Hawai'i Hamilton Library obtained funding to make "selected, heavily used Hawaiian language newspapers available to students throughout the state of Hawaii who have access to the World Wide Web. . . . Alu Like and Bishop Museum are now continuing the newspaper scanning project on the Hawaiian Nupepa Collection web site" (http://libweb.hawai-i.edu/digicoll/newspapers.htm). With these digital images, the Ulukau: Hawaiian Electronic Library (http://nupepa.org) also hosts the more recent, and for research purposes revolutionary, *Ho'olaupa'i* creation of searchable text files extracted from those images.

6. And yet, while clearly documented, the importance of Hawaiian-language newspapers has been obscured by the "discourse of sufficiency" that shaped much research on Hawai'i (Nogelmeier 2–3, 30, 39, 88, 153–54).

7. In her chapter on "Transformations in Language and Power," Elizabeth Buck provides a persuasive overview of how in the nineteenth century "the radical shift from orality to literacy [and] the displacement of Hawaiian by English as the dominant language of discourse . . . altered basic cognitive processes and . . . shaped social consciousness" (*Paradise Remade* 121). In "Disorientation: Unwritable Knowledge," Houston Wood takes a step further and reads Tejaswini Niranjana's *Siting Translation: History, Post-Structuralism, and the Colonial Conquest* as raising "the warning that writing, even when undertaken by Natives, often may further legitimize the colonizer's (literate) traditions at the expense of the Native (oral) alternative" (*Displacing Natives* 57). While I recognize the problem—and this issue has a long tradition of debate in folklore studies, feminist studies, and postcolonial studies—I do not share a position that insists on such a radical or persistent dichotomy between the oral and the written. Nogelmeier presents strong evidence of how the content and form of writings in Hawaiian-language newspapers reflected or inscribed orality (137, 150–53). In an interview with the *Honolulu Weekly* (April 27–May 3, 2005) occasioned by the publication of the third issue of the journal *'Ōiwi: A Native Hawaiian Journal*, editor Ku'ualoha Ho'omanawanui refers to Hawaiians' nineteenth-century "rich literary tradition" as thriving before 1896.

8. The installments of "An Arabian Tale about the Fisherman! The source of Good Fortune" ran from May 1 to July 3, 1875. The first installment of *He Kaao Arabia*—a section of the frame tale—had appeared in that same newspaper on September 26, 1874; two more stories or cycles followed: "Keiki Alii Bedera o Peresia," which appeared in four installments from October 3 to October 24, and the seven "Huakai Holomoku a Sinibada Ka Luina," which the *Kuokoa* ran from October 31 to December 12, 1874 in six installments. For a fuller discussion of these texts, see "*The Arabian Nights* in a Nineteenth-Century Hawaiian Newspaper: Reflections on the Politics of Translation" in *Fabula* (2004). The

Hawaiian-language translation in the *Kuokoa* is from Edward William Lane's 1839–1841 English-language translation of *Alf Layla wa Layla* (The Arabian Nights), that more or less follows the Bulaq edition and was published as *The Thousand and One Nights, Commonly Called in England, The Arabian Nights' Entertainments.*

In addition to the Hawaiian-language texts discussed in that article, there are several other *Arabian Nights* translations in earlier newspapers (*Ka Hoku o ka Pakipika*, starting in 1861 and *Ke Au Okoa* in 1865). It is quite likely that more *Arabian Nights* tales were translated and published in Hawaiian.

9. Arista continues: "Expectations that Arabic-speaking audiences would have had about the roles of women in society, the duties of a King, and what constituted correct and incorrect behavior towards others in society differed radically from what Hawaiian audiences learned from *mo'olelo* (stories). Characters and expectations in the nineteenth-century English-language *Arabian Nights* also differed from Hawaiian *mo'olelo* and cultural practices" (in Bacchilega and Arista 191).

10. "We say this *not* to undermine the importance of Orientalism as a framework for reading *The Arabian Nights* in its many translations; rather the Hawaiian example indirectly confirms the reading of *The Arabian Nights* as a Western fantasy of the 'Orient,' and thereby can constitute an interesting variation within that interpretive narrative" (in Bacchilega and Arista 204).

11. About one of the *Arabian Nights'* translations, Arista writes: "In similar ways, this story and its appended moral are utilized to keep Hawaiians in check and in their place, satisfied with their lot in life as the inheritors of foreign and much greater traditions, religious beliefs, and ways of living" (in Bacchilega and Arista 201).

12. Nogelmeier points out that the same juxtaposition of older oral forms with Western written forms (rather than their replacement by Western forms) is also noted by Jane McCrae in Maori newspapers (141; referring to "'E manu, tena koe!' 'O bird, greetings to you': The Oral Tradition in Newspaper Writing" 44-46)

13. *PCA* (December 11, 1862) as cited in Forbes *Hawaiian National Bibliography* 3: 348.

14. Hale'ole's book was reprinted in a revised edition in 1888, Beckwith informs us (Hale'ole/Beckwith 341). Beckwith's translation and introduction are reprinted in a bilingual book published in 1997 where Malcolm Chun provides some biographical information about Hale'ole.

I am citing from Beckwith's 1919 edition. In the 1919 Annual Report of the Smithsonian Institute, the entire text—which includes Beckwith's introduction and notes—is titled "The Hawaiian Romance of Laieikawai" (285), but the title page for Hale'ole's text is then given as "Laie I Ka Wai: A Hawaiian Romance Translated from the Hawaiian Text of S. N. Haleole" (341).

While I cite the title as *Laieikawai*, I have used current orthography to identify characters' names, including Lā'ieikawai.

15. Green's translation of Hale'ole' Foreword continues: "We have previously had books of instruction on many subjects and also those enlightening us to the right and the wrong; but this is the first book printed for us Hawaiians in story form" (342).

Beckwith refers to this short text as "Hale'ole's foreword" (342), but Sahoa Fukushima has pointed out to me that, echoing the information on the cover page of *Ke Kaao o Laieikawai* "Paiia e Henry M. Whitney," "ka mea nana i pai keia buke" in the Foreword points more to the printer and publisher than to the "editor" of the book; if this is the case, Whitney when writing in Hawaiian was clearly addressing what he believed Hawaiian readers wanted to read. Whether the Foreword was Haleʻole's or Whitney's, two different agendas were at work in the Hawaiian-language presentation of the *Laieikawai* as newspaper series and book.

16. Martha Beckwith, whose translation and study of *Laieikawai* was published in 1919 from her 1917 dissertation, wrote to this effect: "The romance of *Laieikawai* remains the sole piece of Hawaiian imaginative writing to reach book form" (294). While like me Beckwith recognizes Haleʻole's authorship, she stresses its uniqueness as a work of the imagination and also notes its "dullness" (295). In *Native Planters*, "the long and complicated story of Laʻie-i-ka-wai," we are told, "is not an old native legend" (461).

17. I am using "tale of magic" and "tale of wonder" interchangeably to refer to what is more commonly called "fairy tale." In *Laieikawai*, other tale-of-magic elements are dreams; specific motifs, such as the taking away of a woman's clothing while she is bathing so as to hold power over her (which is also found in other Polynesian narratives); doubling (the twins); the journey; and of course magic in an explicitly fictional mode.

18. As Jack Zipes's work in general shows, class matters in Western fairy tales as well, of course, and in particular to the construction of a "good" woman. I agree, but Christian virtue in most cases masks those dynamics and functions as an equalizer. Rapunzel is no princess, but her seclusion in the tower is directly tied to sexual taboo.

19. Briar Rose and Snow White also function symbolically as names to connect these heroines with the natural world, but they seem to symbolize women's abstract nature more than a specific heroine's social status as marked within the natural world as we find in *Laieikawai*.

20. It is not uncommon to find natural helpers in European tales of magic, but those relations are fleeting and more strictly functional.

21. Kawaharada makes the point that "While traditional Hawaiian stories like *Laieikawai* . . . contain motifs similar to those found in European romance (love, lust, deceit, jealousy, betrayal, revenge, justice, and so on), they offer the added benefit of teaching local readers about the place in which they live" ("Alive in Story" 64 and 66). I agree, and my observations seek to flesh out this assertion.

22. John Charlot discusses S. N. Haleʻole's *Laieikawai*, Moses Manu's works, and Moses Kauea Nākuina's two *moʻolelo* as "novels" in the "well developed Hawaiian form of the nineteenth-century novel" (*Nākuina* 34).

23. Not only did Glen Grant (1947–2003) collect and publish a number of volumes of Hawaiʻi's "ghost" and "chicken skin" stories; he also ran what he described as "a small private experiment in cultural tourism called: Honolulu Time Walks" (*Obake Files* xii) as well as weekly radio shows, *Chicken Skin: The Radio Show* and *The Grant Files*. A storyteller in various media, Grant had a doctorate in American Studies and was an educational specialist at Kapiʻolani Community College working with senior citizens for many years. His stories were retold in Standard American English—even though he acknowledged that most of them were told to him in Pidgin or Hawaiʻi Creole English—and were explicitly or implicitly fictionalized for dramatic effect.

24. These kinds of stories have been labeled "urban legends," "contemporary legends," "modern horror myths," and "urban myths." I opt for "contemporary legend" partly because its study has more consistently paid attention to

the supernatural. Scholarship on the contemporary legend is vast, with Gillian Bennett, Jan H. Brunvand, Linda Dégh, Gary Alan Fine, W. F. H. Nicolaisen, and Paul Smith as major proponents since the 1970s of different views of the genre. Recent and valuable perspectives in North America include studies by Bill Ellis, Diane E. Goldstein, Sylvia Grider, Janet Langlois, Cathy Lynn Preston, Elizabeth Tucker, and Patricia A. Turner. For a scholarly overview, see the 1996 *Contemporary Legend*, Linda Dégh's *Legend and Belief* (2001), and the 2005 special issue of the *Journal of American Folklore*. The *Contemporary Legend* journal features a range of international contributions to the field. For stories in North America, see Brunvand's many books—including his *Encyclopedia of Urban Legends*—and the http://www.snopes.com site. There are similar international collections and Web sites.

25. See H. Arlo Nimmo's "Pele, Ancient Goddess of Contemporary Hawaii" for a more expanded reading of Pele narratives in English.

26. A typical bought lunch in contemporary Hawai'i, a mixed plate will include rice, Hawaiian, Japanese, or other "ethnic" foods, vegetables, and macaroni salad.

27. See "Brief Stories of Ghosts and Cunning," a section in *Fornander Collection of Hawaiian Antiquities and Folk-Lore*, vol. 5, pt. II, 418-35.

28. See Pukui and Elbert 194, 36, 32, 186; for older definitions see Lorrin Andrews' *Dictionary*. These concepts are discussed in Pukui, Haertig and Lee *Nānā I Ke Kumu (Look to the Source)* and in Martha Beckwith's *Hawaiian Mythology*.

29. What Grant does also dismisses other cultural differences and spiritual traditions, for instance between Japanese and Filipinos. See also *Ghosts and the Japanese. Cultural Experience in Japanese Death Legends* (1994). Countering a simplified multiculturalism, Diane Goldstein, Patricia Turner, Sylvia Grider, Véronique Campion-Vincent, and Ingo Schneider have produced important studies of contemporary legends mapping out race and culture relations in terms of contestation. My own argument foregrounds the problematic status of Hawaiian belief in Grant's exposition because here I am interested not in how different groups and individuals will interpret these tales, but in taking into account the epistemological framework of Hawai'i's Native people when we approach these stories.

30. "All the stories had one thing in common: they produced a frisson of excitement, that little tingle up and down your spine, or the raised hair on the nape of your neck, that delicious shiver people in Hawai̗i call chicken skin" (Carroll, *Chicken Skin: True Spooky Stories of Hawai̗i* ix). The generic "Chicken Skin" was in the vernacular well before Grant and Carroll used it; however, both Carroll and Bess Press faced a lawsuit because of Grant's "trademark infringement" claim.

31. Rick Carroll offers a different understanding of generic distinctions, but it too ignores historical dynamics and different epistemologies in Hawai'i: "The authors [tellers?], for the most part, turned out to be skeptics who nevertheless had encountered situations in Hawaii they still can't explain. That, alone, is what makes this collection unique and fascinating to me. These aren't old ghost stories or campfire tales or even myths and legends; these are true stories of extraordinary phenomena experienced by ordinary disbelievers" (Carroll, *Chicken Skin: True Spooky Stories* xii).

32. Haluålani's ethnographic approach to "touring the native" (159-169 especially) presents information about what she calls the "Hawaiian spectral" that counters Grant's. By placing stories told by Hawaiian tour guides within

"the larger unseen production context constituting tourism" (141), she shows how their presentation to tourists of the Hawaiian spirits demands "cultural respect" and suggests "that an antagonistic, uncertain, and yet authentic Hawaiian spirit is kept alive" (167). Halualani then refers to "highly priced ghost tours" and top-seller "mainstream books about Hawaiian ghost stories" that have "commodified and politically defused" the Hawaiian spectral's "critical potential to rupture sweeping tourist discourses" (169).

33. Grant writes: "Famed for its Halloweenish setting that invariably creates shrieks of terror just by the very mention of its name, Morgan's Corner consists actually of two sites—one on the Nu'uanu and the other on the Kailua side of the Old Pali Road" (*Chicken Skin Tales* 172). I am focusing on the location on the Nu'uanu side of the cliff.

34. Jan Brunvand (285) refers to Navajo narratives that were studied by Peggy E. Alford, Margaret K. Brady, and Keith and Kathryn Cunningham. While Alford's essay focuses on cross-cultural adaptations in a "cultural border" region, John Ashton's "Ecotypes, Etiology and Contemporary Legend: The 'Webber' Cycle in Western Newfoundland" takes a "regional perspective on the study of contemporary legend" (49) that builds on "tradition ecology" in folklore studies.

Works Cited

Abrams, M. H. "Structure and Style in the Greater Romantic Lyric." In *From Sensibility to Romanticism: Essays Presented to Frederick A. Pottie*, ed. Frederick W. Hilles and Harold Bloom. Oxford: Oxford University Press, 1965. 527–60.

Adams, Linda Kinsey. "Folk Narrative." In *The Emergence of Folklore in Everyday Life: A Fieldguide and Sourcebook*, ed. George H. Schoemaker. Bloomington, Ind.: Trickster Press, 1990. 23–35.

Alford, Peggy E. "Anglo-American Perceptions of Navajo Skinwalker Legends." *Contemporary Legend* 2 (1992): 119–36.

Andrews, Lew. "'Fine Island Views': The Photography of Alonzo Gartley." In *Photography in Hawai'i*. Special issue of *History of Photography*, ed. Lynn Ann Davis. 25, 3 (Autumn 2001): 219–39.

Andrews, Lorrin. *A Dictionary of the Hawaiian Language*. With an introduction to the new edition by Noenoe K. Silva and Albert J. Schütz. Waipahu: Island Heritage Publishing, 2003.

The Annotated Brothers Grimm. Edited with a preface and notes and translated by Maria Tatar. New York: W.W. Norton, 2004.

Appadurai, Arjun. *Modernity at Large: Cultural Dimensions of Globalization*. Minneapolis: University of Minnesota Press, 1996.

Arinaga, Esther. "Harriet Bouslog: Lawyer, Risk Taker, and Champion of the Underdog." In *Biography Hawai'i: Five Lives: A Series of Public Remembrances*. Honolulu: Center for Biographical Research, 2003. 1–3.

Armitage, George T. "Capitalizing Hawaii's Climate." *Hawaiian Annual* (1923): 76–82.

Armitage, George T. and Henry Judd. *Ghost Dog and Other Hawaiian Legends*. Honolulu: Advertiser Publishing, 1944.

Ashton, John. "Ecotypes, Etiology and Contemporary Legend: The 'Webber' Cycle in Western Newfoundland." *Contemporary Legend* n.s. 4 (2001): 48–60.

Bacchilega, Cristina. "Emma Nakuina: A Remarkable Woman of Hawai'i." In *Original Plays & Classic Humanities: A Special Series for Kumu Kahua Theatre (2003–2004 Season)* devoted to Victoria Nalani Kneubuhl's *Fanny and Belle*. March 2004.

———. "Gli spettri e la politica dei luoghi alle Hawai'i." *ÀCOMA* (International Journal of North-American Studies, Milan). Special issue on Hawai'i, ed. Donatella Izzo and Incoronata Inserra. 29–30 (Spring/Fall 2004; pub. in Spring 2005): 106–20.

———. "Hawai'i's Storied Places: Anne Kapulani Landgraf's Re-Vision of Landscape and Illustration." In *Photography in Hawai'i*, Special issue of *History of Photography*, ed. Lynn Ann Davis, 25, 3 (2001): 240–51.

Bacchilega, Cristina and Noelani Arista. "*The Arabian Nights* in a Nineteenth-Century Hawaiian Newspaper: Reflections on the Politics of Translation." *Fabula*. Special issue on *Arabian Nights*. 45, 3/4 (2004): 189–206.

Bal, Mieke. "Figuration." *PMLA* 119, 5 (2004): 1289–92.

————. *Narratology: Introduction to the Theory of Narrative.* 2nd ed. Toronto: University of Toronto Press, 1997.

————. *Travelling Concepts in the Humanities: A Rough Guide.* Toronto: University of Toronto Press, 2002.

Bassnett-McGuire, Susan. *Translation Studies.* London: Methuen, 1980.

Bassnett-McGuire, Susan and André Lefevere, eds. *Constructing Cultures: Essays on Literary Translation.* Philadelphia: Multilingual Matters, 1998.

Bassnett-McGuire, Susan and Harish Trivedi, eds. *Post-Colonial Translation: Theory and Practice.* London: Routledge, 1998.

Bauman, Richard. "Conceptions of Folklore in the Development of Literary Semiotics." *Semiotica* 39, 1/2 (1982): 1–20.

————. "Folklore." In *Folklore, Cultural Performances, and Popular Entertainments. A Communications-Centered Handbook,* ed. Richard Bauman. New York: Oxford University Press, 1992. 29–40.

Bauman, Richard and Charles Briggs. "Poetics and Performance as Critical Perspectives on Language and Social Life." *Annual Review of Anthropology* 19 (1990): 59–88.

————. *Voices of Modernity: Language Ideologies and the Politics of Inequality.* New York: Cambridge University Press, 2003.

Beckley, Fred W. "Voice Culture in Ancient Hawaii." *Paradise of the Pacific,* December 1932, 25–28.

Beckwith, Martha Warren. *Hawaiian Mythology.* 1940. Honolulu: University of Hawai'i Press, 1970.

————. "Introduction." In *The Hawaiian Romance of Laieikawai Translated from the Hawaiian Text of S. N. Haleole, with Introduction and Translation by Martha W. Beckwith.* Annual Report of the Smithsonian Institution 33 (for 1911–1912), 293–340. Washington, D.C.: Bureau of American Ethnology, 1919. Reprinted in *Ka Mo'olelo O Lā'ieikawai, with Introduction and Translation by Martha Warren Beckwith, and Biographical Information by Malcolm Naea Chun.* Honolulu: First People's Production, 1997.

————. "Review." *Journal of American Folklore* 38 (1925): 325–27.

Bendix, Regina. "Capitalizing on Memories Past, Present, and Future. Observations on the Intertwining of Tourism and Narration." *Anthropological Theory* 2, 4 (2002): 469–87.

————. *In Search of Authenticity. The Formation of Folklore Studies.* Madison: University of Wisconsin Press, 1997.

————. "Tourism and Cultural Displays: Inventing Traditions for Whom?" *Journal of American Folklore* 102 (April–June 1989): 131–46.

Bennett, Gillian and Paul Smith, eds. *Contemporary Legend: A Reader.* New Perspectives in Folklore, 4. New York: Garland, 1996.

Bermingham, Ann. *Landscape and Ideology: The English Rustic Tradition 1740–1860.* Berkeley: University of California Press, 1986.

Biography Hawai'i. Documentaries on Maiki Aiu Lake; Harriet Bouslog; Princess Ruth Ke'elikōlani; and Koji Ariyoshi. Directed by Joy Chong-Stannard. Script by Victoria Nalani Kneubuhl. Series Scholar Craig Howes. Center for Biographical Research / PBS Hawaii / Center for Labor Education and Research. 2002–2005.

Bishop, Sereno E. *Beauty Spots: Hawaii.* Variant title: *Scenery in Hawaii.* Honolulu: Hawaii Promotion Committee, 1903.

Brady, Margaret K. *"Some Kind of Power": Navajo Children's Skinwalker Narratives.* Salt Lake City: University of Utah Press, 1984.

Briggs, Charles L. "The Politics of Discursive Authority in Research on the 'Invention of Tradition.'" *Cultural Anthropology* 11, 4 (1996): 435–69.

"Brigham Bellows: Nauseating Rubbish from the Ethnologist." *Independent*, April 13, 1897, 3.

Brunvand, Jan Harold. *Encyclopedia of Urban Legends*. New York: W.W. Norton, 2002.

Buck, Elizabeth. *Paradise Remade: The Politics of Culture and History in Hawai'i*. Philadelphia: Temple University Press, 1993.

Burlingame, Burl. "From a Hawaiian Point of View." *Honolulu Star-Bulletin*, December 20, 1994, B1, B6.

———. "Morgan's Corner Has a Deadly Reputation." In X Marks the Spot column, Travel Section, *Honolulu Star-Bulletin*, May 1, 2005, G3.

Bushnell, Christina (Tina). Class presentation. English 780F: Folklore and Literature. English Department, University of Hawai'i at Mānoa. Fall 2004.

Bushnell, O. A. *The Gifts of Civilization: Germs and Genocide in Hawai'i*. Honolulu: University of Hawai'i Press, 1993.

———. *Ka'a'awa. A Novel about Hawaii in the 1850s*. Honolulu: University of Hawai'i Press, 1972.

Calvino, Italo. *I nostri antenati*. Torino: Einaudi, 1960.

Carroll, Rick. *Chicken Skin: True Spooky Stories of Hawai'i*. Honolulu: Bess Press, 1996.

———. *Hawai'i's Best Spooky Tales. True Local Spine-Tinglers Collected by Rick Carroll*. Honolulu: Bess Press, 1997.

Carter, Angela, ed. *The Virago Book of Fairy Tales*. Ill. Corinna Sargood. London: Virago, 1990.

Carucci, Laurence Marshall. "Elision or Decision: Lived History and the Contextual Grounding of the Constructed Past." In *Cultural Memory: Reconfiguring History and Identity in the Postcolonial Pacific*, ed. Jeannette Marie Mageo. Honolulu: University of Hawai'i Press, 2001. 81–101.

Chapin, Helen G. *Shaping History: The Role of Newspapers in Hawai'i*. Honolulu: University of Hawai'i Press, 1996.

Charlot, John. *The Kamapua'a Literature: The Classical Traditions of the Hawaiian Pig God as a Body of Literature*. Lā'ie, Hawai'i: Institute for Polynesian Studies at Brigham Young University, 1987.

———. *Moses Kuaea Nākuina: Hawaiian Novelist*. Lā'ie, Hawai'i: Pacific Institute, Brigham Young University, Hawai'i. Distributed by University of Hawai'i Press, 2005.

Chauvin, Michael E. "Astronomy in the Sandwich Islands: The 1874 Transit of Venus." *Hawaiian Journal of History* 27 (1993): 185–225.

Cheyfitz, Eric. *The Poetics of Imperialism: Translation and Colonization from* The Tempest *to* Tarzan. Philadelphia: University of Pennsylvania Press, 1997.

Chinen, Joyce N., Kathleen O. Kane, and Ida M. Yoshinaga, eds. *Women in Hawaii: Sites, Identities, and Voices*. Special issue of *Social Process* 38 (1997).

Chock, Eric. "The Neocolonization of *Bamboo Ridge*. Re-Positioning *Bamboo Ridge* and Local Literature in the 1990s." *Bamboo Ridge* (1996): 11-25.

[Church, A. M.]. *Picturesque Cuba, Porto Rico, Hawaii and the Philippines; a Photographic Panorama of our New Possessions . . . .* Springfield, Ohio: Mast, Crowell & Kirkpatrick, 1899.

Coffman, Tom. *Nation Within: The Story of America's Annexation of the Nation of Hawai'i*. Honolulu: EpiCenter, 1998.

Crampon, Louis J. *Hawaii's Visitor Industry, Its Growth and Development*. Honolulu: School of Travel Industry Management, College of Business Administration, University of Hawai'i, 1976.

206   Works Cited

Cresswell, Tim. *Place: A Short Introduction*. Malden, Mass.: Blackwell, 2004.
Crosby, A. W. "Hawaiian Depopulation as a Model for the Amerindian Experience." In *Epidemics and Ideas: Essays on the Historical Perception of Pestilence*, ed. Terence Ranger and Paul Slack. New York: Cambridge University Press, 1992. 175–201.
Cunningham, Keith and Kathryn Cunningham. "The Appearing Hitchhiker: Narrative Acculturation Among Ramah Navajo." In *Questing the Beast*, ed. Gillian Bennett and Paul Smith. Perspectives on Contemporary Legend 4. Sheffield, England: Sheffield Academic Press, 1989. 213–230.
Davis, Lynn Ann. *Nā Pa'i Ki'i: The Photographers in the Hawaiian Islands, 1845–1900*. Honolulu: Bishop Museum Press, 1980.
———. Personal communications during the 2003–2005 period. Honolulu and Kane'ohe, Hawai'i.
———. "Photographically Illustrated Books About Hawai'i, 1854–1945." In *Photography in Hawai'i*, ed. Lynn Ann Davis. Special issue of *History of Photography* 25,3 (Autumn 2001): 288–305.
———, ed. *Photography in Hawai'i*. Special issue of *History of Photography* 25, 3 (Autumn 2001).
De Caro, Frank and Rosan Augusta Jordan. *Re-Situating Folklore: Folk Contexts and Twentieth-Century Literature and Art*. Knoxville: University of Tennessee Press, 2004.
Dégh, Linda. *Legend and Belief*. Bloomington: Indiana University Press, 2001.
De Silva, Kīhei. *The Song of Stones*. Liner notes for Kawai Cockett. 'O Ka'ōhao Ku'u 'Āina Nani. HPCD-203. Honolulu: Ho'olōkahi Productions, 1993.
Denevi, Tim. Class presentation. English 780F: Folklore and Literature. English Department, University of Hawai'i at Mānoa. Fall 2004.
Desmond, Jane C. *Staging Tourism: Bodies on Display from Waikiki to Sea World* Chicago: University of Chicago Press, 1999.
Diamond, Heather. "Capturing Hawai'i: Photographic Subtexts in Early Travel Books on Hawai'i, 1880–1920." Unpublished paper, December 2001.
Dorrance, William H. *O'ahu's Hidden History*. Honolulu: Mutual Publishing, 1998.
Edwards, Elizabeth, ed. *Anthropology and Photography 1860–1920*. New Haven, Conn.: Yale University Press, 1992.
———. "Visuality and History: A Contemplation on Two Photographs of Samoa by Capt. W. Acland, Royal Navy." In *Picturing Paradise: Colonial Photography of Samoa, 1875 to 1925*, ed. Casey Blanton. Daytona Beach, Fla.: Southeast Museum of Photography, 1995. 49–58.
Elbert, Samuel H. "Connotative Values of Hawaiian Place Names." In *Directions in Pacific Traditional Literature. Essays in Honor of Katharine Luomala*, ed. Adrienne L. Kaeppler and H. Arlo Nimmo. Honolulu: Bishop Museum Press, 1976. 117–33.
———, ed. *Selections from Fornander's Hawaiian Antiquities and Folk-Lore*. Ill. Jean Charlot. Honolulu: University of Hawai'i Press, 1959.
Ellis, Bill. *Aliens, Ghosts, and Cults: Legends We Live*. Jackson: University Press of Mississippi, 2001.
Ellis, William. *Narrative of a Tour through Hawaii, or Owhyhee; with Observations on the Natural History of the Sandwich Islands, and Remarks on the Manners, Customs, Traditions, History, and Language of Their Inhabitants*. London, 1826; Honolulu, 1917. First published as *A Journal of a Tour around Hawaii, the Largest of the Sandwich islands*. Boston: Crocker & Brewster; New York, J.P. Haven, 1825.

Emerson, N. B. Letter to Charles R. Bishop. Honolulu, 30 March, 1898. Institutional Records, Bernice Pauahi Bishop Museum, Letters in Bk II, 1897–1898.
———. *Pele and Hiiaka: A Myth from Hawaii.* 1915. Reprint Honolulu: 'Ai Pohaku Press, 1993.
Fabian, Johannes. *Time and the Other: How Anthropology Makes Its Object.* New York: Columbia University Press, 1983.
Feld, Steven and Keith H. Basso, eds. *Senses of Place.* Santa Fe, N.M.: School of American Research Press, 1996.
Forbes, David W. *Encounters with Paradise. Views of Hawaii and Its People, 1778–1941.* Honolulu: Honolulu Academy of Arts, 1992.
———. *Hawaiian National Bibliography 1780–1900.* 4 vols. Vol. 3, *1851–1880.* Honolulu: University of Hawai'i Press, 1998–2003.
Fornander, Abraham. *Account of the Polynesian Race: Its Origins and Migrations, and the Ancient History of the Hawaiian People to the Times of Kamehameha I.* 1878–1885, 1909. Reprint Rutland, Vt.: C. E. Tuttle, 1969. Reprint includes "Index to *The Polynesian Race* by Abraham Fornander," comp. John F. G. Stokes.
Fornander Collection of Hawaiian Antiquities and Folk-Lore: The Hawaiian Account of the Formation of Their Islands and Origin of Their Race, with the Traditions of Their Migrations, etc., as Gathered from Original Sources. Translations revised and illustrated with notes by Thomas G. Thrum. Bilingual edition. Honolulu: Hawai'i: 'Ai Pōhaku Press, 1999. Reprint of *Memoirs of the Bernice Pauahi Bishop Museum of Polynesian Ethnology and Natural History.* v. 4–6. Honolulu: Bishop Museum Press, 1916–1919.
Franklin, Cynthia and Laura Lyons. "Remixing Hybridity: Globalization, Native Resistance, and Cultural Production in Hawai'i." *American Studies Quarterly* 45, 1 (2005): 5–36. Italian version in *ÀCOMA* (International Journal of North American Studies, Milan). Special issue on Hawai'i, ed. Donatella Izzo and Incoronata Inserra. 29–30 (Spring/Fall 2004; pub. in Spring 2005): 134–59.
Fujikane, Candace. "Between Nationalisms: Hawaii's Local Nation and Its Troubled Racial Paradise." *Critical Mass: A Journal of Asian American Cultural Criticism* 1, 2 (1994): 23–58.
———. "Introduction: Asian Settler Colonialism in Hawai'i." In *Whose Vision? Asian Settler Colonialism in Hawai'i,* ed. Candace Fujikane and Jonathan Okamura. Special issue of *Amerasia Journal* 26, 2 (2000): xv–xxii.
———. "Reimagining Development and the Local in Lois-Ann Yamanaka's *Saturday Night at Pahala Theater.*" *Social Process in Hawai'i* 38 (1997): 40–62.
Fujikane, Candace, and Jonathan Okamura, eds. *Asian Settler Colonialism in Hawai'i.* Honolulu: University of Hawai'i Press (forthcoming).
———, eds. *Whose Vision? Asian Settler Colonialism in Hawai'i.* Special issue of *Amerasia Journal* 26, 2 (2000).
Fullard-Leo, Betty. Review of *Nā Wahi Pana O Ko'olau Poko. Hawaii Magazine* (August 1995): 77.
Gegeo, David Welchman. "Cultural Rupture and Indigeneity: The Challenge of (Re)visioning 'Place' in the Pacific." *Contemporary Pacific* 13 (Fall 2001): 491–507.
Glassie, Henry. "Tradition." *Journal of American Folklore* 108 (Fall 1995): 395–412.
Goldstein, Diane. "Welcome to the Mainland, Welcome to the World of AIDS: Cultural Variability, Localization and Contemporary Legend." *Contemporary Legend* 2 (1992). Reprinted in *Contemporary Legend: A Reader,* ed. Gillian Bennett and Paul Smith. New York: Garland, 1996. 209–24.

Gordon, Tamar. *Global Villages*. Documentary video. Tourist Gaze Productions, 2005.

Grant, Glen. *Ghostly Tales for Over the Pali: An Audio Tour Through Hawaii's Supernatural with Glen Grant*. Honolulu: Honolulu Time Walks, 1990.

———. *Glen Grant's Chicken Skin Tales: 49 Favorite Ghost Tales from Hawai'i*. Honolulu: Mutual Publishing, 1998.

———. "Japanese Obake in Hawaii." *Hawaii Herald: A Journal for Hawaii's Japanese Americans*, October 21, 1983, 1.

———. *Obake Files: Ghostly Encounters in Supernatural Hawai'i*. Honolulu: Mutual Publishing, 1996.

Gresham, Melanie Maile. Class presentation. English 780F: Folklore and Literature. English Department, University of Hawai'i at Mānoa. Fall 2004.

Griffith, Lesa. "A Hawaiian Voice: The Journal *'Ōiwi* Continues a Maoli Literary Tradition That Took Root in the 19th Century, Only To Be Silenced in the 1930s." *Honolulu Weekly* (April 27–May 3, 2005): 7–8.

Hale'ole. S. N. *Laie I Ka Wai: A Hawaiian Romance Translated from the Hawaiian Text of S. N. Haleole, with Introduction and Translation by Martha W. Beckwith*. Translated from *Ke Kaao o Laieikawai: Ka Hiwahiwa o Paliuli, Kawahineokaliula*. Honolulu: Henry M. Whitney, 1863. Annual Report of the Smithsonian Institute 33 (for 1911–1912), 285–666. Washington, D.C.: Bureau of American Ethnology, 1919.

Hall, Lisa Kahaleole Chang and Kēhaulani Kauanui. "Same Sex Sexuality in Pacific Literature." In *Asian American Sexualities*, ed. Russell Leong. New York: Routledge, 1996. 113–18.

Halualani, Rona Tamiko. *In the Name of Hawaiians: Native Identities & Cultural Politics*. Minneapolis: University of Minnesota Press, 2002.

Hamasaki, Richard. "Mountains in the Sea: The Emergence of Contemporary Hawaiian Poetry in English." *Readings in Pacific Literature*, ed. Paul Sharrad. Wollongong, Australia: New Literatures Research Center, University of Wollongong, 1993. 190–207.

Handy, E. S. Craighill, Elizabeth Green Handy, and Mary Kawena Pukui. *Native Planters in Old Hawaii: Their Life, Lore, and Environment*. Honolulu: Bishop Museum Press, 1972.

Handy, E. S. Craighill, and Mary Kawena Pukui. *The Polynesian Family System in Ka-'u, Hawai'i*. Wellington, N.Z.: Polynesian Society, 1950 and 1958. Reprint Honolulu: Mutual, 1998.

Hanlon, David and Geoffrey M. White. *Voyaging Through the Contemporary Pacific*. New York: Rowman & Littlefield, 2000.

Haring, Lee. "Pieces for a Shabby Hut." In *Folklore, Literature, and Cultural Theory. Collected Essays*, ed. Cathy Lynn Preston. New York: Garland, 1995. 187–203.

Harjo, Joy. Writings. In *The Pueblo Imagination: Landscape and Memory in the Photography of Lee Marmon*, with works by Leslie Marmon Silko, Joy Harjo, and Simon Ortiz. Boston: Beacon Press, 2003.

Hau'ofa, Epeli. "Our Sea of Islands." 1993 and 1994. Reprinted in *InsideOut: Literature, Cultural Politics, and Identity in the New Pacific*, ed. Vilsoni Hereniko and Rob Wilson. New York: Rowman & Littlefield, 1999. 27–38.

———. "Pasts to Remember." In *Remembrance of Pacific Pasts: An Invitation to Remake History*, ed. Robert Borofsky. Honolulu: University of Hawai'i Press, 2000: 453–471.

Hawaii, a Primer: Being a Series of Answers to Queries and *Letters from Hawaii*. Honolulu: Hawaii Promotion Committee, 1905.

Hereniko, Vilsoni and Rob Wilson, eds. *Inside Out: Literature, Cultural Politics, and Identity in the New Pacific.* New York: Rowman & Littlefield, 1999.

Hobsbawm, Eric and Terence Ranger. *The Invention of Tradition.* Cambridge: Cambridge University Press, 1983.

Hodge, Clarence L. and Peggy Ferris. *Building Honolulu: A Century of Community Service.* Honolulu: Chamber of Commerce, 1950.

Holo mai Pele (Pele Travels). DVD or VHS. Co-production of International Cultural Programming, Thirteen/WNET New York, and Pacific Islanders in Communications. Produced by Dominique Lasseur and Catherine Tatge. Directed by Catherine Tatge. PBS Great Performances/Dance in America special. New York, N.Y.: Thirteen WNET, 2001.

Ho'omanawanui, Ku'ualoha. "He Lei Ho'oheno no nā Kau a Kau: Language, Performance, and Form in Hawaiian Poetry." *Contemporary Pacific* 17, 1 (2005): 29–81.

———. "Ka Ola Hou 'Ana o ka 'Ōlelo Hawai'i i ka Ha'i 'Ana o ka Mo'olelo i Kēia Au Hou: The Revival of the Hawaiian Language in Contemporary Storytelling." In *Traditional Storytelling Today: An International Sourcebook,* ed. Margaret Read MacDonald. Chicago: Fitzroy Dearborn, 1999. 160–70.

———. "'This Land Is Your Land, This Land Was My Land': Kanaka Maoli Versus Settler Representations of 'Āina in Contemporary Literature of Hawai'i." Forthcoming in *Asian Settler Colonialism in Hawai'i,* ed. Candace Fujikane and Jonathan Okamura. Honolulu: University of Hawai'i Press.

Ho'oulumāhiehie. *Ka Moolelo o Hiiakaikapoliopele: The Epic Tale of Hi'iakaikapolio-Pele.* Trans. and ed. by Puakea Nogelmeier. Honolulu: Awaiaulu Press, forthcoming.

Hori, Joan. "Background and Historical Significance of *Ka Nupepa Kuokoa.*" Hamilton Library, University of Hawai'i at Mānoa online resource at http://libweb.hawaii.edu/digicoll/nupepa_kuokoa/kuokoa_htm/kuokoa.html (accessed 8/20/2005).

Hufford, Mary. "Context." *Journal of American Folklore* 108 (1995): 528–549.

Hutchins, Wells A. *The Hawaiian System of Water Rights.* Honolulu, 1946.

Hyde, Charles McEwen. "Hawaiian Poetical Names for Places. *Hawaiian Annual* (1887): 79–82.

Imada, Andria L. "Hawaiians on Tour: Hula Circuits Through the American Empire." *American Quarterly* 56, 1 (March 2004): 111–149.

Ing, Tiffany Lani. "To Be or Not To Be, That Was Not the Question: A Rhetorical Study of Kalākaua's *Legends and Myths of Hawaii: The Fables and Folk-Lore of a Strange People.*" M.A. project. English Department, University of Hawai'i at Mānoa, 2003.

Inserra, Incoronata (Nadia). Class presentation. English 780F: Folklore and Literature. English Department, University of Hawai'i at Mānoa. Fall 2004.

Iwasaka, Michiko and Barre Toelken. *Ghosts and the Japanese: Cultural Experience in Japanese Death Legends.* Logan: Utah State University Press, 1994

James, Van. *Ancient Sites of O'ahu.* Photographs by Michael Weidenbach. Honolulu: Bishop Museum Press, 1991.

Jarves, James J. *History of the Hawaiian or Sandwich Islands: Embracing Their Antiquities, Mythology, Legend.* London 1843.

Johnson, Rubellite K., ed. *Kūkini 'Aha'ilono. [Carry on the News]: Over a Century Of Native Hawaiian Life and Thought from The Hawaiian Language Newspapers of 1834 to 1948.* Honolulu: Topgallant Press, 1976.

Jolly, Margaret. "Specters of Inauthenticity." In *Voyaging Through the Contempo-

rary Pacific, ed. David Hanlon and Geoffrey M. White. New York: Rowman & Littlefield, 2000. 274–97.

Kaeppler, Adrienne and H. Arlo Nimmo, eds. *Directions in Pacific Traditional Literature. Essays in Honor of Katharine Luomala*. Honolulu: Bishop Museum Press, 1976

Kahiolo, G. W. *He Moolelo no Kamapua'a: The Story of Kamapuaa*. Text from *Ka Hae Hawaii*, 1861. Trans. by Esther Mookini and Erin Neizman, with the assistance of David Tom. Honolulu: Hawaiian Studies Program at the University of Hawai'i at Mānoa, 1978.

Kaho'olawe: na Leo o Kanaloa: Chants and Stories of Kaho'olawe. Photographs by Wayne Levin et al. Honolulu: 'Ai Pōhaku Press, 1995.

Kaho'olawe Aloha 'Āina. VHS. Produced by Protect Kaho'olawe 'Ohana and written by Rodney Morales, Davianna Pōmaika'i McGregor, and Joan Lander. Honolulu, Hawai'i: Nā Maka o ka 'Āina, 1992.

Kaipu, Emma. "The Legend of Na-Iwi-O-Pae." *Paradise of the Pacific*, August 1898, 117–118.

Kalākaua, David. *The Legends and Myths of Hawaii: The Fables and Folk-Lore of a Strange People. By His Hawaiian Majesty Kalakaua. Ed. and with an Introduction by Hon. R. M. Daggett*. New York: Charles L. Webster, 1888.

Kamahele, Momiala. "'Īlio'ulaokalani: Defending Native Hawaiian Culture." *Amerasia Journal* 26, 2 (2000): 38–65.

Kamakau, Samuel Mānaiakalani. *Ka Po'e Kahiko: The People of Old*. Translated from the Newspaper *Ke Au Okoa* by Mary Kawena Pukui. Arranged and edited by Dorothy B. Barrère. Illustrated by Joseph Feher. Honolulu: Bishop Museum Press, 1964.

———. *Nā Mo'olelo a ka Po'e Kahiko: Tales and Traditions of the People of Old*. Translated from the Newspapers *Ka Nupepa Kuokoa* and *Ke Au Okao* by Mary Kawena Pukui. Edited by Dorothy B. Barrère. Honolulu: Bishop Museum Press, 1991.

———. *Ruling Chiefs of Hawaii*. Rev. ed. Honolulu: Kamehameha Schools Press, 1992.

Kame'eleihiwa, Lilikalā K., trans. and ed. *A Legendary Tradition of Kamapua'a, the Hawaiian Pig-God: He Mo'olelo Ka'ao o Kamapua'a*. Honolulu: Bishop Museum Press, 1996.

———. *Native Land and Foreign Desires: Pehea Lā E Pono Ai?* Honolulu: Bishop Museum Press, 1992.

Kanahele, Pualani Kanaka'ole. *Holo Mai Pele*. With translations by Ku'ulei Higashi, ed. by D. Māhealani Dudoit. Honolulu: Pacific Islanders in Communications; and Hilo: Edith Kanaka'ole Foundation, 2001. Distributed by Native Books.

Kanahele, Pualani Kanaka'ole and Duke Kalani Wise. *Ka Honua Ola: The Living Earth*. Honolulu: Center for Hawaiian Studies, University of Hawai'i at Mānoa, 1992.

Kanaka'ole, Edith. Interview with Homer Hayes. Pt. 2. Videocassette and transcripts. Hilo: Hawai'i Foundation for History and the Humanities, 1978. Wong Audiovisual Center, University of Hawai'i at Mānoa Library, Honolulu, Hawai'i.

Kawaharada, Dennis. "Alive in Story." In *Wao Akua: Sacred Source of Life*. Honolulu: Division of Forestry and Wildlife, 2003. 53–68.

———, ed. *Ancient O'ahu: Stories from Fornander & Thrum*. Honolulu: Kalamakū, 1996.

———. *Local Geographies: Essays on Multicultural Hawai'i*. Honolulu: Kalamakū, 2004.

————. "Local Mythologies, 1979–2000." *Hawai'i Review* 56 (2001): 185–225.

————, ed. *Nanaue the Shark Man & Other Hawaiian Shark Stories by Emma M. Nakuina and Others.* Honolulu: Kalamakū Press, 1994.

————. *Storied Landscapes: Hawaiian Literature & Place.* Honolulu: Kalamakū, 1999.

————. "Toward an Authentic Local Literature of Hawai'i." In *ReViewing Paradise: Contemporary Photography from Hawai'i.* Honolulu, 1995. 13–17.

Kelly, Marion and Nancy Aleck. *Mākua Means Parents: A Brief Cultural History of Mākua Valley.* Honolulu: American Friends Service Committee, Hawai'i Area Program, 1997.

Kepler, Angela Kay. *Hawaiian Heritage Plants.* Honolulu: University of Hawai'i Press, 1998.

Kimura, Larry. "Native Hawaiian Culture." In *Native Hawaiians Study Commission Report.* Washington, D.C.: U.S. Department of the Interior, 1983. 1: 173–97.

Kingston, Maxine Hong. *Hawai'i One Summer.* Honolulu: University of Hawai'i Press, 1998.

Kirshenblatt-Gimblett, Barbara. *Destination Culture: Tourism, Museums, and Heritage.* Berkeley: University of California Press, 1998.

————. "Mistaken Dichotomies." *Journal of American Folklore* 101 (April–June 1988):140–155.

Knaefler, Tomi K. "Haunted Hawai'i." *Honolulu* (October 1991): 46–49, 77–80.

Kneubuhl, Victoria N. "Emma Metcalf Beckley Nakuina: Hawai'i's First Woman Judge." *Kaulike.* Judiciary History Center of Hawai'i, 1998.

Krauss, Beatrice H. *Plants in Hawaiian Culture.* Ill. by Thelma F. Greig. Honolulu: University of Hawai'i Press, 1993.

Kuykendall, Ralph S. "Thomas George Thrum: A Sketch of His Life." *Hawaiian Annual* (1933): 43–47.

Lam, Margaret M. "Six Generations of Race Mixture in Hawaii." Master's thesis. Hamilton Library, University of Hawai'i, 1932.

Landgraf, Anne Kapulani. "Ē Luku Wale Ē . . . Devastation upon Devastation." *'Ōiwi: A Native Hawaiian Journal* (1998): 137–142.

————. *Nā Wahi Kapu o Maui.* Honolulu: 'Ai Pōhaku Press, 2003.

————. *Nā Wahi Pana O Ko'olau Poko. Legendary Places of Ko'olau Poko.* Trans. Fred Kalani Meinecke. Honolulu: University of Hawai'i Press, 1994.

Langton, Elinor A. "Give the Tourists More Variety." *Paradise of the Pacific,* March 1905, 15.

Lane, Melia. "Cross-Reference of Descriptions of Kaliuwa'a Valley." Typescript "Religion 482B, for J. Charlot," 1979. Honolulu, 1980. Hamilton Library, University of Hawai'i at Mānoa.

Langlois, Janet L. "'Celebrating Arabs': Tracing Legend and Rumor Labyrinths in Post-9/11 Detroit." *Journal of American Folklore* 118 (Spring 2005): 219–36.

Laws of the Republic of Hawaii Passed by the Legislature at Its Session, 1896. "Act 57." Honolulu: Hawaiian Gazette Company's Print, 1896. 181–95.

Lefebvre, Henri. *The Production of Space.* Trans. Donald Nicholson-Smith. Oxford: Blackwell, 1991.

Leib, Amos Patten. "Hawaiian Mythology in English Translation." M.A. Thesis. University of Hawai'i, 1947.

Leib, Amos Patten and A. Grove Day. *Hawaiian Legends in English: An Annotated Bibliography.* Honolulu: University of Hawai'i Press, 1979.

Letters from Hawaii: Documents in Evidence. Honolulu: Hawaii Promotion Committee, 1905.

Lippard, Lucy R. *The Lure of the Local: Senses of Place in a Multicentered Society.* New York: New Press, 1997.

Lucas, Paul M. "'E Ola Mākou I Ka 'Ōlelo Makuahine: Hawaiian Language Policy and the Courts." *Hawaiian Journal of History* 34 (2000): 1–28.

Lum, Darrell. "Local Genealogy: What School You Went?" In *Growing Up Local: An Anthology of Poetry and Prose from Hawai'i*, ed. Eric Chock, James R. Harstad, Darrell H. Y. Lum, and Bill Teter. Honolulu: Bamboo Ridge Press, 1998. 11–12.

———. "Local Literature and Lunch." In *The Best of Bamboo Ridge*, ed. Eric Chock and Darrell H. Y. Lum. Honolulu: Bamboo Ridge Press, 1986. 3.

Luomala, Katharine. "Creative Processes in Hawaiian Use of Place Names in Chants." *Laographia* 22 (1965): 234–247.

———. "Disintegration and Regeneration, the Hawaiian Phantom Hitchhiker Legend." *Fabula* 13 (1972): 20–59.

———. "A Dynamic in Oceanic Maui Myths: Visual Illustration with Reference to Hawaiian Localization." *Fabula* (1961): 137–162.

Lüthi, Max. *The European Folktale: Form and Nature.* 1974. Translated by John D. Niles. Bloomington: Indiana University Press, 1987.

Lyons, Paul. *American Pacificism.* New York: Routledge, 2005.

———. "Pacific Scholarship, Literary Criticism, and Touristic Desire: The Specter of A. Grove Day." *boundary 2* 24, 2 (1997): 47–78.

———. "'They Will Eat Us Up': Remembering Hawai'i." *American Literary History* 16, 3 (2004): 543–57.

MacCannell, Dean. *Empty Meeting Grounds: The Tourist Papers.* London: Routledge, 1992.

———. *The Tourist: A New Theory of the Leisure Class.* New York: Schocken Books, 1976.

Mākua Valley: Yesterday and Today, What About Tomorrow? Video recording. Hawai'i: Henry Paoa and Jude Dady, 1996.

Malo, David[a]. *Hawaiian Antiquities (Moolelo Hawaii).* 1898. Trans. Nathaniel B. Emerson. Honolulu: Bishop Museum Press, 1951.

Manu, Moses. *Keaomelemele.* Trans. by Mary Kawena Pukui, ed. Puakea Nogelmeier. Honolulu: Bishop Museum Press, 2002.

Marzolph, Ulrich. "Re-locating the *Arabian Nights*." In *Philosophy and Arts in the Islamic World. Proceedings of the Eighteenth Congress of the Union Européenne des Arabisants et Islamisants held at the Katholieke Universiteit Leuven (September 3–10, 1996)*, ed. U. Vermeulen and D. De Smet. Louvain: Uitgverij Peeters, 1998. 155–63.

Matsuda, Mari J. "Harriet Bouslog." In *Called from Within: Early Women Lawyers of Hawai'i*, ed. Mari J. Matsuda. Honolulu: University of Hawai'i Press, 1992. 148–71.

Maxwell, Anne. *Colonial Photography & Exhibitions: Representations of the 'Native' and the Making of European Identities.* London: Leicester University Press, 1999.

McClintock, Anne. *Imperial Leather: Race, Gender and Sexuality in the Colonial Context.* London: Routledge, 1995.

McCrae, Jane. "'E manu, tena koe!' 'O bird, greetings to you': The Oral Tradition in Newspaper Writing." In *Rere Atu, Taku Manu! Discovering History, Language & Politics in the Maori-Language Newspapers*, ed. Jenifer Curnow, Ngapare Hopa, and Jane McRae. Auckland: Auckland University Press, 2002. 43–59.

McDonald, Marie A. and Paul R. Weissich. *Nā Lei Makamae: The Treasured Lei.* Honolulu: University of Hawai'i Press, 2003.

McGregor, Davianna Pōmaika'i. "Waipi'o Valley, a Cultural *Kīpuka* in Early 20th Century Hawai'i." *Journal of Pacific History* 30, 2 (1995): 194–209.

McQuire, Scott. *Visions of Modernity: Representation, Memory, Time and Space in the Age of the Camera.* London: Sage, 1998.

Mele aloha 'āina songs and hula of Hawaiian resistance. Video recording. Washington, D.C.: Smithsonian Institution, 2002

Men of Hawaii: A Biographical Reference Library, Complete and Authentic, of the Men of Note and Substantial Achievement in the Hawaiian Islands. 5 vols. Ed. J. W. Siddall (vols. 1–2, 1917–1921) and George F. Nellist (vols. 3–5, 1930–1935). Honolulu: Honolulu Star-Bulletin, 1917–35.

Merry, Sally Engle. *Colonizing Hawai'i: The Cultural Power of Law.* Princeton, N.J.: Princeton University Press, 2000.

Meyer, Manulani Aluli. "Our Own Liberation: Reflections of Hawaiian Epistemology." *Contemporary Pacific* 13,1 (Spring 2001): 124–148.

Minerbi, Luciano. "Sanctuaries, Places of Refuge, and Indigenous Knowledge in Hawai'i." In *Land Use and Agriculture: Science of Pacific Island Peoples*, vol. 2, ed. John Morrison, Paul Gerahty, and Linda Crowl. Suva, Fiji: Institute of Pacific Studies, 1994. 89-128.

Mookini, Esther K. *The Hawaiian Newspapers.* Honolulu: Topgallant, 1974.

Mookini, Esther K. and Sarah Nākoa, trans. *The Wind Gourd of La'amaomao*, by Moses K. Nakuina. Honolulu: Kalamakū Press, 1990.

Morais, Dawn. Class presentation. English 780F: Folklore and Literature. English Department, University of Hawai'i at Mānoa. Fall 2004.

Morales, Rodney. *Ho'iho'i Hou: A Tribute to George Helm and Kimo Mitchell.* Honolulu: Bamboo Ridge Press, 1984.

———. "Literature in Hawai'i—A Contentious Multiculturalism." In *Multicultural Hawai'i: the Fabric of a Multiethnic Society*, ed. Michael Haas. New York: Garland, 1998. 107-129.

Morris, Robert J. "Translators, Traitors, and Traducers: Perjuring Hawaiian Same-Sex Texts Through Deliberate Mistranslation." *Journal of Homosexuality*, forthcoming.

Naithani, Sadhana. "The Colonizer Folklorist." *Journal of Folklore Research* 34, 1 (1997): 1–14.

———. "Prefaced Space: Tales of the Colonial British Collectors of Indian Folklore." In *Imagined States: Nationalism, Utopia, and Longing in Oral Cultures*, ed. Luisa Del Giudice and Gerald Porter. Logan: Utah State University Press, 2001. 64–79.

———. "To Tell a Tale Untold: Two Folklorists in Colonial India." *Journal of Folklore Research* 39, 2/3 (2002): 201–16.

Nakuina, Emma Kaili Metcalf Beckley (Nakuina, Emma Metcalf). "Ancient Hawaiian Water Rights and Some of the Customs Pertaining to Them." *Hawaiian Annual* (1894): 79–84.

———(Nakuina, Emma Metcalf). *Hawaii: Its People, Their Legends.* Honolulu: Hawaii Promotion Committee, 1904.

———(Beckley, Emma Metcalf). *Hawaiian Fisheries and Methods of Fishing with an Account of the Fishing Implements Used by the Natives of the Hawaiian Islands.* Honolulu: Foreign Affairs, 1883.

———(Nakuina, Emma M. B.). "Hawaiian Sharks." *Paradise of the Pacific*, June 1893, 82.

———(Kaili). "Hiiaka: A Hawaiian Legend by a Hawaiian Native." *Pacific Commercial Advertiser*, August 25–October 13, 1883.

————(Nakuina, Emma). "Historical Catalogue of the [Hawaiian National] Museum." Bishop Museum ms. HI.H.112. (188–?; filed as 1891.01). 20 handwritten pages.

————(Beckley, Emma Metcalf). "Kahalaopuna: A Legend of Manoa Valley." *Saturday Press*, December 8, 1883.

————(Nakuina, E. M. B.). "Kahalaopuna, Princess of Manoa," "The Punahou Spring," "Oahunui," "Ahuula: A Legend of Kanikaniula and the First Feather Cloak," and "The Shark-Man, Nanaue." In *Hawaiian Folk Tales*. Comp. Thomas. G. Thrum. Chicago: A.C. McClurg, 1907.

————(Beckley, Emma Metcalf). "The Legend of the Fishhook, Called Na-iwi-o-Pae, Now in the Government Museum." *Hawaiian Annual* (1884): 39–40.

————(Nakuina, Emma K.). "The Legend of Kalaipahoa, the Famous Poison God of Molokai." Copyrighted by Emma M. Nakuina. *Paradise of the Pacific*, May 1920, 31.

————(Nakuina, Emma K.). "The Legend of Kawaiahao Stone." *The Friend* (August 1919): 181–182.

————(Nakuina, E. M. B.). "The Legend of Oahunui." *Hawaiian Annual* (1897): 90–95.

————(Nakuina, E. M. B.). "The Legend of the Shark-Man, Nanaue." *HHSAR* (1896): 10–19. Rpt. *Hawaii's Young People* 7 (October 1902), 50–53; *Hawaii's Young People* 20 (April 1915), 243–248.

————(Beckley, Emma Metcalf). "Mrs. Beckley's Report on the Library" and "Mrs. Beckley's Report on the Museum." Honolulu: Report of the Minister of Foreign Affairs, 1884.

————(Beckley, Emma Metcalf). "Mrs. Beckley's Report on the Library and Museum" and "Mrs. Beckley's Report on Her Visit to Molokai" (appendix R). Honolulu: Report of the Minister of Foreign Affairs, 1886.

————(Nakuina, E. M. B.). "The Punahou Spring: A Legend." *Hawaiian Annual* (1893): 101–4. Rpt. *Hawaii's Young People* 6 (Sept. 1901), 14–16; *Paradise of the Pacific*, March 1917, 23–24.

————(Nakuina, Emma). "The Royal Arms of Hawaii, to be Presented in Features of Program for Kauikeaouli Centenary." *PCA* (March 15, 1914): 1.

————(Nakuina, Emma K.). "Springs of Wailele." *The Friend* 93 (April 1923), 81–82.

Nakuina (Beckley, Emma Metcalf) and Harriet Green, trans. *He Buke No Ke Ola Kino No Kamalii*. Trans. Dr. William De Witt Alexander's work by Emma M. Beckley and Harriet Green under the superintendence of W. D. Alexander. Honolulu, 1887.

Nakuina, Moses K. "Native Chiefs of Honolulu." In *Picturesque Honolulu*. Honolulu: Hawaii Gazette, 1907. 1–4.

————. *The Wind Gourd of La'amaomao*. Trans. Esther K. Mookini and Sarah Nākoa. Honolulu: Kalamakū Press, 1990.

Nee-Benham, Maenette K. P. and Ronald H. Heck. *Culture and Educational Policy in Hawai'i: The Silencing of Native Voices*. Mahwah, N.J.: Lawrence Erlbaum, 1998.

Nicolaisen, W. F. H. "Maps of Space—Maps of Time." *Names* 32, 4 (1984): 358–66.

————. "The Past as Place: Names, Stories, and the Remembered Self." *Folklore* 102,1 (1991): 3–15.

Nimmo, H. Arlo. "Pele, Ancient Goddess of Contemporary Hawaii." *Pacific Studies* 9,2 (1986): 121–79.

Niranjana, Tejaswini. *Siting Translation: History, Post-structuralism, and the Colonial Context.* Berkeley: University of California Press, 1992.

Nogelmeier, Puakea M. "Mai Pa'a I Ka Leo: Historical Voice in Primary Materials, Looking Forward and Listening Back." Ph.D. dissertation, University of Hawai'i at Mānoa, 2003.

'Ōiwi: A Native Hawaiian Journal. 3 vols. Honolulu: Kuleana 'Ōiwi Press, 2001–2003.

Okamura, Jonathan Y. "The Massie-Kahahawai Case and Race Relations in Hawai'i in the 1930s." *Original Plays and Classic Humanities: A Special Series from Kumu Kahua Theatre for Its 2003–2004 Season.* Honolulu, 2004.

Osorio, Jonathan Kay Kamakawiwo'ole. *Dismembering Lāhui: A History of the Hawaiian Nation to 1887.* Honolulu: University of Hawai'i Press, 2002.

Paki, Pilahi. *Legends of Hawaii. O'ahu Yesterday.* Photographs by Francis Haar. Honolulu: Victoria, 1972.

Paliko'olauloa, M. K. "Na Wahi Pana o Kaliuwa'a." *Ka Hoku o ka Pakipika*, November 14, 1861.

Peterson, Barbara Bennett, ed. *Notable Women of Hawaii.* Honolulu: University of Hawai'i Press, 1984.

"Place Names." *New Alu Like Connection* video. Dir. Jason Beique. Prod. Kaleo Woo. Honolulu: Oceanic, 1990.

"Police Seek One Man in Murder of Mrs. Wilder: Kamaaina Woman Is Strangled in Her Home on Nuuanu Pali Rd." *Honolulu Star-Bulletin*, March 16, 1948, 1.

Pratt, Mary Louise. *Imperial Eyes: Travel Writing and Transculturation.* London: Routledge, 1992.

——. "Scratches on the Face of the Country; or, What Mr. Barrow Saw in the Land of the Bushmen." In *"Race," Writing, and Difference*, ed. Henry Louis Gates, Jr. Chicago: University of Chicago Press, 1986. 138–62.

Pukui, Mary Kawena. *'Ōlelo No'eau: Hawaiian Proverbs and Poetical Sayings.* Bernice P. Bishop Museum Special Publication 71. Honolulu: Bishop Museum Press, 1983.

Pukui, Mary Kawena and Samuel H. Elbert. *Hawaiian Dictionary.* Rev. enlarged ed. Honolulu: University of Hawai'i Press, 1986.

Pukui, Mary Kawena, Samuel H. Elbert, and Esther T. Mookini. Rev. ed. *Place Names of Hawaii.* Honolulu: University of Hawai'i Press, 1974.

Pukui, Mary Kawena, E. W. Haertig, and Catherine A. Lee. *Nānā I Ke Kumu (Look to the Source).* 1979. Reprint Honolulu: Hui Hānai, an auxiliary of Queen Lili'uokalani Children's Center, 2001.

Pukui, Mary Kawena and Alfons L. Korn, trans. and eds. *The Echo of Our Songs: Chants and Poems of the Hawaiians.* Honolulu: University of Hawai'i Press, 1973.

ReViewing Paradise: Contemporary Photography from Hawai'i. Booklet published in conjunction with an exhibit of the photography of Kimo Cashman et al. at Honolulu Advertiser Gallery, April 27, 1995–June 28, 1995. Honolulu, 1995.

Rose, Jan. "Opening the Way to Respect the Land." Review of *Nā Wahi Pana O Ko'olau Poko. Honolulu Advertiser*, Nov. 27, 1994, G7.

Rose, Roger. *Hawai'i: The Royal Isles.* With an introductory essay by Adrienne L. Kaeppler and photographs by Seth Joel. Special publication 67. Honolulu: Bishop Museum Press, 1980.

——. *A Museum to Instruct and Delight: William T. Brigham and the Founding of Bernice Pauahi Bishop Museum.* Honolulu: Bishop Museum Press, 1980.

——. *Symbols of Sovereignty: Feather Girdles of Tahiti and Hawaii.* Pacific Anthropological Records 28. Honolulu: Bishop Museum Press, 1978.

Rumsey, Alan and James F. Weiner, eds. *Emplaced Myth: Space, Narrative, and Knowledge in Aboriginal Australia and Papua New Guinea*. Honolulu: University of Hawai'i Press, 2001.

Schmitt, Robert C. and Ronn Ronck. *Firsts and Almost Firsts in Hawai'i*. Honolulu: University of Hawai'i Press, 1995.

Schultz, Susan M., ed. *TinFish: Journal of Experimental Poetry from the Pacific*. Honolulu: TinFish Press.

Schweizer, Niklaus R. *Hawai'i and the German Speaking Peoples*. Honolulu: Topgallant, 1982.

———. "Kahaunani: 'Snow White' in Hawaiian: A Study in Acculturation." *East Meets West: Homage to Edgar C. Knowlton, Jr.*, ed. Roger L. Hadlich and J. D. Ellsworth. Honolulu: University of Hawai'i Press, 1988. 283–289.

———. *Turning Tide: The Ebb and Flow of Hawaiian Nationality*. Berne: Peter Lang, 1999.

Shaffer, Marguerite S. *See America First: Tourism and National Identity, 1880–1940*. Washington, D.C.: Smithsonian Institution Press, 2001.

Shuman, Amy. "Dismantling Local Culture." *Western Folklore* 52 (1993): 345–364.

Siikala, Anna-Leena. "Oral History and Landscape: Narratives in the Southern Cook Islands." Paper presented at the American Folklore Society meeting, Austin, Texas, October 1997.

Siikala, Anna-Leena and Jukka Siikala. *Return to Culture: Oral Tradition and Society in the Southern Cook Islands*. FFF Communications 287. Helsinki: Suomalainen Tiedeakatemia Academia Scientiarum Fennica, 2005.

Silko, Leslie Marmon. *Yellow Woman and a Beauty of the Spirit: Essays in Native American Life Today*. New York: Touchstone, 1996.

Silva, Noenoe. *Aloha Betrayed: Native Hawaiian Resistance to American Colonialism*. Durham, N.C.: Duke University Press, 2004.

———. "Kanaka Maoli Resistance to Annexation." *'Ōiwi: A Native Hawaiian Journal* (1998): 40–75.

———. "Pele, Hi'iaka, and Haumea: Women and Power in Two Hawaiian Mo'olelo." In *Women Writing Oceania: Weaving the Sails of Vaka*, ed. Caroline Sinavaiana and Kēhaulani Kauanui. Special issue of *Pacific Studies* 29, 1 (2006).

Skinner, Charles Montgomery. *Myths and Legends of Our New Possessions & Protectorate*. Philadelphia: J.B. Lippincott, 1900.

Skinner, H. D. "Ancient Hawaii." Review of *Hawaiian Historical Legends* and *More Hawaiian Folk Tales*. *Journal of Polynesian Society* 33 (1924): 141–42.

Smith, Bernard. *European Vision and the South Pacific: A Study in the History of Ideas*. New Haven, Conn.: Yale University Press, 1985.

Smith, Linda Tuhiwai. *Decolonizing Methodologie: Research and Indigenous Peoples*. New York: Zed Books; Dunedin, N.Z.: University of Otago Press, 1999.

Spahr, Juliana. *2199 Kalia Road*. Photographs by Candace Ah Nee. Honolulu: Subpoetics, Self-publish or Perish, 2003.

———. *Dole Street*. Honolulu: Subpoetics, Self-publish or Perish, 2001.

Spivak, Gayatri Chakravorty. *A Critique of Postcolonial Reason*. Cambridge, Mass: Harvard University Press, 1999.

———. *Death of a Discipline*. New York: Columbia University Press, 2003.

———, trans. and ed. *Imaginary Maps: Three Stories by Mahasweta Devi*. New York : Routledge, 1995.

———. "The Politics of Translation." In *Outside in the Teaching Machine*. New York: Routledge, 1993. 179–200.

————. "Questioned on Translation: Adrift." *Public Culture* 13, 1 (2001): 13–22.

————. "Translation as Culture." In *Translating Cultures*, ed. Isabel Carrera Suárez et al. Oviedo, Spain: KRK Ediciones; Hebden Bridge, England: Dangaroo, 1999. 17–30.

————. "Translating into English." In *Nation, Language, and the Ethics of Translation*, ed. Sandra Bermann and Michael Wood. Princeton, N.J.: Princeton University Press, 2005. 93–110.

Stannard, David E. *Before the Horror: The Population of Hawai'i on the Eve of Western Contact.* Honolulu: Social Sciences Research Institute and University of Hawai'i Press, 1989.

————. *Honor Killing: How the Infamous "Massie Affair" Transformed Hawai'i.* New York: Viking, 2005.

————. "The Massie Case: Injustice and Courage." *Honolulu Advertiser*, October 14, 2001, B1, B4.

Sterling, Elspeth Press and Catherine C. Summers. *Sites of Oahu.* Revised ed. Honolulu: Bishop Museum Press, 1978.

Stevens, John Leavitt and W. B. Oleson. *Picturesque Hawaii: A Charming Description of Their Unique History, Strange People, Exquisite Climate, Wondrous Volcanoes, Luxurious Productions, Beautiful Cities, Corrupt Monarchy, Recent Revolution and Provisional Government.* Philadelphia: Hubbard Publishing, 1894.

Stillman, Amy Ku'uleialoha. "'Nā Lei O Hawai'i': On Hula Songs, Floral Emblems, Island Princesses, and *Wahi Pana.*" *Hawaiian Journal of History* 28 (1994): 87–108.

————. "Of the People Who Love the Land: Vernacular History in the Poetry of Modern Hawaiian Hula." *Amerasia Journal* 28, 3 (2002): 85–108.

————. "Re-Membering the History of the Hawaiian Hula." In *Cultural Memory: Reconfiguring History and Identity in the Postcolonial Pacific*, ed. Jeannette Marie Mageo. Honolulu: University of Hawai'i Press, 2001. 187–204.

Sullivan, Robert. Poetry reading. Korean Studies Center, University of Hawai'i at Mānoa, January 30, 2003.

Sumida, Stephen H. *And the View from the Shore: Literary Traditions of Hawai'i.* Seattle: University of Washington Press, 1991.

Taylor, Clarice B. "Tales About Hawaii: Caretaker Emma Metcalf Nakuina." *Honolulu Star-Bulletin*, May 17, 1961, 46.

————. "Tom Thrum Knew All About Hawaii." *Honolulu Star-Bulletin*, July 24, 1954, mag. sec. 8,1.

Tenbruggencate, Jan. "Book Gives Voice to Windward Oahu." Review of *Nā Wahi Pana O Ko'olau Poko* by Anne Kapulani Landgraf and of *The Hawaiian Monk Seal* by Patrick Ching. *Honolulu Advertiser*, February 12, 1995, D6.

Testa, F. J. "The Sacred Pavement of Liloa." *Paradise of the Pacific*, November 1890, 2.

Thrum, Thomas G. *Hawaiian Folk Tales: A Collection of Native Legends.* Comp. Thos. G. Thrum. Chicago: A. C. McClurg, 1907. Reprint *Hawaiian Folk Tales*, intro. Glen Grant, Honolulu: Mutual, 1998.

————. "Hawaiian Place Names." Appendix to Lorrin Andrews's *Dictionary of the Hawaiian Language*, as revised by Henry H. Parker. Honolulu: Board of Commissioners of the Public Archives of the Territory of Hawaii, 1922. 625–74.

————. *Hawaiian Traditions: Stories of the Menehunes.* Collected and translated by Thos. G. Thrum (from *Hawaiian Folk Tales*) [variant title: *Menehunes*]. Chicago: A. C. McClurg., 1910.

————. *More Hawaiian Folktales. A Collection of Native Legends and Traditions.* Compiled by Thomas G. Thrum. Chicago: A. C. McClurg, 1923.

————. "Story of the Race of People Called the Menehunes, of Kauai (A Hawaiian Tradition)." *Journal of the Polynesian Society* 19,2 (1920): 70–75.

————. *Tributes of Hawaiian Traditions: The Pali and Battle of Nuuanu; Kaliuwaa Falls and Kamapuaa, the Demigod.* Revised from the *Hawaiian Annual* and *Hawaiian Folk Tales* by Thos. G. Thrum. Honolulu, 1920.

————. *Tributes of Hawaiian Verse.* Honolulu: Thrum 1882.

Thurston, Lorrin A., ed. *Vistas of Hawaii: Paradise of the Pacific and Inferno of the World.* St. Joseph, Mich.: W.F. Sessor for Kilauea Volcano House Company and the Oahu Railway and Land Company, 1891.

Tobin, Jeffrey. "Cultural Construction and Native Nationalism: Report from the Hawaiian Front." *boundary 2* 21, 1 (1994): 111–133.

Toelken, Barre. *The Dynamics of Folklore.* Rev. exp. ed. Logan: Utah State University Press, 1996.

Trask, Haunani-Kay. "Decolonizing Hawaiian Literature." In *Inside Out: Literature, Cultural Politics, and Identity in the New Pacific,* ed. Vilsoni Hereniko and Rob Wilson. New York: Rowman & Littlefield, 1999. 167–82.

————. *From a Native Daughter: Colonialism and Sovereignty in Hawai'i.* 1993. Rev. ed. Honolulu: University of Hawai'i Press, 1999.

————. *Night Is a Sharkskin Drum.* Honolulu: University of Hawai'i Press, 2002.

————. "Politics in the Pacific Islands: Imperialism and Native Self-Determination." *Amerasia* 16 (1990): 246–49.

————. "Settlers of Color and 'Immigrant' Hegemony: 'Locals' in Hawai'i." In *Amerasia. Whose Vision? Asian Settler Colonialism in Hawai'i,* special issue, ed. Candace Fujikane and Jonathan Y. Okamura, 26, 2 (2000): 1–24.

————. "Writing in Captivity: Poetry in a Time of Decolonization." In *Inside Out: Literature, Cultural Politics, and Identity in the New Pacific,* ed. Vilsoni Hereniko and Rob Wilson. New York: Rowman & Littlefield, 1999. 17-26.

Tuan, Yi-Fu. *Topophilia: A Study of Environmental Perception, Attitudes, and Values.* Englewood Cliffs, N.J.: Prentice-Hall, 1974.

Ty-Tomkins, Nikki. "The Hawaiian Eye." Review of *Nā Wahi Pana O Ko'olau Poko. Honolulu Weekly,* November 30, 1994, 8.

Ulele, S. K., trans. "He Kaao Arabia! No ke Kanaka Lawaia! Ke Kumu o ka Pomaikai." *Ka Nupepa Kuokoa,* May 1–July 3, 1875.

Venuti, Lawrence. *The Scandals of Translation: Towards an Ethics of Difference.* London: Routledge, 1998.

————. "Translation, Community, Utopia." In *The Translation Studies Reader.* London: Routledge, 2000. 468–88.

————, ed. *The Translation Studies Reader.* London: Routledge, 2000.

Warner, Marina. *Fantastic Metamorphoses, Other Worlds.* Oxford: Oxford University Press, 2002.

Wendt, Albert. "Towards a New Oceania." In *Readings in Pacific Literature,* ed. Paul Sharrad. Wollongong, Australia: New Literatures Research Center, University of Wollongong, 1993. 9–19.

Westervelt, W. D. *Around the Poi Bowl and Legend of Paao.* Honolulu: Paradise of the Pacific, 1913.

————. *Hawaiian Historical Legends.* New York: Fleming H. Revell, 1923.

————. *Hawaiian Legends of Ghosts and Ghost-Gods.* Rutland, Vt.: Tuttle, 1963.

————. *Hawaiian Legends of Old Honolulu.* Rutland, Vt.: Tuttle, 1963.

————. *Hawaiian Legends of the Volcanoes.* Boston and London: Geo. H. Ellis, 1916.

————. *Legends of Gods and Ghosts.* Boston and London: Geo. H. Ellis, 1915.

————. *Legends of Ma-ui—A Demi God of Polynesia and of His Mother Hina.* Honolulu: Hawaiian Gazette, 1910.

————. *Legends of Old Honolulu.* Boston and London: Geo. H. Ellis, 1915; 1916.

"Westervelt, Veteran Isle Figure, Dead." *Honolulu Star-Bulletin,* March 9, 1939, 1 and 6.

Whitney, Caspar W. *Hawaiian America: Something of Its History, Resources, and Prospects.* New York: Harper & Brothers, 1899.

Whitney, Henry M. *The Hawaiian Guide Book, for Travelers.* Honolulu: H. M. Whitney, 1875.

Williams, Raymond. *Marxism and Literature.* Oxford: Oxford University Press, 1977.

Wilson, Rob. *Reimagining the American Pacific: From "South Pacific" to Bamboo Ridge and Beyond.* Durham, N.C.: Duke University Press, 2000.

————. "Shark God on Trial: Symbolic and (Ill)Legal Acts of Landscape Possession in Postmodern Hawaii." *Tamkang Review* 26, 1–2 (1995): 220–34.

Winduo, Steven Edmund. "Unwriting Oceania: The Repositioning of the Pacific Writer Scholars within a Folk Narrative Space." *New Literary History* 31 (2000): 599–613.

Wittig-Harby, Bill. "A Stroll with the Ghosts of Honolulu." *Honolulu* (October 1990): 52–56, 63.

Wong, Laiana. "Authenticity and the Revitalization of Hawaiian." *Anthropology and Education Quarterly* 30,1 (1999): 94–115.

Wood, Houston. *Displacing Natives: The Rhetorical Production of Hawai'i.* Boulder, Colo.: Rowman & Littlefield, 1999.

————. "Hawaiian Texts in an American Context: The Example of Moses K. Nakuina's *Moolelo Hawaii o Pakaa a me Ku-a-Pakaa.*" *Not English Only. Redefining "American" in American Studies,* ed. Orm Øverland. Amsterdam: VU University Press, 2001. 163–177.

Wright, A. R. Review of *Legends of Ma-ui—A Demi God of Polynesia and of His Mother Hina. Folklore* 23 (1912): 520–521.

Yamanaka, Cedric. "Ghost Stories." *Honolulu* (October 2004): 31–35, 44–47.

Zipes, Jack. *Breaking the Magic Spell: Radical Theories of Folk and Fairy Tales.* Austin: University of Texas Press, 1979.

————. *Fairy Tales as Myth/Myth as Fairy Tale.* Lexington: University Press of Kentucky, 1994.

Index

Acknowledgments

In Chapter 1, I introduce the people and writings that have shaped my thinking about Hawai'i and made serious demands on it; therefore my acknowledgments here are of a more personal or institutional nature. My deepest gratitude is to those who, early on in this project, humbled and challenged me through conversation, comments, example, dedication, and knowledge: foremost, Lynn A. Davis, Candace Fujikane, Ku'ualoha Ho'omanawanui, Donatella Izzo. While all errors are mine alone, I have also greatly benefited from feedback on conference papers, specific chapters, or the whole manuscript offered by Gillian Bennett, Regina Bendix, Marjorie Edel, Esther Figueroa, Sahoa Fukushima, Lee Haring, Lilikalā Kame'eleihiwa, Anne Kapulani Landgraf, Janet Langlois, Uli Marzolph, Sadhana Naithani, Bill Nicolaisen, Puakea Nogelmeier, Cathy Lynn Preston, John Rieder, Reina Whaitiri, and John Zuern. Students in my undergraduate classes—especially the English 380s I taught in 1998 and 2004—motivated me to pursue my project. The graduate class English 780F in Fall 2004 stands out in my mind as a true seminar or site for exchange and discussion, and I thank all sixteen participants for their engaged participation. In particular, Tina Bushnell, Thuy Da Lam, Jeff Mexia, Melanie Ried, and Nani Ross gave me much to think about; I am also indebted, as documented in Chapter 4, to specific in-class comments by Tim Denevi, Nadia Inserra, Maile Gresham, and Dawn Morais for my discussion of Nakuina's book. Without Craig Howes—his example, energy, critical questions, and friendship—I am not sure I could have finished the book. Walking with Cindy Franklin, Esther Figueroa, and Laura Lyons; dancing with Kristin McAndrews, Reina Whaitiri, and my other hula sisters; kayaking with Lynn Davis; and being part of Coline Aiu's *hālau* replenished me, body and heart. My friendships with Donatella Izzo and Ravi Palat have been more long-distance but just as nurturing. And I am fortunate to have had unwavering support from my department; in particular, I thank Mark Heberle, Judith Kellogg, Laura E. Lyons, Glenn Man, Gayle Nagasako, and Joe O'Mealy, whose leadership, generosity, and trust made all the difference.

I acknowledge with gratitude the support of the John Simon Guggenheim Memorial Foundation, the University of Hawai'i's Research Council, and the University of Hawai'i at Mānoa College of Languages, Linguistics, and Literature for granting me in 2001 precious and focused time away from teaching responsibilities and service as department chair. Additionally, University of Hawai'i URC Research Relations grants allowed me to benefit from the research and translation skills, knowledge, and cooperation of Sahoa Fukushima and—for a related project—Noelani Arista.

My thanks go to the staff at Bancroft Library at the University of California-Berkeley, Bishop Museum, Pacific Collection at the University of Hawai'i-Mānoa Hamilton Library, Hawai'i State Archives, and Honolulu Mission Houses for helpful references and technical support. Joan Hori greatly facilitated my work with early issues of *Paradise of the Pacific.* DeSoto Brown, Deanne DuPont, Ron Schaeffer, and Charles Myers helped me greatly at Bishop Museum Archives. For use of photographic images, I am especially grateful to Lynn A. Davis, Anne Kapulani Landgraf, the University of Hawai'i Press, Hamilton Library, Bishop Museum, and the Bancroft Library; my thanks also to Huanani-Kay Trask and the University of Hawai'i Press for permission to quote her poetry.

At the heart of my inquiry stands Emma Kaili Metcalf Beckley Nakuina, a remarkable Hawaiian woman and writer. Individuals who were particularly helpful in gathering information about her include: Mercy and Monica Kaili Bacon, two of Emma's descendants from her first marriage; Lynn Davis, Head of Preservation at the University of Hawai'i at Mānoa Hamilton Library; David Forbes; Maile Gresham, Punahou alumna and doctoral candidate at the University of Hawai'i at Mānoa; Victoria Nālani Kneubuhl; Noenoe Silva, Director of the Indigenous Politics Program in the University of Hawai'i at Mānoa Political Science Department; Luella Holt Kirkjian at the Hawai'i State Archives; Joan Hori of the University of Hawai'i at Mānoa Hamilton Library; Judith Kearney, when she was at the Bishop Museum Archives; Ann S. Koto of the Supreme Court Law Library of Honolulu; Helen Y. Lind via Meda Chesney-Lind of Women's Studies at the University of Hawai'i at Mānoa.

It is my pleasure to thank Jerry Singerman, at the University of Pennsylvania Press, for ably shepherding the project from start to end and proving at every turn to be an attentive and dedicated editor. I am also thankful to the anonymous readers whose questions propelled me to sharpen my vision and refine my rhetoric; to Managing Editor Alison Anderson and copyeditor Jennifer Shenk.

Through storms and quiet, John Rieder has been my steadfast *compagno.* I may not offer such a calm place of respite in return, but he has my love.

www.ingramcontent.com/pod-product-compliance
Lightning Source LLC
Chambersburg PA
CBHW020347270326
41926CB00007B/340